# If . . . Then . . . Curriculum: Assessment-Based Instruction, Grades 6–8

Lucy Calkins with Colleagues from the Teachers College Reading and Writing Project

*Photography by Peter Cunningham*

HEINEMANN ◆ PORTSMOUTH, NH

DEDICATED TO TEACHERS™

*first*hand
An imprint of Heinemann
361 Hanover Street
Portsmouth, NH 03801–3912
www.heinemann.com

Offices and agents throughout the world

The authors and publisher wish to thank those who have generously given permission to reprint borrowed material:

Reprinted with permission from the book *National Geographic Readers: Deadliest Animals* by Melissa Stewart. Copyright © 2011 National Geographic Society.

Cataloging-in-Publication data is on file with the Library of Congress.

ISBN: 978-0-325-05952-5

Production: Elizabeth Valway, David Stirling, and Abigail Heim
Cover and interior designs: Jenny Jensen Greenleaf
Series photographs by Peter Cunningham and Nadine Baldasare
Composition: Publishers' Design and Production Services, Inc.
Manufacturing: Steve Bernier

Printed in the United States of America on acid-free paper
18 17 16 15 14 PAH 1 2 3 4 5

# Contents

*IF your students have not previously been part of writing workshop classrooms and they have not had any experience writing informational texts, THEN you may want to teach this unit. This unit provides foundational teaching and learning about information writing that students will need before attempting more complex units such as research-based information writing. This unit invites students to draw from their own areas of personal expertise to create lively, voice-filled information books. Choose this unit if you'd like your students to experience firsthand that information writing need not be bland or tedious to create; it can be filled with opportunities for choice, engagement, and exploration. This unit will support all middle school writers in reaching for the demands of the Common Core in information writing.*

*IF your sixth-grade students display a solid understanding of personal narrative writing, and you want them to develop their skills in writing realistic fiction, THEN you may want to teach this unit. This unit will support sixth-grade writers in learning to craft and revise integral scenes, to create well-developed characters that respond to conflict in realistic ways, and to use tension and pacing to draw readers into their unfolding plot. If you choose to teach this alongside fiction reading, this unit will particularly build reading–writing connections. This unit will support all middle school writers in reaching for the demands of the Common Core in narrative writing.*

*IF your students are new to the genre of argument writing, or if they would benefit from additional practice in writing persuasively, THEN you may want to teach this unit. This unit introduces students to the foundational skills of persuasive writing and then quickly builds on those in more ambitious ways, with the invitation to students to learn from source-based material and to produce argument essays that draw on that research. The work this unit covers sets the stage for the literary essay writing unit that is detailed in each of the full-length books for sixth (The Literary Essay: From Character to Compare/Contrast), seventh (The Art of Argument: Research-Based Essay), and eighth (The Literary Essay: Analyzing Craft and Theme) grades. It could as easily follow these, especially with a greater focus on the final bends.*

*IF you want to teach a unit that will tap into students' motivation because it is especially personal, and that can also show students that structure follows content and that authors decide upon their structure as they figure out what they want to say, THEN a unit on memoir is a good choice. Such a unit can extend the personal narrative work your students experienced in sixth grade, bringing the power of that unit to seventh grade, while also adding a new spin to it. Choose memoir if your students need to engage with their lives and each other in the curriculum, to build a cohesive community of writers, and if you'd like their writing to be more reflective, purposeful, and disciplined.*

## Historical Fiction: Weaving Together Fact and Fiction • 59

*IF your students have already experienced a realistic fiction writing unit and display a solid understanding of personal narrative writing, THEN this unit would be a good choice. This unit will especially appeal to your budding historians. Many teachers accompany this unit with social studies research, though you could teach it in isolation if your students have in-depth knowledge of a particular time period. Either way, the work is challenging in that it calls on students to weave historically accurate details through a well-crafted, fictional narrative; the unit also invites students to incorporate informational text through an accompanying prelude or endnote. Especially (but not only) if you choose to teach this alongside historical fiction reading, this unit will particularly build reading–writing connections.*

## Poetry: Immersion and Innovation • 75

*IF the language with which your students write tends to be social rather than literary, and you'd like to build their sense of playfulness, their love of words, their ability to make reading–writing connections, and their engagement with writing, THEN poetry gets teen writers writing up a storm. If you have students who struggle with stamina or writing long, poetry allows them to be successful as writers and therefore to build positive relationships with writing. When studying poetry, writers can mine mentor texts closely and repeatedly, so this unit provides you with a powerful opportunity to teach students to apprentice themselves deeply to the craft and form of writers they admire.*

## Documentaries: Bringing History to Life • 88

*IF your students know enough about topics to teach others, and you'd like to see their informational writing have more voice, authenticity, and craft, THEN the invitation for them to produce historical documentaries gives students an opportunity to practice the essential skills of information writing such as organizing information, writing with both ideas and information, and highlighting a perspective. This unit also allows students to compose multimedia digital texts in a short, nine-session unit. To do this work, students need access to research sources, time to research, and opportunities to teach each other digital media.*

## Literary Essays: A Mini-Unit on Analyzing Complex Texts for Meaning, Craft, and Tone • 106

*IF you want a quick, minor unit to hone students' skills with text-based writing, and to support their engaged reading, THEN writing literary essays will give students an opportunity to explore how theme and craft are related in the stories they read. Literary essays will also strengthen students' skills with analyzing text evidence and elaborating their thinking about complex texts. Choose literary essays to sustain a trajectory of writing about reading, analyzing texts, and illuminating complexity.*

## Fantasy: Writing within Literary Traditions • 121

*IF your students are game to build upon their experience writing fiction with a unit that extends that work, THEN you'll want to teach them to write fantasy. This will be especially perfect if you teach students who are fairly strong readers and who love fantasy and dystopian novels. A unit on writing fantasy will give these avid readers the chance to create their own worlds; work with archetypes, quest structures, and universal themes; and generally to revel in complexity. A unit on fantasy will particularly build reading–writing connections.*

# PART TWO: Differentiating Instruction for Individuals and Small Groups: If . . . Then . . . Conferring Scenarios

## INTRODUCTION/RATIONALE • 134

## NARRATIVE WRITING • 136

### Structure and Cohesion • 136

*If the writer is new to the writing workshop or this particular genre of writing.*
*If the writer seems to paragraph randomly or not much at all.*
*If the story lacks tension.*
*If the beginning of the piece is lacking story elements or does not hint at larger issues or tension.*

# Introduction

I N MIDDLE SCHOOL, students are in the throes of adolescence. Given the opportunity, very few of us would want to relive those days—tortured by everything from bad skin and body image, friends and peer groups, to the pressure to succeed and the pressure to conform. For students lucky enough to have it, a writing curriculum can make all the difference. A strong writing workshop will harness their interests and give voice to their troubles, all the while helping them to move fast and steadily toward long-term academic goals. It can help them grow not just as writers who will be asked to meet ever more demanding standards, but as people and citizens.

Chances are that your students do a lot of writing throughout their lives, mostly digital and through the use of social media. Douglas Reeves reminds us that twenty years ago, many students didn't write outside of school and didn't write after they graduated. Now that has all changed, and kids are writing all the time. They also have near constant access to the songwriters of their generation, so they are immersed in words nonstop. They write to plan, to create an identity, to say, "I was here." They write to collect and synthesize lyrics, texts, images, and ideas. The world of texting, Facebook, Twitter, and email and the world of the classroom may seem very disparate, but they needn't be. You'll see that we've woven writing from a variety of sources through this curriculum—writing from students' own lives, writing from the literature they read, writing from the content they are studying, and writing in response to the cultural and social worlds they inhabit.

Middle-schoolers are tough critics. They can look at their writing with judgmental eyes, noting ways it works and doesn't work, sizing up their writing against the writing that others do. Their ability to be hard on themselves and to self-critique can be turned into a source of strength because your students want to be competent. As their skills grow, they'll likely want to continue that trajectory of progress.

Despite all this, it won't surprise you to hear that middle-schoolers can be all over the map in terms of their attitudes toward writing, their attitudes toward school, and their attitudes toward themselves. That means that it will be important for you to keep your finger on the pulse of your writers' skills *and* engagement with writing. Without engagement, you won't get far, and without skills, engagement means little.

## ON-DEMAND ASSESSMENTS WILL HELP YOU PRIORITIZE WRITING INSTRUCTION AND ADJUST YOUR CURRICULUM

So, first things first. Before determining what units you will teach, and in what order, you'll want to gather baseline data on each of your writers to learn what they can do in narrative, information, and argument writing. We recommend beginning by having students complete one (or more) of the on-demand writing assessments found in the book *Writing Pathways: Performance Assessments and Learning Progressions, Grades 6–8*. You'll need one writing period to complete each of these assessments, but the information you will get about your students will be priceless. Watch them as they write. Are students struggling to come up with a topic to write about? Disinterested in the task at hand? Flying down the page so they produce two pages in fifty minutes of writing time? Their challenges—and their strengths—will be immediately evident. Then look at the work they produce, and look at it in relation to a progression of expected achievements K–8. As you mull over the results, realize that if students have not received instruction in writing and opportunities to write, their progress can be dazzling as you move through this curriculum. They can improve before your eyes—and theirs. But that sort of development requires a wholehearted commitment to the teaching of writing, so we urge you to think seriously about your commitment to writing this year.

Depending on how much time students have to write—how often and for how long your writing workshop extends—you'll probably be able to teach four or five writing units across your year. This means that in addition to the *Units of Study* full-length books, you'll create at least one and perhaps two of your own units. This book is designed to help you with that effort.

You may question this commitment to writing instruction. If your students' writing meets the ambitious standards of the Common Core State Standards without a fair amount of practice and instruction, you may decide to teach just two or three writing units and then to use writing as a tool within the rest of your curriculum. If students' on-demands are strong, you will see the power instruction has had on them. You'll see them writing with purpose, intention, and an appreciation for structure, craft, and detail.

We generally find, however, that for students to meet the ambitious standards set forth by the CCSS, they do need to write every bit as much as they need to read. The need for students to devote time to writing—and for you to teaching writing—will be especially imperative if your initial on-demand assessments show that students are already behind. Time and again we've seen teachers turn an entire class of writers around in dramatic ways, but this requires ironclad resolve to prioritize writing and then intense commitment that comes with that choice.

The gap between the fifth- and sixth-grade standards is not large, and yet there is a giant leap to be made when moving from the sixth- to the seventh-grade standards, and seventh- to eighth-grade standards. Because the expectations accelerate, we suggest teachers of sixth grade aim to reach as many of the seventh-grade standards as they can reach. This, then, allows your students the time they need to reach those ambitious levels.

## WHAT TO EXPECT FROM THE SIXTH-, SEVENTH-, AND EIGHTH-GRADE UNITS OF STUDY AND HOW TO MAKE CHOICES IN AN IF . . . THEN . . . CURRICULUM PARADIGM

### Sixth Grade: The Full-Length Books and Recommendations for "If . . . Then . . ."

Because your sixth-graders will come to you from a variety of backgrounds and experience with writing workshop, you will have a bit of a balancing act to perform, especially at the start of the year. Certainly, you will want to rely on the formal and informal assessments you conduct to understand your students' strengths and challenges in writing. You will likely want to begin with *Personal Narrative: Crafting Powerful Life Stories*, the first full-length unit in this strand, because it is designed both for students who have had experience writing narratives and for those who have had little, if any, chance to give this kind of writing a go. Whatever their entry point, they will leave the unit with a solid understanding of what it means to craft shapely, meaningful narratives. You may later opt to extend their narrative work through the *If . . . Then . . .* unit, "Fiction Writing," which builds directly on narrative writing skills, while also extending these through new lessons in craft. Because this is a favorite of many students, you can expect that your kids' enthusiasm will lead to spurts in writing skills.

The second full-length unit in sixth grade, *The Literary Essay: From Character to Compare/Contrast*, like *Personal Narrative*, is designed to offer your sixth-graders foundational essay skills before extending their expertise with more sophisticated work. The unit begins with an essay writing "boot camp," a fast-paced shared writing activity that will quickly get students up to speed on the foundational skills they need to generate a claim and supports and to craft an essay that incorporates both. From there, the unit moves into instruction designed to build in sophistication across its bends, moving from a focus on character to a focus on theme and ending with the challenge to compare and contrast two texts, incorporating understanding of character and theme. By the end of the unit, students will be well versed in the elements of literary essay writing and in the qualities of writing that this genre demands. Though this unit offers considerable support and challenges for a wide range of writers, if your preassessments show that most of your students are working at a third- or fourth-grade level, we suggest you first teach the *If . . . Then . . .* unit, "Persuasive Essays."

You and your students are in for a treat with the final full-length unit in sixth grade, *Research-Based Information Writing: Books, Websites, and Presentations*. What's special about this unit is its focus on kids who have done remarkable things to fight for causes that matter to them. Meanwhile, students will learn the skills that will position them to join these kids in the endeavor of researching, writing persuasively, and eventually going public with the information they've gathered about a topic and cause about which they care, now as teen activists themselves. This unit spotlights writing within a carefully selected structure with focus, detail, elaboration, and meaning.

In the final bend, students will also be exposed to technology as they turn their research projects into digital presentations, either as digital slideshows or websites. If your informational preassessments show that most of your students are writing at a third- or fourth-grade level, we urge you to precede this work with the *If . . . Then . . .* unit, "Writing Information Books on Topics of Personal Expertise."

Another enrichment option for your sixth-grade curriculum is the *If . . . Then . . .* "Poetry: Immersion and Innovation" unit. This was designed with any of the middle grades in mind, so if you opt to teach it, you will certainly want to confer with seventh- and eighth-grade teachers in your school. If they intend to teach poetry too, you will want to find ways to distribute the teaching so that there is something new for each grade and so that the instruction students receive each year builds in sophistication.

Of course, before making any final decisions about your individual course of study, you will want to meet with your colleagues teaching sixth, seventh, and eighth grade, to decide on a pathway that builds in sophistication across all three grades. There are more than enough units outlined in this book to add variety and engagement to each of the middle school grades' writing curriculum.

### Seventh Grade: The Full-Length Books and Recommendations for "If . . . Then . . ."

In an ideal world, your seventh-graders will have come to you from the sixth-grade units of study. This means that the first unit, the unit on fiction writing, can stand on the shoulders of the sixth-grade unit on narrative craft. If your seventh-graders do not have that background and you have time enough this year to teach two narrative units, my first suggestion would be to conduct the on-demand narrative assessment, and if students' writing is at the third-grade level, I'd suggest you borrow the full-length unit, *Personal Narrative: Crafting Powerful Life Stories* from a sixth-grade colleague and teach that unit prior to teaching *Writing Realistic Fiction: Symbolism, Syntax, and Truth*. If your students' on-demands are closer to the fourth- or fifth-grade level, I wouldn't be too concerned about their ability to run with *Writing Realistic Fiction*. I'd dive in. This is an enormously popular unit with students, and their energy for fiction writing will make it far easier for you to teach.

The second full-length unit in seventh grade, *Writing About Reading: From Reader's Notebooks to Companion Books*, does not require a background

in either information writing or in writing about reading. It's a high-level book—you and I would enjoy working with the challenges that are given to students—but it is also an elastic unit that can support writers and readers at many levels.

The final full-length unit in seventh grade, *The Art of Argument: Research-Based Essays*, is the most challenging, and before students embark on that unit they do need some background in essay writing. If your students' on-demand argument work is solidly at the fourth-grade level, you can embark on this unit, but if they have not yet learned to write well-structured essays with a thesis that is then advanced across the text, they'll benefit from learning that work before embarking in this unit. They could get that background from even just an abbreviated version of one of the full-length sixth-grade units in this series: *The Literary Essay: From Character to Compare/Contrast* or *Research-Based Information Writing: Books, Websites, and Presentations*.

Most of the units in *If . . . Then . . . Curriculum*, then, are designed as enrichment units. If your students need more instruction and practice in solid nonfiction writing, you may want to teach the *If . . . Then . . .* unit "Documentaries: Bringing History to Life." This unit gives students the opportunity to hone the skills necessary for good nonfiction writing, but it also engages the interest of your technology-minded students by encouraging them to combine historical research, informational writing, images, and music into a digitally delivered documentary. If your students don't have a lot of experience with information writing, the *If . . . Then . . .* unit "Writing Information Books on Topics of Personal Expertise" will provide them with the necessary foundational skills for future success in this genre.

If you and your students enjoyed the full-length unit *Writing Realistic Fiction*, and if your teaching aims to create a close community of learners and to engage students in reflecting on their own lives, then you will love the *If . . . Then . . .* unit "Memoir: Writing to Reflect on Experience and Suggest Thematic Connections." The overview of this unit (and all the units in this book) follow. Then again, especially if your students are ravenous readers of fantasy and if they thrived under the invitation to write fiction, the *If . . . Then . . .* unit "Fantasy: Writing within Literary Traditions" is an all-time favorite. "Historical Fiction: Weaving Together Fact and Fiction" is a sophisticated *If . . . Then . . .* unit in which students have the opportunity not only to sharpen their narrative writing skills, but also to learn about a time period. Consider teaching this unit later in the year when students have some content from social studies or history class under their belts. Most secondary schools wisely devote a unit to poetry, and the *If . . . Then . . .* unit "Poetry: Immersion and Innovation" can help you teach that unit well. We also suggest you draw on some of the books by Georgia Heard. Finally, we've included a fairly accessible *If . . . Then . . .* unit in "Literary Essays: A Mini-Unit on Analyzing Complex Texts for Meaning, Craft, and Tone." If your students didn't study this in sixth grade, or if their high-stakes tests require strong literary essays, you could easily follow the full-length *Writing About Reading* unit with this *If . . . Then . . .* one. Then again, you could borrow the sixth-grade unit and teach that to your seventh-graders, if for some reason they missed it last year.

### Eighth Grade: The Full-Length Books and the Recommendations for If . . . Then . . . Units

Whether your students arrive in your classroom having had years in a writing workshop or are new to this instruction, they'll feel welcomed into the first full-length unit, *Investigative Journalism*, and be able to thrive within it. It's a motivating unit, too, so you'll find everything is easier. If your students thrive in that unit and want more opportunities to extend that sort of work, the *If . . . Then . . .* unit "Documentaries: Bringing History to Life" is a perfect extension.

The second full-length unit for eighth grade, *The Literary Essay: Analyzing Craft and Theme*, expects that students have been writing about reading prior to the unit. If you have some students whose skills are low, they'll be able to catch up within that unit, and you will not need to teach them the *If . . . Then . . .* unit "Literary Essays: A Mini-Unit on Analyzing Complex Texts for Meaning, Craft, and Tone." The unit will provide the background your students will need for the full-length unit *Position Papers: Research and Argument*.

The only narrative unit in the eighth-grade books is *Investigative Journalism*, but the *If . . . Then . . .* units offer more opportunities to teach your students narrative writing. How your eighth-graders would love the opportunity to write fantasy! Using the *If . . . Then . . .* unit "Fantasy: Writing within Literary Traditions" will let them explore the world of fantasy while keeping their work grounded in solid literary practice. The *If . . . Then . . .* unit "Historical Fiction: Weaving Together Fact and Fiction" provides yet another opportunity for students to sharpen their narrative writing skills, this time while immersed in the study of a historical time period. This unit works particularly well when paired with a social studies unit. Poetry will be equally important to eighth-graders—especially if you connect poetry to song writing using the "Poetry: Immersion and Innovation" *If . . . Then . . .* unit and allow for a coffee house as the form of publication. And as your eighth-graders move toward the end of their middle-school years, we encourage you to teach them the *If . . . Then . . .* unit "Memoir: Writing to Reflect on Experience and Suggest Thematic Connections," because this is a sophisticated genre that requires students draw on both narrative and expository writing skills. Some teachers call this "The College Essay" to help students grasp that this will, in fact, be some of the most high-stakes writing they ever do.

# Writing Information Books on Topics of Personal Expertise

## RATIONALE/INTRODUCTION

If you teach sixth grade and your students have not had a prior introduction to information writing, and if you have time during the year to teach several information writing units, then rather than diving into *Research-Based Information Writing: Books, Websites, and Presentations*, you may instead opt to begin with a unit in which students learn the ins and outs of information writing by taking on topics of personal expertise. If you teach seventh grade, you will have noticed that there is no traditional information-writing course in the full-length units, and you may therefore be eager to teach this one to make up for that.

Because each student will write about a topic of his own choosing, and a topic on which he already has knowledge, your students can focus on developing the organizational, elaboration, and language techniques they need to produce strong informational writing. While there will be opportunities to include research, the main thrust of this unit is to learn the structures to convey information well.

This unit, in conjunction with the teaching you'll do later in *Research-Based Information Writing: Books, Websites, and Presentations* (sixth grade) or *Writing About Reading* (seventh grade), is specially designed to help students meet the rigorous Common Core State Standards (CCSS) for informative/explanatory writing. The unit is particularly designed to meet the challenges of the sixth-grade standards, but it holds important foundational skills for seventh-graders as well. In sixth grade, students are expected to "introduce a topic; organize ideas, concepts, and information, using strategies such as definition, classification, comparison/contrast, and cause/effect; include formatting (e.g., headings), graphics (e.g., charts, tables), and multimedia when useful to aiding comprehension" (W.6.2a). By seventh grade, the expectations become loftier, because students are expected not only to be expert at the challenges set out by the sixth-grade standards, but also to introduce the topic clearly and preview what is to come (W.7.2a). This unit helps students to become experts at structuring their writing in the ways called for by the sixth-grade standards, upon which the seventh-grade standards are built.

In this unit, students write about topics they know intimately, ones they find fascinating. This means their engagement will skyrocket, and the volume of writing they do will also increase exponentially. You'll help your students learn to plan for their writing using a variety of text structures and to use text structures to convey information clearly. They'll also learn to elaborate using a variety of techniques. Although students will begin by writing about their own expert topics, they'll progress toward doing research that extends their knowledge on these topics, and as part of that research will learn to weave outside information into their own writing.

Last but not least, you will teach your students to read information texts as insiders, noticing the choices that other authors have made and developing theories about the effects those craft moves are meant to have on readers. Students will learn that craft is as important in nonfiction as in narrative writing and that nonfiction writers draw on a variety of craft moves to highlight both central ideas and the significance of their content. Students will use these same moves to illuminate concepts and convey information in their own writing.

Let's get started.

## A SUMMARY OF THE BENDS IN THE ROAD FOR THIS UNIT

**In Bend I (Drafting and Revising to Teach What You Know)**, you will help your students know that information writers don't just plow into writing. They'll take a bit of time to consider their organizational structure, doing this before writing a large text (such as a book) and also before writing smaller portions of that text (such as a chapter). Students will spend time considering several ways to divide their topics into smaller subtopics (or chapters), finally choosing one way that they deem would best teach readers. From that day on, your teaching each day will highlight a different quality of good information writing. Students will use what you teach as they draft new chapters and revise old ones, proceeding in that fashion to produce a nonfiction chapter book and to build a good understanding of the essentials of information writing.

**In Bend II (Using Brief Research to Supplement and Extend Books)**, you will convey to students that strong writers keep their audience in mind. Students will learn how to analyze their writing to determine what additional chapters, subchapters, and information will make their texts more compelling to readers. You will then coach your students on simple research methods so that they can learn what they need to know to write those portions of their text.

**In Bend III (Using Mentor Texts to Lift Writing to the Next Level)**, you will guide students to examine the work of expert authors and to generate ideas for how to make their final pieces come alive for readers. During this bend, students will also celebrate their published pieces and reflect on all they will take with them as they move beyond this unit. Some of the key understandings students will hopefully garner are that smaller, more focused topics allow the writer to dig deeper, that information can be presented in many different formats, and most of all, that good information writers work to make a topic more compelling. The goal of the unit is to provide the foundation writers need to write well about information for the rest of their lives.

## GETTING READY

Before this unit even starts, you'll want to hook your students into the excitement of writing to teach others by inviting them to "get geeky" about a topic on which they are already knowledgeable. Encourage them to think of a small list of "expert topics" that they might choose to write about, and then to begin focusing those topics. The smaller the topic, the bigger the writing, so guide students to write about topics like "The Threatened Animal: What's Happening to Frogs?" rather than "Animals." By channeling students to settle on topics before the unit even begins, you will be able to launch right into the heart of your teaching without taking time at the start for students to generate topic ideas. We have found that students rarely need a whole writing session to settle on a topic, anyhow. You will also create plenty of buzz about the upcoming unit.

## BEND I: DRAFTING AND REVISING TO TEACH WHAT YOU KNOW

Now that students have selected a topic, they will consider many different ways of organizing their content. Once they settle on a structure, they will begin drafting and revising to create a nonfiction chapter book.

### Bend I, Session 1: Considering Different Structures

The Common Core expects that sixth- and seventh-graders, by the end of the school year, should be able to "organize ideas, concepts, and information, using strategies such as definition, classification, comparison/ contrast, and cause/effect" (W.6.2a; W.7.2a ). Today you'll be teaching students that any information text can be structured in one of a variety of ways and that it helps to ponder possible ways to organize a piece before starting to write. Your teaching point might sound like, "Today I want to teach you that writing an information book is similar to teaching—and one of the things a teacher does is break down a topic into smaller topics so it is easier for the learner to grasp the content. Teachers and writers, both, try to think of a logical way to organize the information for learners."

To provide an example of this, you might explain that every topic has subtopics, and there are ways subtopics "go together." A book on gardening might contain planting, fertilizing . . . and then what? Harvesting. That book will be following a chronological structure. A book on dogs might contain chapters such as collies, beagles, and poodles; this book would be structured like a list. That list would have more of a logical structure if it addressed the most common dogs and went in sequence from the least to the most. Or the book on dogs could contain both good things about dogs as pets and problems (in which case it would be organized into pros and cons).

You could introduce a chart, "Ways Nonfiction Can Be Organized," jotting:

## Ways Nonfiction Can Be Organized

- Chronological
- Ranked list
- Pros and cons
- Similarities and differences

You might then invite your class to consider a shared topic—say, "Being a Middle School Student"—and to try dividing this topic into subtopics that fall into each of the four structures you've introduced. You could quickly divide your class into groups, right in the meeting area, and assign each group a structure to consider. Perhaps one cluster would come up with ways to write that book so that the chapters followed a chronological structure (such as grade levels or periods in the day); another cluster of students could take a moment to imagine a list of pros and cons or similarities and differences (perhaps in comparison to elementary or high school).

As your minilesson ends, suggest that students spend today planning alternative tables of contents for the topics they are considering writing, imagining that topic divided into various chapters. As they go off to write, urge them to try several structures, even if they feel they know right away which one they would like to use.

In a mid-workshop teaching point, you might suggest that once a writer has decided on at least a tentative table of contents for her book, it helps to jot notes under the chapter titles as reminders of the information that might go into that topic. As a writer does this, she is thinking, "Do I have enough to say for this to be a whole chapter?" or "Do I have so much to say that this really needs to be two chapters?" A mid-workshop teaching point such as this pushes students toward greater volume in their writing, which could very easily be lacking in a session such as this if students spend the entire time only jotting tables of contents.

During the share, encourage students to consider which chapter they'll write first—presumably one addressing a topic they know especially well—and suggest they take a few minutes to teach their partner about the topic. Informational writing is writing to teach, so it makes sense to start the unit by positioning the authors as teachers. You'll find that students launch into teaching these chapters without thinking for a minute about the organizational structure of the chapter—forgetting that the minilesson for the day was not just angled to today's writing but instead, to all information writing (or teaching) they ever do. Remind kids that they will need to think about the structure of their chapter just as they thought of the structure for their book as a whole. Their homework for the evening can involve planning out the chapter they'll write in class on the second day of the workshop.

### Bend I, Session 2: Studying Qualities of Good Information Writing to Write Well Right from the Start

Today your students will begin drafting the information book that they will work on throughout this unit. They will hopefully arrive in your class having already thought about the organizational structure for their first chapter and will be well positioned to begin drafting. Today's session, then, is designed to lift their energy for this important work and to position them so that their writing is as good as it can be right from the start.

You might, therefore, say to your students, "Today I want to teach you that although information writers are mostly fastening information onto the page so that others can learn it, their goal is the same goal that fiction writers have—to write well, to write in ways that get through to their readers. Two ways that information writers do this is to read the work of other information writers and to write with their readers in mind, thinking, 'How can I make this really good?'"

To demonstrate this two-pronged teaching point, choose a snippet of wonderful information writing for your class to study. Some nonfiction writers that we particularly admire are Seymour Simon, Gail Gibbons, and Joy Hakim. A small section of the text should be sufficient. Ask, "What do you notice about this text? What has this writer done that really helps readers to learn about the topic?" This work will yield a short list of qualities of good information writing, from which you could generate the beginnings of an important chart, based on what your students say, for example:

### Qualities of Good Information Writing

- Sections are focused on one subtopic
- Has ideas, not just facts
- Includes a variety of examples, such as stories, quotes, statistics
- Uses "expert language": words and phrases important to the topic, with definitions for many
- Some information taught using words, some taught with images, captions, or charts

Then, for your link, encourage your writers to consider this list of qualities as they write and to think about how they can incorporate as many of them as they can to best teach readers.

Expect that students will draft at least an entire chapter today, perhaps moving on to their next chapter, and that a chapter will be approximately two pages in length. It will be helpful to convey those expectations explicitly to the class. As students write, offer voiceovers such as "By now you should be about halfway done with your first page. Plan on your chapter being two or three pages and on finishing it today."

### Bend I, Session 3: Working on Self-Assessment, Goal-Setting, and Revision

Your students will have written at least a chapter, so today is a good time to remind them that writers always draw on all they know. Channel students to bring out the Information Writing Checklist for the grade level below yours and to assess whether they have done everything on that checklist. Remind students that this checklist should already be familiar to them, and the goal is just to make sure they drew on all they already know how to do. You won't give your students this year's checklist until you have taught most of the new items on it. Checklists are to reinforce previous learning, not for learning new content.

## Information Writing Checklist

| | Grade 5 | NOT YET | STARTING TO | YES! | Grade 6 | NOT YET | STARTING TO | YES! |
|---|---|---|---|---|---|---|---|---|
| | **Structure** | | | | **Structure** | | | |
| **Overall** | I used different kinds of information to teach about the subject. Sometimes I included little essays, stories, or how-to sections in my writing. | ☐ | ☐ | ☐ | I conveyed ideas and information about a subject in a well-structured text. Sometimes I incorporated arguments, explanations, stories, or procedural passages. | ☐ | ☐ | ☐ |
| **Lead** | I wrote an introduction in which I helped readers get interested in and understand my subject. I let readers know the subtopics that I would later develop as well as the sequence. | ☐ | ☐ | ☐ | I wrote an introduction in which I interested readers, perhaps with a quote or significant fact. I let readers know the subtopics that I would develop later and how my text would unfold. | ☐ | ☐ | ☐ |
| **Transitions** | When I wrote about results, I used words and phrases like *consequently, as a result,* and *because of this.* When I compared information, I used words and phrases such as *in contrast, by comparison,* and *especially.* In narrative parts, I used phrases that go with stories such as *a little later* and *three hours later.* In the sections that stated an opinion, I used words such as *but the most important reason, for example,* and *consequently.* | ☐ | ☐ | ☐ | I used transitions to help readers understand how different bits of information and different parts of my writing fit together. I used transitions to help connect ideas, information, and examples, and to imply relationships such as when material exemplifies, adds on to, is similar to, explains, is a result of, or contrasts. I used transitions such as *for instance, such as, similarly, therefore, as a result, in contrast to,* and *on the other hand.* | ☐ | ☐ | ☐ |
| **Ending** | I wrote a conclusion in which I restated the main points and may have offered a final thought or question for readers to consider. | ☐ | ☐ | ☐ | I wrote a conclusion in which I restated the important ideas and offered a final insight or implication for the reader to consider. | ☐ | ☐ | ☐ |

Be sure that you approach this self-assessment work with a big emphasis on kids becoming their own coaches. A good coach is hard on his players—pushing relentlessly for them to do their best work. A good coach wouldn't say, "Well, you know how to do that even though it isn't here on the page," or "Well, you kinda did that, so we'll check 'yes.'" A good coach has the utmost expectations and doesn't step back from those.

The purpose of self-assessment is for writers to reflect on goals they need to tackle and to make those goals into a big deal. Suggest that students reread the mentor text from yesterday to watch the way *that* writer did whatever it is that the student hasn't yet aced. Suggest students get help from other classmates who have different strengths and that they revise with extra power because of the checklists.

### Bend I, Session 4: Writing with Specifics

As you plan your teaching, it will help you to keep in mind that the two areas of focus in this unit are elaboration and structure, and it is important to maintain a balance of both. For example, you will have already taught a number of lessons on structure, so it makes sense now to focus on elaboration. Look at students' writing and assess what they are doing in the way of writing with content. First, notice if, in fact, their information writing is chock-full of information. Do you see examples, facts, quotes, statistics, observations, and descriptions, or do you find a sort of bland, chatty style of summary? If you can't identify and box out the chunks of information that comprise a good information text, then you'll want to teach the rather obvious thing, that information writing is built with detail—and that details need to be specific, precise, and factual. You might say to your students, "Today I want to teach you that, in information writing, perhaps more so than in any other genre, specifics matter. Expert writers know it's not enough to write, 'Dogs eat a lot.' Instead, they write with specifics: 'Large dogs usually eat a cup and a half of kibble, twice a day. Smaller dogs eat far less, perhaps only half a cup, twice a day.'"

After this minilesson, send your students off to write, inviting them to consider how they can draft their upcoming chapters differently, armed with this new teaching. Remind them to remember all you have taught them about structure as they focus on writing with information.

In a mid-workshop teaching point, you might channel students to consider not only drafting more chapters but also reflecting on what they've already written. Remind them that any new writing moves they learn can also be a lens for revision. Invite students to reread chapters they wrote earlier and revise those chapters to reflect whatever they now know about good information writing.

## Bend I, Session 5: Selecting Appropriate Content

One thing you will certainly want to teach your writers is to carefully consider the selection of their material, which is a key expectation of the Common Core for middle school writers. Your teaching point might sound like, "Writers give careful attention to the content they include in their pieces, deciding not only what should go in each section, but also what might be excluded." Demonstrate this concept with a snippet from the class book, prepared in advance with some information that doesn't quite fit in a particular section. Then, send students off to write, encouraging them to do two things as they continue drafting new chapters—devote special attention to determining whether the content fits together and turn a critical eye on chapters they have already written.

On this day you may want to rely on partnerships so that students have extra support and practice making these decisions. Perhaps in a mid-workshop teaching point, you might channel partners to rehearse sections with each other, discussing what information is most relevant and powerful and what information doesn't fit, as well as how information might be better organized to convey it clearly. When students go off to write, they can revise or even restart chapters after these conversations, aiming to ratchet up the level of their work.

## Bend I, Session 6: Creating Cohesion Using Transition Words

Certainly, you will want to teach a session on the importance of making connections within and across categories of information. Often, students get so focused on one section, or one chapter, that they write with laser focus, as if that part of the project were an isolated effort. The Common Core expects sixth-graders to "use appropriate transitions to clarify relationships among ideas and concepts" (W.6.2c); the expectation is for seventh-graders to use transitions to create cohesion as well (W.7.2c). You could say to students, "An important skill for an information writer is to create cohesion across a piece of writing. Parts of a text—paragraphs, sections, or chapters—are like links in a chain. Each subsection of a text must be linked with the ones before it and the ones after it. Otherwise, the chain (the cohesion of the whole book) will be broken." Send writers off to work, suggesting that they continue to use linking words and phrases they know, paying particular attention to how these phrases work to create a feeling of cohesion across the piece.

During a mid-workshop teaching point, you could point out that transitions alone are not enough to create cohesion; the information itself needs to be logically ordered, with each part of the book building on the one before it. If there is an introductory paragraph to a section, it should foreshadow the content that follows, and it should also contain any background information the reader needs to fully understand the content. Remind students that as they consider the information to include in a chapter, as well as the logical order for laying out that information, they should factor in what preceded the section so that each piece in it connects to what came before.

### Bend I, Session 7: Developing Text Features to Teach Information and Ideas

You might find that your students are itching to start adding in-text features. They might have already begun gathering images or creating charts or adding a glossary. To push your students toward deeper intellectual work and the Common Core's recommendation that text features be used to "aid in comprehension," you might say to your students, "Writers, today I want to teach you that text features are more than just pictures that go with the words on the page. Text features can be used to teach additional information or convey information more quickly in a better format than words." Then, demonstrate how you might take a snippet of your class book, perhaps a section about using lockers in middle school, and you might think about additional information that could be conveyed using text features, such as a diagram depicting the parts of a locker.

On this day during independent writing time, ensure that your writers not only create text features, but also continue to write; you don't want them to spend the entire session drawing or searching for images. In a mid-workshop teaching point, you might point out that text features can also be used as a way to convey *ideas*, not just facts. Creative subtitles are one way writers can present ideas. For an information book about the film *Return of the Jedi*, for example, a subtitle such as "The Worst Star Wars Movie Ever Made" would certainly convey the writer's stance on the topic.

# BEND II: USING BRIEF RESEARCH TO SUPPLEMENT AND EXTEND BOOKS

By now your students will have generated fairly lengthy drafts that include a table of contents, chapters organized according to a deliberately selected structure, and text features highlighting important information. The next step is to help your students progress from using information they already know to conducting research to find and include additional relevant information. Research is crucial to information writing and is also a skill the Common Core expects of middle school students. While the research you'll set students up to do will be light, you may still find that students need some additional guidance during this stage. Certainly, you will help them make plans for what further information they need to research, what sources they might use to find it, and where in these sources the information they gather might live.

## Bend II, Session 1: Researching to Find New Information that Bolsters Writing

You might frame this bend by explaining that information writers often find themselves asking questions that they can't answer without turning to research. Then say, "Today I want to teach you that one way information writers set out to research is to think about *kinds* of research they need to do to find the information they need, such as interviewing an expert, using books or online sources, or creating a survey. Then, keeping their deadline and audience in mind, writers make smart decisions about what kind of research makes the most sense for their project."

You might model how to generate questions about the shared class topic—being a middle school student. Point out that statistics would strengthen your chapter on the differences between elementary students and middle-schoolers. Suppose that one claim that you make in your book is that middle school students have considerably more homework than elementary students. You know this, vaguely, but wonder how you might support it. So you pose the question: How much more homework do middle school students have than elementary students? Then you could invite students to brainstorm with you about how you'd get this information. Typical suggestions might be to survey a sample of elementary and middle school students to find out how much time they spend on homework each night or how many pages of reading and writing they are required to do each week. Reinforce your teaching by pointing out that readers are much more likely to buy into their ideas if they can bolster these ideas with concrete, statistics-based facts, such as "On average, middle school students say they have around 1.2 more hours of homework per night than elementary students."

Send your students off to research and to write. Remind them in a link that they should be alternating between researching and writing today. Of course, the research your students will do relies largely on the sources you have available. Depending on these, you could steer your students toward a library or use a mid-workshop teaching point to show students how to search the Internet for reliable sources or how to conduct a successful survey. You'll need to decide which research skills will best suit your class, given the topics students are addressing, the things they know and still need to learn, and the way your room is set up. After students have spent some time researching, you may want to use a second mid-workshop teaching point to channel them toward adding some of their newfound information to their drafts.

In a share session, you might encourage your writers to share with each other some of the interesting information they uncovered. Consider grouping your students with others that have similar topics in the hope that they might collect more information for their books in addition to celebrating the work of the day.

### Bend II, Session 2: Quoting Experts

According to the Common Core Standards, sixth-graders are expected to assess the credibility of sources, quote or paraphrase the conclusions of others, and provide basic bibliographic information in their writing (W.6.8). By seventh grade, students are expected to do all of this as well as follow a standard format for citation (W.7.8). This session is designed to support all of this work. To support students in bolstering their writing with quotations from published sources, you might say to your class, "Information writers often draw on the testimony of experts to support their writing. They research, on the lookout for 'juicy quotes' that they can incorporate into their writing, quotes that capture precisely what the writers are hoping to say or that support a fact or idea they've included in their writing." Demonstrate for your students how you carefully draw information from a source, making sure to record the words exactly as they appear, to put beginning and end quotation marks around the words you select, and show that you cite the source, giving proper credit. As a tip, you might say, "One way to identify expert testimonies you want to include is when, as you're reading, you think, 'That's the perfect way to say that!'"

To support plenty of writing volume in this session, remind students that it is not enough to just plop quotes into their drafts. They must also provide some explanation about why the quotes are relevant and how they connect to the writer's own ideas about the topic. Tailor your share for the grade you teach, using it as an opportunity to teach your students how to format a bibliographic section, depending on the expectations of the Common Core for your grade.

### Bend II, Session 3: Including Expert Language or Content Vocabulary

To build on yesterday's session, you might teach students the importance of adding expert language or content vocabulary. All middle school information writers are expected to use "precise and domain-specific vocabulary," according to the Common Core. Your teaching point might sound like, "Because information writers teach others, they make sure they are using the technical vocabulary that distinguishes them as experts and that informs others about their topic." Explain that if a writer is teaching about chameleons, for example, she won't write that chameleons *blend in* when, in fact, there is a precise technical term for this function: *camouflage*. Likewise, it doesn't do to refer to the *jaws* of an insect when the correct term is *mandibles*. You'll want to convey to your students that part of their job as information writers is to "talk the talk" of their topics, thinking always, "How can I teach others about this in ways that they will learn more than they already know—so that they, too, can sound like insiders on the topic?"

In a link, to support productive, independent writing time, you might remind students to continue their research and writing, this time with an eye for expert vocabulary words to add to their pieces. You might use the mid-workshop teaching point as an opportunity to remind them that most expert words are important enough to be discussed at several points in a text. Encouraging students to weave important terms throughout a text will help to support elaboration and consistency.

For a share, students might take turns showing off some of the new expert terms they have picked up, perhaps using these in sentences and then seeing if their classmates can guess what they mean.

## Bend II, Session 4: Using Diagrams and Illustrations to Convey Information

For extra work on text features that supports research, you might consider a minilesson in which you convey, "Today I want to teach you that information writers look for opportunities to use a diagram or illustration from a source that would be just right in their own writing. Often this is one that visually illustrates—and thus clarifies—a larger point or idea in a way that words alone cannot. When writers insert an image from another text, they are careful not only to reference it, but to explain it as well."

If you haven't done so already, you might now create a chart that spotlights the purposes for incorporating different kinds of information, so that your students see the value of including varied information. You might start with the types of information listed in the Common Core grade-specific standards: "relevant facts, definitions, concrete details, quotations, or other information and examples" and add to this list, showing students that conducting interviews or including quotes can give information writing a more personal feel, while facts and statistics gives the writing an authoritative feel.

You might also make a large T-chart with "Type of Visual Information" on one side and "How We Can Use It in Our Writing" on the other. Then you could record for students how and why to use visual features to aid the comprehension of the reader. In doing this you will again be addressing work that the Common Core considers pivotal to middle school: "using formatting (e.g., headings), graphics (e.g., charts, tables), and multimedia when useful to aiding comprehension" (W.6.2, W.7.2).

You might kick off independent writing time with a call to action: today is nearly the last session in this bend, and the last real opportunity students will have to research during writing workshop. Encourage your students to use their time industriously, because there isn't a moment to lose. During the share (or in a small group if only a handful of your students need this work), you might teach summarizing or paraphrasing. Alternatively, you might remind writers to keep an up-to-date list of the sources they have used.

## Bend II, Session 5: Self-Assessing and Setting Goals

Note that while this bend introduces research, it simultaneously emphasizes rehearsing and revising. And, of course, the goal is always to emphasize these two parts of the writing process during *any* bend. At this point in the unit, your writers will have drafted many sections and chapters of their texts. You will want to continue to raise the level of their work as well as charge them with transferring and applying all they have learned each time they create a new section.

Then too, each revision strategy and editing strategy you teach can be applied not just to a current section, but to every section. In this way, your writers are continually accumulating and building on all they have learned. This is a good time to bring out the Information Writing Checklist for your grade level, because you will have taught most of the skills on the checklist. Encourage your students to consider their goals alongside their latest work, studying to be sure that all they have learned—or set out to try to do really well—is reflected in their work. They can use the checklist to revise, and you can involve the whole class in creating mentor pieces of writing that you can annotate together, labeling specific sections for qualities that match parts of the checklist for writers to reference as they work.

## BEND III: USING MENTOR TEXTS TO LIFT WRITING TO THE NEXT LEVEL

By now, your students have experimented with organizational structures, drafted, revised, added text features, and elaborated using research found in expert texts on their topic. Most students should have a text of about seven to twelve pages that are crossed out and scribbled on. At the start of this unit, you briefly studied mentor texts together, mining them for qualities of good information writing. In this final bend, you'll steer students toward mentor texts once more, this time with the intention of examining them for potential structures and elaboration ideas to borrow as students make final revisions to their own writing before publishing a final draft.

### Bend III, Session 1: Using Mentor Texts for Ideas on Presenting Information and Structuring Texts

You might begin this final bend with a lesson in which you convey that writers often look to other writers not just for information itself, but for how that information is presented—in other words, how the text is structured. You might begin by modeling how you examine a nonfiction book to determine its overall structure. For example, if the book begins with a narrative structure and then delves into more factual writing, you might say that this particular way of beginning is effective because it pulled you into the topic—it got you "hooked," so that you wanted to read on to learn more. You could then model how you could borrow that structure for the class's shared topic, by introducing

**Information Writing Checklist**

| | Grade 6 | NOT YET | STARTING TO | YES! |
|---|---|---|---|---|
| | **Structure** | | | |
| Overall | I conveyed ideas and information about a subject in a well-structured text. Sometimes I incorporated arguments, explanations, stories, or procedural passages. | ☐ | ☐ | ☐ |
| Lead | I wrote an introduction in which I interested readers, perhaps with a quote or significant fact. I let readers know the subtopics that I would develop later and how my text would unfold. | ☐ | ☐ | ☐ |
| Transitions | I used transitions to help readers understand how different bits of information and different parts of my writing fit together. I used transitions to help connect ideas, information, and examples, and to imply relationships such as when material exemplifies, adds on to, is similar to, explains, is a result of, or contrasts. I used transitions such as *for instance, such as, similarly, therefore, as a result, in contrast to,* and *on the other hand.* | ☐ | ☐ | ☐ |
| Ending | I wrote a conclusion in which I restated the important ideas and offered a final insight or implication for the reader to consider. | ☐ | ☐ | ☐ |
| Organization | I chose a focused subject. | ☐ | ☐ | ☐ |
| | I used subheadings and/or clear introductory transitions to separate sections. | ☐ | ☐ | ☐ |
| | I made deliberate choices about how to order sections and about the sequence of information and ideas within sections. I chose structures such as compare-and-contrast, categories, and claim-and-support to organize information and ideas. Some sections are written as argument, explanation, stories, or procedural passages. | ☐ | ☐ | ☐ |
| | **Development** | | | |
| Elaboration | I included varied kinds of information such as facts, quotations, examples, and definitions. | ☐ | ☐ | ☐ |
| | I used trusted sources and information from authorities on the topic and gave the sources credit. | ☐ | ☐ | ☐ |
| | I worked to make my information understandable and interesting. To do this, I may have referred to earlier parts of my text, summarized background information, raised questions, and considered possible implications. | ☐ | ☐ | ☐ |

the book with a short excerpt of "a day in the life of a middle-schooler." Share out at least a few different effective structural decisions that mentor authors have made, so students see a variety of options to add to their repertoire.

Continue to lead your class in this inquiry work, guiding them to name a few more presentation moves the author made that they could try, too. For instance, they might look at how the writer links different parts of a text in creative ways (this, of course, builds off of the teaching you did in Bend I on linking parts to create a cohesive whole).

You might then send students off in small groups, allotting five or ten minutes for them to study mentor texts in the room to get ideas for how to prepare their own books for publication, perhaps borrowing from several authors. Encourage students to think especially about how structural choices can showcase content—and to make decisions for their own books accordingly.

After about ten minutes of students studying mentor texts, you could use your mid-workshop teaching point to move students toward trying out some of the presentation moves they discovered in their own texts.

### Bend III, Session 2: Analyzing Texts by Published Authors, Asking, "What Makes This Text So Effective at Conveying Information?"

This day of teaching builds off of yesterday's teaching. Where the teaching in yesterday's session emphasized structure, today's teaching emphasizes elaboration. Set up this session by saying to your students, "Yesterday we noticed ways that published authors structured their information texts. Today we can study these texts with an eye on how these authors packed their texts with tons of great information. We can study our texts and ask, 'What makes this so effective at conveying information?'"

You might launch this session with a brief demonstration, showing your students a section from a mentor text that models a particular technique you think would benefit them. For example, you could share this bit of text by Melissa Stewart:

"Hippopotamuses are usually gentle giants. During the day, they lounge and snooze in shallow water holes. At night, they lumber onto land and munch on grasses and leaves. But if a boat gets between a hippo and the deep water or between a mother and her calf, the animal will panic. It may tip over the boat and attack the passengers with its powerful jaws.

Then you might say, "Hmm . . . it's almost like she's written a setup sentence for readers—'Hippopotamuses are usually gentle giants'—which she then follows with information that shows exactly what she means by this. And here's what's interesting. She could have followed this first sentence with a few straightforward facts. But instead, she uses visual imagery and strong, descriptive words to convey facts in this particular section. This isn't poetry or narrative writing; it's expository. But the way that Melissa Stewart uses descriptive words, it almost feels like a story! I don't know about you, but for me, this brings those hippos to life. It's as if I can see them as I read. That's a really smart elaboration move that you could try in your writing, too."

Then, send students off to inquire and explore. Listen in and record their observations to create a quick chart of all that they noticed. If they do not notice ways a writer has elaborated on information, you will certainly want to help them to notice this, whispering in as they work.

After ten minutes or so of inquiry, gather your students to share what they noticed and also raise the level of that work—or teach into what they did *not* notice during their inquiry that they might have picked up on, given the books they selected, perhaps spotlighting key work that the Common Core highlights. For example, you might point out ways that the informational writers whose work they've admired use the language of experts. Earlier, you taught your writers that including domain-specific vocabulary is key (W.6.2, W.7.2). Now, you might teach them to look at how writers explain domain-specific vocabulary so that terms become crystal clear to readers. Authors might choose to define words using appositives right in the text or using sidebar definitions, or perhaps they might choose not to define words directly but instead to provide enough context that readers can glean the definitions. Your students can make decisions about how to define vocabulary words based on their assessments of the words' importance and difficulty.

If students don't comment on this themselves, you might point out the formal, authoritative style that many published information writers adopt, a style that the Common Core expects middle school students to emulate: "Establish and maintain a formal style" (W.6.2e, W.7.2e). Additionally, you might remind students to include text features that will contribute to their readers' understanding, and you might share with them a mentor text that includes multimedia features, perhaps channeling some or all of your writers to create electronic informational books.

Be sure to leave some time in this session for your students to try in their own writing some of the moves they learned studying mentor authors. Make a big deal of homework on this day. Let your students know that this is the last chance they have to make large-scale revisions on their pieces before making final edits to ready them for publication.

## Bend III, Session 3: Readying Writing for Presentation

In this session, you could say to your writers, "Think about how you would feel if a teacher of yours taught a lesson filled with bad grammar and incomplete sentences. You would have a hard time learning what that teacher was trying to teach, wouldn't you? It's the same with information writing. For information writing to be most effective, it must be accurate and clear. It must be free of grammatical errors." Certainly, you will want to remind your writers to edit in meaningful ways, looking carefully at where best to create paragraphs, examining their use of pronouns, punctuation, and spelling, and making sure to incorporate all they know about the conventions of grammar. They might also consider varying their sentence structures for meaning, style, and reader engagement. Remind your writers to check that they used the most precise language they could (rather than writing in generic ways) and that they maintained a consistent style or tone.

As you send students off to work, channel them to study their writing with the language section of the Information Writing Checklist in hand, using the checklist to make corrections to their own writing. Then, invite your students to trade their writing with a partner and to act as editors for one another.

In a mid-workshop teaching point, you might spotlight some of the grammatical errors that students are catching and fixing that are particularly important to this kind of writing, such as punctuation of embedded quotations and commas around appositives.

You might end this session with a share in which you invite students to practice reading parts of their pieces as a way to prepare for the final celebration. If some of your students' pieces are particularly long, you might encourage them to choose just a section or two to share with their audience in the next session.

At the end, students should have a text that includes information based on their own expertise on the topic as well as information they have collected through research, features, structures, and craft moves they have never before tried, and a new understanding of what makes for a strong information text.

## Bend III, Session 4: Sharing Published Pieces with the World

We encourage you to find some time, even if it is short, to allow students to share their hard work with classmates. In addition to celebrating what students have accomplished, a celebration serves as a reminder to students that they are writing for an audience, which inevitably guarantees that the level of each student's work will be lifted.

You might conduct what in writing workshop classrooms is often dubbed an "expert fair," in which your writers serve as experts on their chosen topics. Organize students' desks into a square around the periphery of the room while your writers set up on the outside of the square. Direct them to sit at desks side by side, with their writing and any artifacts they would like to share during the presentation set up in front of them. Half the class—or any audience you choose to invite, such as another class or parents—might move around inside the square, visiting writers' stations, asking questions, offering feedback, and giving compliments. Your goal is that your writers feel like true masters of the information they worked so hard to collect and present, and that they leave this unit more fired up about being authors of information texts than when they started the unit.

# Fiction Writing

## RATIONALE/INTRODUCTION

This unit is designed to follow the sixth-grade unit, *Personal Narrative: Crafting Powerful Life Stories*. You'll find that fiction is the genre your students want worst to write—and are the worst at writing! They'll be eager to write with tremendous volume and high levels of engagement, and this makes this unit a terrific forum for teaching students to engage in large-scale revision. The Common Core Standards for narrative writing in grade 6 are challenging, and you'll see that this unit, in combination with the first narrative unit, allows you to bring students to those high levels. They will learn to write narratives using "effective technique," "relevant descriptive details," and "well-structured event sequences." They will learn to craft and revise integral scenes, to create well-developed characters that respond to conflict in realistic ways, and to use tension and pacing to draw readers into their unfolding plot.

More than this, however, this unit allows your students to develop a deep understanding of Standards 4, 5, and 6 in reading. That is, by adjusting the language, structure, and perspectives in their own narratives to achieve specific purposes, students will learn to read published literature with an eye for the decisions that authors have made. They will learn to recognize when an author of a mentor text has used symbols and metaphors to convey larger meanings, asking, "Why might the author have made this choice?" And more importantly, they'll add symbols and metaphor into their own drafts. In the same way, writers will learn the power of figurative language and other narrative techniques. This unit, then, is in a sense a unit on text interpretation—from the inside out.

## A SUMMARY OF THE BENDS IN THE ROAD FOR THIS UNIT

**In Bend I (Collecting and Rehearsing Story Ideas While Checking In on Writing Goals)**, you will teach students to collect multiple story ideas, blurbs, and scenes in their notebooks, drawing on what they know about strong narrative writing. They will learn that writers often focus on issues in the world to come up with ideas for the conflicts their characters might experience. Will their story tell about peer pressure? About tensions between home and school? About a young person who is driven to be a perfectionist and can't forgive her own vulnerability? Students will spend time developing their characters, settings, and plots and rehearsing how their stories might go.

**In Bend II (Drafting with a Strong Purpose and Revising in Deep, Meaningful Ways)**, you will invite students to draft a first version of their stories, and you will teach them that writers revise in large, meaningful ways as they write, not waiting until a draft is completed before engaging in revision. As part of this, students will study mentor texts, noticing the qualities of good writing in them, and they will give special attention to the scene in a story that introduces the central conflict of that story. Students will try out different leads and, especially, endings, exploring different ways that the central conflict in a story could be resolved.

**In Bend III (Revising and Editing with an Eye toward Publication)**, students will continue to revise their stories, this time in smaller, more nuanced ways. You will teach them that writers craft setting, convey the passage of time, and write dialogue to convey meaning, mood, and tension. Students will also learn revision and editing techniques as they prepare their pieces for publication.

**In Bend IV (Publishing and a Celebration)**, you'll teach students the process that fiction writers follow when preparing stories for publication. As part of this process, students will consider who their audience is and let that answer guide their choices about how and where they will publish their writing. Then they will publish and celebrate their writing.

## BEND I: COLLECTING AND REHEARSING STORY IDEAS WHILE CHECKING IN ON WRITING IDEAS

During this first phase of the unit, students will fill their notebooks with possible fictional entries that feature particular conflicts or issues that matter to them. The bend begins with students collecting possible story ideas through writing story blurbs and small scenes. A few sessions later, students will choose a seed idea, an entry that stood out. The bend ends with a variety of development strategies—multiple ways to develop the seed idea through work on characters, plot, and setting.

### Bend I, Session 1: Collecting Possible Story Ideas by Writing Story Blurbs and Small Scenes

Right away, you will launch your students into writing stories. You'll of course need to teach them strategies for generating and weighing ideas for possible stories they could write, but we caution you against letting that work consume more than two days. Writers learn to write by writing. Slowing down their choice of story just long enough (two days) gives you the chance to make sure that no student chooses a story that will be impossibly long or in which you can already see signs of incoherence.

You will probably want to start the unit by teaching possible ways that fiction writers generate ideas for stories. You might spotlight that writers often generate fiction ideas by looking at moments of trouble from their lives and then projecting those onto a character. This way, students will find ideas for fiction that are born out of the trouble they've experienced in their own lives. You might say, "Writers return to moments of trouble in their own lives. They get ideas for fiction, just as they get ideas for personal narratives and essays, by paying attention to the moments and issues in their own lives." Then point out the important difference between personal narrative writing and fiction by saying, "But in *fiction*, writers get to create characters who may deal with the moment of trouble in a different way than they themselves might, or to create a plot twist through which the moment of trouble ends differently."

In the teaching component of your minilesson, you might offer them a model about a character you are creating based on a situation you experienced when you were their age: "When I was your age, a kid named Chris called me names in the art room. Maybe I could write a story about a boy who also gets called names, and like me, he doesn't do anything about it. Or maybe I could write a story about a boy who gets called names but who gets the courage to stand up for himself and eventually . . . Or maybe I could write a story about a boy who is a bully and discovers he is alienating himself. Or maybe . . ." Demonstrate the process of imagining several scenarios, so students will see that fiction writers try on ideas for size before settling on the one that feels right.

If students are collecting story ideas in their writer's notebooks, you might point out that the blurbs on the back covers of novels can be mentor texts for what a writer might do to envision a story—only when writing short stories, as these students will be doing, they'll probably limit themselves to two to three characters and two to three scenes. A story blurb might start, "My character wants to have a new best friend, because her old best friend has moved away. She tries to make new friends by trying out for a soccer team because a lot of the kids in her class are also trying out. But then . . ." Blurbs help writers map out the arc of their story idea, exploring how the story might begin, imagining the trouble, and creating a resolution. To help students plan the arcs of their stories in their blurbs, you could teach them the template "(Someone) wanted . . . but . . . and so . . . Finally . . ." as a shorthand for thinking through how any story idea might go.

You probably won't want students spending a full day's workshop just writing story blurbs for possible stories they could write, so you might, in your mid-workshop teaching point, let students know that sometimes writers try out various ideas by writing just a scene from one, then another, to see which story idea feels especially right.

You will not want to actually write scenes out in front of your students (especially during a mid-workshop teaching point), but you could "write-in-the-air," dictating the sort of thing you might write if you had the time. To write a fictional scene (or in this instance, to dictate one), you may want to take something real that happened to you and then switch the narrator from first person (I) to third person, giving that person a name (Chris), and then dictate the fiction scene so that it starts right before the moment of trouble.

Simply showing how to change the narrator from first person to third person can help your sixth-graders get started. Often the trouble scene is a good one to try, because it crystallizes what a story is really about. In *On Writing*, Stephen King (2001) writes that the easiest way for writers to get a plot is to put their character in a "situation." You will only need to dictate a few sentences, remembering as you do, that when you and your students write personal narratives it helps to start with dialogue or small actions.

## Bend I, Session 2: Collecting Ideas for Conflicts that Characters Face

Another way you might steer students to begin collecting is to write story ideas rooted in characters tackling issues or conflict that they and their peers face, such as bullying, parental divorce, or pressures about physical appearance. This taps into the writing advice many authors give young writers and that they themselves follow. Many authors address issues in their fictional narratives that they or their readers face. Conflict is at the heart of good fiction—and at the heart of a character's journey toward change. If you visit the Reading Rockets website and scroll through the video interviews and transcripts of well-known children's book authors, you will find that many share their stories of writing inspiration, which often addresses issues close to their hearts.

Teach your students that fiction writers often set up their characters to face tough issues as a central part of a story's plot. You might say, "When I was young, I thought fiction writers dreamed at night and imagined make-believe stories about castles and dragons. And of course, some do! But many fiction writers—James Howe, Walter Dean Myers, Angela Johnson, Gary Paulsen, and Christopher Paul Curtis, to name just a few—start by thinking about the urgent issues that shape kids' lives. These writers look at the cruelties and challenges that people are dealt, the issues that individuals and groups of kids face, and turn those into stories." You might gather some kids who need more support coming up with ideas, and remind them, "Sometimes writers think about which issues have factored into their own lives (fitting in, divorce, loss, and so on.) They can then brainstorm small moment episodes in which they've experienced one of those issues and use that small moment as grist for a story idea."

In a teaching share, you might remind students to apply the narrative skills they know to their collection of possible story scenes. For example, remind them that writers use the narrative craft they know to "show, not tell" as they write, using dialogue, detail, inner thinking, and action to craft the scene. By the end of the second day, your students will have generated four or five half-page-long story blurbs as well as a number of small scenes. For the share, you might say, "When choosing which story idea to develop, it's often helpful for writers to tell a couple of story contenders to others—a partner, someone at home—and for the writer and the listener to think about whether the story draws in the listener, whether there is a clear problem, whether there is rising tension." By the third session, you'll want writers to have a story idea in hand.

## Bend I, Session 3: Rehearsing How Stories Might Go, Using Planning Tools

By now, students will be ready to start rehearsing and planning more specifically. We don't recommend students make flowcharts or webs, because those do not reflect story structure. We also don't recommend they write timelines of their story plans, because that strategy leads them to generate too many scenes. The goal is two or three scenes at the most. Story mountains can do the same, sometimes. You might, then, want to teach students that writers often think of a story in terms of three major parts: in the first part, readers meet the characters and discover the setting, as well as hints of the problem; in the second part, the problem is developed and choices are made; and in the third part, change and resolution occurs. It's often helpful to have students do quick mini-sketches in boxes of the three parts of their story, in which they label the setting, the characters, and the action that is occurring. This work gives you a chance to quickly circulate, making sure kids are composing stories they'll be able to write. Storytelling the planned stories also works well, and revising those stories to make them more detailed, more specific, more "show, not tell" works also.

You may want to set a few constraints on writers to serve as helpful boundaries to draw students into the work of the unit. You can choose whatever constraints make sense to you, but we have found that these constraints work:

### Short Stories Work Best When . . .

- The characters are approximately the same age as the writer
- There are no more than two or three main characters (and very few others)
- None of the names used (or characters developed) are those of students in the class
- The stories can be told within two or three major scenes or small moments, at the most, each involving not more than approximately an hour of time.

Of course, that list is open to debate, and you will need to decide if these make sense for your classroom. Here is our rationale for each one. When characters are approximately the same age as the writer, they are drawn more realistically, and you avoid the possibility of students writing long, drawn-out stories about people getting married, having quintuplets, and doing other things that students likely have no personal experience with. When students focus on just two or three main characters, they are able to spend some time developing these characters so that they become interesting, realistic, three-dimensional characters, rather than flat ones who are a dime a dozen. By leaving out the names (and personas) of kids in the class, you avoid the risk of kids writing stories that hurt feelings or offend others. Finally, by limiting stories to just two or three major scenes, you encourage students to develop these with detail and meaning. Stories that go on endlessly are less likely to succeed.

### Bend I, Session 4: Writing Entries to Develop Plot, Setting, and Characters

You probably have heard that in the younger grades, students take time to develop their characters before launching into draft one. They write entries about the external features and the internal features of a character. They jot about the characters' hopes and fears. They write about how a character walks. They bring that character to life with her best friend.

Now that students are in middle school, you may suggest they do this preparatory writing to develop not only their characters, but also their plot and their setting. You might begin by saying, "Today I want to teach you that once writers have a story idea in mind, they often do some writing to develop aspects of a story's plot, setting, or characters." You might suggest students go back to a scene they may have written earlier, when trying out this story idea, and this time rewrite it with more developed characters or a more developed setting.

For example, if you originally had written this:

> Sierra painted after school. Chris was snickering about her in the hallway. She got up to move closer to hear what he was saying. "Look at Sierra! She can't find anyone to hang out with after school, so she paints bad flowers over and over again."

You could show students that you tried rewriting in ways that brought out the setting:

> Sierra painted in the art room after school. She heard Chris snickering out in the hallway. She got up to move closer and hear—so she stood by the sink, washing the brushes. Chris said, "Look at Sierra! She can't find anyone to hang out with after school, so she paints bad flowers over and over again." Sierra looked around the room, wondering if there was somewhere to go, to hide, anywhere other than the hallway where Chris stood with her friends.

You could say to students that you might rewrite that same episode to show that the art room is a safe place for Sierra:

> The quiet in the art room kept Sierra's mind focused on her painting, instead of thinking about the comments she'd heard Chris say from the hallway. Others worked near her, so she didn't feel alone.

Then again, instead of writing entries about the setting, a writer could write about the internal and external traits of the central character or write small scenes to bring out the personality of the main character by showing not only what she did, but how she did it. If I want to show Sierra being creative and true to herself, I might write:

> Sierra moved the paintbrush along the edge of the paper, making a bold green line outlining the vase of flowers. It was different—and she liked that.

The writer might consider the objects that help define the main character. For example, the writer might write a little scene showing the character opening her locker, shuffling past the . . . what? What is in there?

If the character is reaching into her locker to get something, what is that thing the character wants? The objects that the writer puts into that locker will reveal something about the character. You might remind students that they can reveal their character through objects this way, too.

## BEND II: DRAFTING WITH A STRONG PURPOSE AND REVISING IN DEEP, MEANINGFUL WAYS

In this bend, students will create a rough draft of their story while engaging in large-scale, on-the-go revision. They will tackle specific scenes with a focus on experimentation, trying them one way, then another, then another. You'll invite students to write and rewrite their scenes, each time with a different angle or purpose. In this way, you set students up to engage in more intentional, deep revision that requires revisiting larger swaths of text, rather than inserting just small changes into a single rough draft. A big goal of this bend is that students obtain a high writing volume, while writing, too, with intention and the ability to revise on the go.

You'll probably want students to begin by making themselves blank books with two to three pages for the beginning scene and the same for the next two scenes.

### Bend II, Session 1: Diving In: Drafting the "Problem Scene" First

Often, students begin drafting with energy and zeal, and while their first scene is developed (and sometimes overly developed), by the time they turn to the next scenes, their writing tank is low, and the result is anemic or shallow writing. It can help to teach students to draft their "problem scene" first. You could say, "Today I want to teach you that writers develop a sense of when they're ready to start drafting parts of a story. As important scenes crystallize in their imaginations, they are eager to get them on paper. Sometimes writers set themselves the task of drafting their 'problem scene' first—the one in which the character faces the central problem."

You'll want to leave maximum time for writing today, so that students get an entire two- to three-page scene written, fast and furious. Students' writing will be more coherent and, usually, more intense if it is written in a flash, with writers imagining the scene and dramatizing it in their mind's eye as they write to capture the drama on the page. In the link of the minilesson, then, you can invite students to start with either the first scene or the problem scene. You might convey these tips to them:

- In the first scene, the reader will expect an introduction to the main character, and to discover what she wants, to understand the character's motivation.

- In the problem scene, the character faces the central problem, and things get worse and worse. The protagonist really wants to win the prize, pressure is intense . . . and then, to make matters worse a crew of reporters shows up to capture the results (or her long-lost grandmother arrives from a cross-country trip, come to see the protagonist's victory).

Make sure that whatever scene students choose to write, they draw on all they learned from personal narrative writing. These are small moments. The Narrative Writing Checklist should be front and center.

You might, then, have students reread the pages on which they developed their seed idea, close their notebooks, and use their writing plan to draft the problem scene, writing fast and furiously. This enables students to outgrow previous bits of writing and bring their freshest ideas to the page.

## Bend II, Session 2: Walking in the Footsteps of Favorite Stories: Using Mentor Texts to Draft

You will find that once students have an idea for how their story will go and have written a scene, they will want to race ahead and write the *entire* story (all in a day!). This is a good time to raise the stakes by showing them texts that resemble those you hope they will write. You might say, "Today I want to remind you that writers often spend a bit of time studying some texts—ones that resemble the kind of thing they aim to write. Writers notice and jot lists of the moves these other writers have made, and then they try out similar moves in their own writing."

During your demo, you will then have an opportunity to highlight craft moves that you know will make your students' writing stronger. Scores of teachers remark that the best resources for them have been the student writing samples from the CD-ROM, included in the series *Units of Study in Opinion, Information, and Narrative Writing* (Heinemann, 2013). Or you might use some of your past students' writing, the entries from collecting, or mini-booklets from planning. Above all, be sure to use writing samples that represent different ability levels so that you are differentiating your instruction.

Whatever mentor texts you select, bear in mind that your students are writing very short stories. Try to find texts that are centered around just two or, at the most, three small moments (or episodes). If the texts you use as mentors race through too many events, your students will do so as well, and their stories will very likely become summaries rather than stories.

Then perhaps students will jot a list of the qualities of strong fictional writing. The list might go like this:

**Narrative Writing Checklist**

| | Grade 6 | NOT YET | STARTING TO | YES! |
|---|---|---|---|---|
| **Structure** | | | | |
| Overall | I wrote a story that has tension, resolution, realistic characters, and also conveys an idea, lesson, or theme. | ☐ | ☐ | ☐ |
| Lead | I wrote a beginning that not only set the plot/story in motion, but also hinted at the larger meaning the story would convey. It introduced the problem, set the stage for the lesson that would be learned, or showed how the character relates to the setting in a way that matters in the story. | ☐ | ☐ | ☐ |
| Transitions | I not only used transitional phrases and clauses to signal complicated changes in time, I also used them to alert my reader to changes in the setting, tone, mood, point of view, or the time in the story (such as *suddenly, unlike before, if only she had known*). | ☐ | ☐ | ☐ |
| Ending | I wrote an ending that connected to what the story is really about. I gave the reader a sense of closure by showing a new realization or insight, or a change in the character/narrator. I might have shown this through dialogue, action, inner thinking, or small actions the character takes. | ☐ | ☐ | ☐ |
| Organization | I used paragraphs purposefully, perhaps to show time and setting changes, new parts of the story, or to create suspense for readers. I created a logical, clear sequence of events. | ☐ | ☐ | ☐ |
| **Development** | | | | |
| Elaboration | I developed realistic characters, and developed the details, action, dialogue, and internal thinking that contribute to the deeper meaning of the story. | ☐ | ☐ | ☐ |
| Craft or Language | I developed some relationship between characters to show *why* they act and speak as they do. I told the internal, as well as the external story. | ☐ | ☐ | ☐ |
| | I wove together precise descriptions, figurative language, and some symbolism to help readers picture the setting and actions, and to bring forth meaning. | ☐ | ☐ | ☐ |
| | I used language that fit my story's meaning and context (for example, different characters use different kinds of language). | ☐ | ☐ | ☐ |
| **Conventions** | | | | |
| Spelling | I used resources to be sure the words in my writing are spelled correctly. | ☐ | ☐ | ☐ |
| Punctuation and Sentence Structure | I used punctuation such as dashes, parentheses, colons, and semicolons to help me include extra detail and explanation in some of my sentences. | ☐ | ☐ | ☐ |
| | I used commas and quotation marks or italics or other ways to make clear when characters are speaking. | ☐ | ☐ | ☐ |

## Qualities of a Strong Fictional Draft

- Setting establishes what kind of world the characters live in.
- Details pull readers in to the story.
- Conflict between or within characters shows us what's at stake in the story.
- Actions and dialogue reveal characters' traits, emotions, and motivations.
- Dialogue tags imply emotion with which a character speaks.

As you send students off to write, you could challenge them to return to their "problem scenes" and redraft these, incorporating some of the writing moves they noticed in the mentor texts. Students can lay the scenes they wrote during the last session alongside their revised versions, post–mentor text work. This before/after snapshot provides a concrete model for students and a reminder of the level of revision they will aim to maintain during the course of the entire bend.

During the mid-workshop teaching or share, you might suggest that students can read like writers any time they need inspiration. In particular, suggest that they can search for a place in a mentor text that stands out to them (because it moves them or makes them think or gives them goose bumps or brings the setting or characters to life), and they can then name *what, specifically*, the author is doing and then find other places in the text in which the author replicates that same move. Authors use craft moves to create particular effects; it is important that students can determine these purposes, rather than just learning the moves themselves, so that they continue to think intentionally about the craft they incorporate in their own stories.

### Bend II, Session 3: Writing (and Rewriting) Different Leads for Each Scene, Especially Opening Scenes

Having been immersed in the language and structure of published stories, students will now have the momentum to draft lots of leads, and to recognize that each one sets up a different version of the same story. You might say to writers, "Today I want to teach you that as writers draft the scenes of a story, they try out different leads—not just for the opening scene, but for *each* scene. Writers do this knowing that different leads can spur new thinking and help them develop the meaning of a story or the characters or the setting." By spotlighting the importance of experimenting with the lead of each scene, you'll remind writers that they have not one but two or three first images to pull the audience in—the beginning of each of their scenes.

You will probably want to hold many small-group conferences during this time so that you see—and push—more students to get off to a strong start. It is important that students launch into their scenes with a variety of craft moves—using dialogue, action, description of setting, internal thinking, conflict, and so on. Chances are that many students will need help incorporating back-information (so the story can stand on the shoulders of imagined previous events) into their storyline. Or you might pull out some leads of scenes from mentor texts your class knows well, such as *The Misfits*, to study the different ways scenes begin. Above all, you'll want to be sure that students understand the difference between storytelling and summarizing.

Expect that the day on which you teach students to try out different leads will become the day on which students settle on one lead and continue drafting their entire first scene! By the end of the day, you will probably find that half or two thirds of your class is already a page into the draft of the first scene. The problem is that very soon, each of these students will have invested so much energy into this first draft of the first scene that he will be gung ho to keep writing, rather than reflecting on the impact of the other leads. Therefore, you would be wise to give a mid-workshop teaching point that steers students to try different leads for their first scene—that is, to draw a line under all they have written and to start the scene again. This way, students will try several different "starts" or leads to their first (or second or third) scene and can then step back and choose the best one. Of course, you'll coach writers to lift the level of their work each time, so the next draft is vastly better than the first. Convey that the revision you expect—which you know students are capable of doing—is large scale. It involves writing version one, version two, and version three of the same scene. This will help writers grow exponentially.

### Bend II, Session 4: Considering Endings that Resolve Conflict in Realistic Ways

Oftentimes in student drafts, a character magically receives her fondest dream in the form of a solution that flies in out of nowhere, like Superman. The main character wants to win the award, to be invited to the party, to get back to normal with his best friend—and lo and behold, it happens!

In this session, you may decide to teach students to consider whether life always turns out that way. Do people always win the awards? Receive the wanted gift? Become the most popular person? Chances are, your students will realize right away that this isn't the case. Here, then, is your opportunity to teach them an important reality that fiction writers know well: when life doesn't turn out as we hoped, that's when the real inner action occurs. According to the standards, by sixth grade students should be able to "provide a conclusion that follows from the narrated experiences or events" (W.6.3e). By encouraging your students to rethink easy endings, you will not only teach them about writing-to-discover, but you will also teach them the valuable lesson that people grow through times of difficulty, that whenever a door closes, often there is a window somewhere that remains open.

You might, then, initiate this session by saying, "Today I want to teach you that writers consider various endings. They are cautious of fairy tale endings in which everything is solved perfectly. Instead, they ask themselves, 'How might this turn out in real life? What is realistic, yet also conveys what I want to teach about this particular issue?'" You might model going back to your demonstration writing from Bend I, Session 4 about the resolution or perpetuation of an issue. Encourage writers to consider the possibility that their message may have shifted through the process of drafting.

With your help, students will see that the solutions tend to be more an emotional realization than a big change in action. You could share, "You know, right now in my story the problem is solved because

Sierra and Chris have this heart-to-heart, and he swears never to put Sierra down again. But I'm thinking that may be too fairy tale-like. Maybe the story ends with Sierra just telling Chris what she is feeling, and Chris saying nothing. But the next day at school when someone outside the art room is making fun of her again, Chris says to cut it out."

A helpful small-group lesson might be to study the writing rubric or revisit students' goals as they finish drafting. This way, students see possible next steps for their writing as they finish their drafts. Coach students to make sure scenes are glued together with transitions; the plot unfolds with a variety of craft moves, such as alternating dialogue, inner thinking, and description; the beginning of the story orients the reader to the setting and the characters; the plot has a logical progression, and the like.

During a teaching share, you might remind students that in all narrative writing, writers focus their pieces not only by narrowing the time frame in which they write, but also by deciding on the meaning that they want to highlight across the story. They ask themselves, "What is this story really, *really* about? What do I want my reader to take away?" and then they craft every part of the story—the beginning, the middle, the end—to spotlight what it is they are especially trying to convey. A story about a boy learning to fit in will unfold very differently if it's angled to be about a boy overcoming the differences of his physical disability, versus a boy who is new to a school and doesn't have any friends yet. The final scene—the resolution—should convey what the author thinks the story is, at its heart, about.

## BEND III: REVISING AND EDITING WITH AN EYE TOWARD PUBLICATION

In this bend, students dive into their drafts to revise and edit. They will read their drafts through different lenses to focus their efforts on setting, dialogue, grammar, and punctuation.

### Bend III, Session 1: Developing a Sense of Time and Place

In this session, you teach students a lens they can use to reread and revise their writing. Because setting is so important in the books students are reading, we recommend you suggest students reread their drafts and think about what they can do to make better use of the setting. By the time students are in sixth grade, the books they are reading have settings that operate almost as a secondary character. The settings in books like *Hatchet*, *Nightjohn*, and *The Lightning Thief* convey mood and tone, contain symbols, and mirror the main character's emotional journey.

You might say something like, "Today I want to teach you that writers craft settings on purpose. They may make it thunder outside to show that a character is growing angry on the inside. They may make the scenery be sinister to foreshadow problems. Once writers know what they really want to say in a story, they return to their draft and revise the setting so that it helps to advance the larger meanings."

You might also teach students that writers sometimes use settings to show shifts in time. "It was getting dark when . . ." "The table was set before . . ."

## Bend III, Session 2: Using Dialogue as a Powerful Story Element

Chances are, your students will benefit from support with dialogue. Typically, middle school writers insert a lot of dialogue. They tend to think the goal is to include everything a character says (or thinks). You'll want to teach students to be more deliberate, including relevant dialogue as outlined by the CCSS (W.6.3). You could say, "Today I want to teach you that skilled writers use dialogue sparingly, intentionally. They may use dialogue to bring out the conflict in a story or to show a character's most revealing traits."

You might model this by showing a video clip of a popular (or formerly popular) television show that contains a banter of dialogue between characters. The conversation between Will Schuester and Sue Sylvester in *Glee* (a show that many of your students will likely know), for example, offers powerful mini-transcripts of mentor dialogue. These exaggerated characters speak in ways that reveal their most defining traits and extreme emotions.

While working with a small group of proficient writers, you could share that writers often create dialogue in which what characters say or do contradicts what they think or do—which serves to create more tension in a story. For instance, a character might be feeling nervous on the inside, but when he speaks, his voice is filled with confidence and strength. You might encourage students to role-play a conversation between characters, because drama can play up this dynamic.

## Bend III, Session 3: Revising

As students begin to shift from revision to editing, one topic they'll want to consider is paragraphing. You might launch a quick inquiry, sending students back to their mentor texts to figure out when and why authors generally insert new paragraphs in fiction. It won't take them long to figure out that paragraphs are used when the setting or time changes, when a new character speaks, or when the action or mood changes. Before students set out to type or copy their pieces, they can reexamine them through the lens of paragraphs.

You might say, "Today, writers, I want to teach you that it is important to also reconsider your paragraphs. Writers know that narrative paragraphs often mark important moments of change in a story. They are like a street sign for a reader. A new narrative paragraph indicates a change in setting or time, in action or in mood, or when a new character speaks." A helpful way to demonstrate this is by writing a narrative that is absent of paragraph indentations. Then, as a class, you can work together to reformat the text into multiple paragraphs. Alternatively, you could find a series of paragraphs from one of your mentor texts, retype it without indentations, and follow the same format, with your class working together to correct it.

## Bend III, Session 4: Using Punctuation while Editing for Clarity and Variety

By sixth grade, students will have knowledge of a growing number of punctuation marks—commas, semi-colons, dashes, ellipses, and the like—with which they will now experiment as they write. Chances are that they will often "use and confuse" many of these new marks (after all, many adults continue to confuse them, too!). You may want to study a mentor text for examples of these punctuation marks, explicitly naming each one you spot and also exploring its use(s) through inquiry, before you give students a go at using it themselves during the minilesson.

For instance, you might say, "I want to remind you about something you already know: writers have a variety of punctuation marks to use in their writing: commas, dashes, ellipses, oh my! As writers learn about these marks, it can help to study how mentor authors use them in their writing. Writers name how the mark is used in a sentence—what it's function is—and then experiment with using it in their own writing in those same ways."

Students will most likely juggle the names of multiple characters and the pronouns they substitute for their names across the story. But quickly, the overuse of pronouns can lead to a lack of clarity. As the draft progresses, rounds of *he*, *she*, *they*, and *them*, might be in quick rotation, with the reader left wondering, "Wait, what character is speaking? Who is he again?"

Also, encourage writers to edit for clarity around which characters are speaking or interacting, and with whom. You might suggest, "Today I want to teach you something writers play close attention to as they revise; writers make sure their readers don't get lost or confused with all the *he*, *she*, *it*, *they*, *them* words that float around a story! These words are called *pronouns*, and they act as substitutes for a character's name or for a group of people. But, writers, here's where you need to be careful! If you don't make sure these short words closely follow the character's name or the group of people they are replacing, your reader will get confused!"

If you find that your students struggle with grammar as they revise and edit, you might steer them toward helpful grammar lessons. Some that your students may find particularly helpful include Mary Ehrenworth and Vicki Vinton's *The Power of Grammar* (2005), Elisa Zonana and Chantal Francois's *Catching up on Conventions* (2009), Mignon Fogarty's *Grammar Girl's Quick and Dirty Tips for Better Writing* (2008) and her #1 ranked *Grammar Girl* podcast.

## BEND IV: PUBLISHING AND A CELEBRATION

As you enter this final bend, students will have had multiple chances to draft and revise, and to set and meet writing goals. Through it all, they will have honed their narrative writing skills and learned some important fiction craft moves along the way. They will have strong drafts that they feel proud of—ones they are ready to publish and share with the world. You have some choices to make about how to celebrate.

### Bend IV, Session 1: Preparing for Publication

At the conclusion of this session, you'll want to create opportunities for your writers to rethink their writing in light of the checklist and make final revisions based on that rethinking. They will also want to think about the form for publication. You may decide to invite students to publish their stories as illustrated books, in which case you can give some time now to study illustrated books and the role of the images in capturing the tone of a page (when the pages are abstract), in illustrating a pivotal moment, and in extending the text. Or you may invite writers to sort their stories into thematic short-story anthologies, which will then be available in the classroom for read-aloud and independent reading.

You might say, "Today I want to teach you something you probably already know: fiction writers, like all other writers, think carefully about how to publish their writing. Depending on the choices they make (publishing their work as short stories, anthologies, or podcasts, for example), they set final goals for themselves as writers."

Or you might say, "Today I want to teach you that writers seek help when they strive to meet publishing deadlines. They help each other with editing, copying, or typing, in other words, fancying up writing to get it ready for publication. They work within a community of writers to meet everyone's goals."

## Bend IV, Session 2: Giving Feedback and Holding a Celebration

This may be one of the last writing celebrations of the year! Make it a special one. Perhaps you will organize small groups of personal readings, in which four to six students read their stories to their peers. Of course, you might offer all writers center stage in the classroom, in which they read excerpts of their stories to the entire class or to an audience of a neighboring class. If the weather is nice, you might take a walk to a park for an outdoor reading series. Some teachers have been known to work with a local coffee shop, diner, or library and to host a reading series for a larger audience.

Alternatively, you might let your kids show off in a different way. Up until now, they've done a lot of writing and some deep revision. Students know a lot about how to come up with ideas for realistic fiction, how to rehearse and plan, and how to draft wisely and revise thoughtfully. You could give kids two or three class periods to do just this. You might lean on Colleen Cruz's *Independent Writing* (2004) and organize writing groups so that kids can support each other. These days will give you a chance to identify what your kids have become independent at—and they'll have an opportunity to show off their skills. Consider this final piece a kind of "on-demand" fiction narrative. Your students and you can put it next to your preassessment and revel in what they've learned.

You might say, "Today I want to teach you that writers welcome opportunities to show off their skills. They carry everything they can forward, so that each piece they write is more fluent and skillful than the one before. They sometimes take everything they know and put it to use right away, writing another very fast story, so that they put all their skills to use."

Whichever option feels right for you and your students, encourage your young community of writers to give feedback to each other, because feedback is a powerful tool that will help them grow and develop as writers. You might say, "Today I want to teach you that writers are thoughtful in the feedback they give other writers. Writers know that fellow writers appreciate hearing what especially worked!" This feedback could then be verbal or recorded on pieces of paper that become a written scroll of feedback the writer can take away.

# Persuasive Essays

## RATIONALE/INTRODUCTION

This unit on argument writing will likely be predominantly used in sixth grade and precede or follow the argument unit that is detailed in the full-length book, *The Literary Essay: From Character to Compare/Contrast*. However, if you have seventh-graders with no essay experience, they may benefit from doing this unit prior to the seventh-grade full-length book, *The Art of Argument: Research-Based Essays*. This unit does not assume that students enter it with strengths in writing thesis-driven essays. Both this unit and the sixth-grade literary essay unit take students on an ambitious, fast-paced journey into the land of source-based persuasive writing. So the timing of this unit is your decision entirely. It should not be your first unit of the year (we hope you rely on the sixth-grade unit, *Personal Narrative: Crafting Powerful Life Stories*, for that), but you can teach this unit at any other time within the year.

The title of this unit, "Persuasive Essays," reflects the fact that the unit supports the Common Core standards for argument. As part of a long tradition of helping students write persuasive essays, we have taken special care to meet all the CCSS for argumentation, which will give this unit a special flavor, making it slightly different from a traditional persuasive writing unit. Whatever the name, the unit aims to support your students in getting better at writing logical, compelling, and persuasive arguments about topics that feel relevant to them. Students will learn to harness their own expertise on a topic, to incorporate a bit of added research, and to tailor their arguments for specific audiences.

Your students are not short on opinions; they have opinions on music groups, on school policies, and on what is fair and unfair. Adolescents sometimes feel that the adults in their lives do not take them seriously. They believe they have opinions that could help their schools, their communities, but to adult ears their opinions sometimes come off as lists of demands or as complaining rants more than as thoughtful suggestions. The ability not just to have an opinion, but to support it clearly and persuasively is a powerful life skill. Entire industries are built around persuasion, convincing the public that *this* politician is the one to trust, or *this* car is the one to buy, or *this* cause is worth fighting for.

## A SUMMARY OF THE BENDS IN THE ROAD FOR THIS UNIT

**In Bend I (Developing a Plan for a Persuasive Essay)**, you will teach or remind students of the structure of an essay through essay "boot camp," a shared writing experience during which the class co-constructs a simple essay to quickly warm up for the work that goes into this kind of writing. From this point forward, students will choose an issue that matters to them and decide their stance on it. They will grow more ideas about the topic by writing entries in their notebooks, and they will learn the various parts and structure that make up an argument essay. Finally, they will spend some time developing a claim and supports.

**In Bend II (Drafting and Revising a Persuasive Essay)**, students will draft and then revise their essays as they learn ways to make these more persuasive and more powerful. You'll teach them that essayists shift between reasons and illustrative anecdotes, that they angle stories to make points, and that they pay special attention to how they begin and end their essays, introducing a counterargument and concluding by revisiting this counterargument and making a plea for an action plan. Students will learn, too, to study famous persuasive speeches, using these as models for how to revise their essays so that they are more convincing. This bend ends with students checking the work they've done on their essays against the Argument Writing Checklist, setting goals for what they can do better.

**In Bend III (Try it Again, with a Twist: Research and Persuasive Essays)**, you will set students up to choose a second topic from the list they generated in Bend I and to plan and write a second essay, this time with a focus on research. Students will learn how to develop and organize their new essay plan, weighing evidence and finding angled stories that best support their claims. They will put their energy into writing and revising with greater sophistication, considering their audience, word choice, and tone, and aiming especially to lift the level of their persuasiveness.

### Argument Writing Checklist

| | Grade 6 | NOT YET | STARTING TO | YES! | Grade 7 | NOT YET | STARTING TO | YES! |
|---|---|---|---|---|---|---|---|---|
| | **Structure** | | | | **Structure** | | | |
| **Overall** | I explained the topic/text and staked out a position that can be supported by a variety of trustworthy sources. Each part of my text helped build my argument, and led to a conclusion. | ☐ | ☐ | ☐ | I laid out a well-supported argument and made it clear that this argument is part of a bigger conversation about a topic/text. I acknowledged positions on the topic or text that might disagree with my own position, but I still showed why my position makes sense. | ☐ | ☐ | ☐ |
| **Lead** | I wrote an introduction to interest readers and help them understand and care about a topic or text. I thought backwards between the piece and the introduction to make sure that the introduction fit with the whole. | ☐ | ☐ | ☐ | I interested the reader in my argument and helped them to understand the backstory behind it. I gave the backstory in a way that got the reader ready to see my point. | ☐ | ☐ | ☐ |
| | Not only did I clearly state my claim, I also told my readers how my text would unfold. | ☐ | ☐ | ☐ | I made it clear to readers what my piece will argue and forecasted the parts of my argument. | ☐ | ☐ | ☐ |
| **Transitions** | I used transitions to help readers understand how the different parts of my piece fit together to explain and support my argument. | ☐ | ☐ | ☐ | I used transitions to link the parts of my argument. The transitions help the reader follow from part to part and make it clear when I am stating a claim or counterclaim, giving a reason, or offering or analyzing evidence. These transitions include terms such as *as the text states, this means, another reason, some people may say, but, nevertheless,* and *on the other hand.* | ☐ | ☐ | ☐ |
| | I used transitions to help connect claim(s), reasons, and evidence, and to imply relationships such as when material exemplifies, adds on to, is similar to, explains, is a result of, or contrasts. I use transitions such as *for instance, in addition, one reason, furthermore, according to, this evidence suggests,* and *thus we can say that.* | ☐ | ☐ | ☐ | | | | |

# GETTING READY

It would be wonderful if this unit could be taught at the same time as a unit in reading high-interest non-fiction texts, because if students will have access to articles, books, and digital texts on the topic or issue they select, they'll be able to incorporate more research into their argument essays. The third bend of this unit depends on students being able to do a bit of topic-based research. However, if that is not possible, you can also lop off that portion of the unit.

You will also want to decide at the outset, and after looking at their on-demand pieces, how much time to spend on each bend of the unit. If your students' on-demands lack the basic structure of a claim, some reasons that support the claim, and some evidence that supports the reasons, then you may choose to spend more time in Bends I and II, using Bend III as a source of small-group lessons for your stronger writers. The third bend focuses on bringing research into persuasive essays. This portion of the unit supports students moving beyond the basics of essay—the skinny five-paragraph essays—to do the more writerly work of convincing people through the strength of argument and the power of writing.

Notice, from the start, that we suggest you make a big deal of the publishing/celebration event that culminates the unit, perhaps by inviting your students to make an iMovie/YouTube clip/PSA. This way, they can be working toward authentic publishing goals throughout the unit.

# BEND I: DEVELOPING A PLAN FOR A PERSUASIVE ESSAY

Beginning this unit you have two goals: first, to engage and inspire your students to want to do the work ahead, and second, to get your class on the same page concerning what an essay is at its most basic level—structure. These goals can feel inconsistent because the structure of a basic essay is not the most engaging thing about this kind of writing, but you can achieve both goals with a little finessing.

## Bend I, Session 1: Reminding Students about Basic Essay Structures through "Boot Camp"

To kick off the unit, you might play a YouTube clip of a powerful argument, like a clip from the 2007 film, *The Great Debaters*, or from some school-appropriate YouTube rant. You might say, "When you argue for your point of view, you want to be heard. You want people to nod in understanding. This means that you have to have a careful balance of emotion—the heat of the argument—and logic—the brains behind it." But you will quickly want to shift and teach or remind students of the structure of an essay. If you lead a one- or two-day boot camp on writing essays, you can use that time to remind students who have written many essays about what they already know, while at the same time "whipping into shape" those students whose writing does not yet meet grade level expectations of essayists in sixth grade. (Know, of course, that with your eagle teacher's eye you will also in this time identify some of your small groups for differentiation.)

If you teach sixth grade and have already taught *The Literary Essay: From Character to Compare/Contrast*, you'll be familiar with the concept of a writing boot camp. Additionally, if your students grew up within the K–5 *Units of Study* series, they'll also be familiar with this. Essentially, what we refer to as a boot camp is a shared writing experience that allows you to model and help students practice the writing work that they will need for the unit ahead of them. Because it is highly guided, it serves a different purpose than your on-demand, which assesses what your students know. Your boot camp is not a time for assessment; rather, it is a time to get your class onto the same page by front-loading instruction.

To begin on Day One, you might then say something like, "Writers, today we are going to work on an essay together, to make sure that you have some of the basic essay moves down. So just for today, we are all going to work with the same argument: gossiping is the worst thing you can do to a friend." Of course, you could choose a different claim entirely. Just be sure to choose a claim that will resonate with your students.

Reveal chart paper on which you write the claim inside a box. While adding bullets under the box, you might say, "I'm going to think of reasons to support this claim. I think gossiping is the worst thing you can do to a friend because . . ." Pause for a minute and look up to the ceiling. ". . . because it spreads lies." Write "because it spreads lies" next to the first bullet. "Now it's your turn. Think of more reasons to support this opinion, this claim. To do this, what I do (and many writers do) is we say the claim to ourselves like this: 'Gossiping is the worst thing you can do to a friend because . . . A. Gossiping is the worst thing you can do to a friend because . . . B. And most of all, gossiping is the worst thing you can do to a friend because . . . C.' What will reasons B and C be?"

You will continue in this way through the course of your shared essay. Coach students to start their first body paragraph by restating the first reason for the claim ("One reason that gossiping is the worst thing you can do to a friend is that it spreads lies"), and then include transition language, such as "For example . . ." and then present evidence. After the evidence is included, the writer discusses why that evidence supports the topic sentence, before shifting into a second bit of evidence, which is handled in a similar fashion.

Once you have gone through the steps of one part of an essay together, you can ask your class to write the rest of the essay themselves, repeating the same main moves for the next two body paragraphs (actually each is probably more than one paragraph). At the end of your first day of essay boot camp, students will have produced a well-structured essay defending the claim that gossiping is the worst thing you can do to a friend.

### Bend I, Session 2: Choosing an Issue to Address and Developing Voice on That Issue

Your teaching point might be, "Today I want to teach you that persuasive essay writers often have a few issues that they care deeply about or that they think are important in the world. They think about these issues, and explore them through talk and writing, to find out what they really believe." During the workshop, writers might spend a couple of minutes generating possible topics and then freewriting thoughtful entries about those possible topics to try them on for size (and to let you glimpse the material the writers have to bring to bear on a topic). As students do that freewriting, keep in mind that a reasonable goal for sixth- and seventh-graders is that they can produce in one sitting (say, one class period) at least two pages in their notebooks. When one researcher studied SAT essays, he saw that you could accurately predict the grade a student received on his essay from looking at the length of it across the room.

## Bend I, Session 3: Writing Entries to Grow Ideas about the Issue

Your students will be ready to frame out their persuasive essays just as they did during boot camp, but we recommend that you rein them in, suggesting they take some time to grow the most insightful ideas and to gather some material before diving into their essays. Today's teaching point may be, "Today I want to teach you that instead of diving into drafting a plan for an essay, writers know that it pays off to spend time collecting materials and writing ideas to rethink the essay plan. Front-end work always saves time."

Then, in your teaching portion of the minilesson, you could share with students two different ways of collecting: by gathering detailed vignettes that pertain to their topic and by writing generalizations. You might convey that you already collected some Small Moment stories, some anecdotes, about your topic (don't bother to write these publicly), and then you can show them that you take any one of these vignettes and write "off from it," generating big ideas that come to mind. The important thing is that here, again, you freewrite entries in your notebook that help you consider the issue your essay will address. This is a terrific exercise for developing bigger, more sophisticated ideas about an issue, so your demonstration will set students up to do similar work. Students should be able to write two or three of these annotated moments during the workshop and will hopefully gain greater clarity about their thinking and their evidence as they do this.

## Bend I, Session 4: Developing an Image of an Argument Essay

In *Visible Learning* (2008), John Hattie points out that one of the best ways to accelerate students' progress is to provide them with crystal clear images of whatever it is they are aiming to do. In this session, you draw on Hattie's suggestion by reminding writers that it helps to study an example of the kind of writing they themselves aim to write, to get a clear image of strong work in that genre.

During the teaching component of your minilesson, you can show students an essay, giving them copies of it to annotate. They can then look for the essay's component parts, noticing things like the fact that the claim is supported by reasons, and the reasons by a variety of evidence. They should see, too, that the author sets up the evidence and then unpacks it with analysis and that each reason links to the one before it in a way that makes sense.

If you study one essay together, or part of one essay, students can study a second essay afterward or study drafts of essays to suggest what would have made these stronger. They may also begin the process of making a quick boxes-and-bullets plan of their own essay, using their work with the mentor texts as a guide.

## Bend I, Session 5: Rethinking a Claim and Supports

Today you can teach students to use all they know to draft several alternative boxes-and-bullets plans for an essay. You might say, "Essayists draft and revise their claims, trying to say what they mean exactly and playing with the wording of the claim so that it has 'punch.'" Students will need to hold on to what they learned in boot camp, remembering that there are predictable problems to essay plans. Sometimes writers write reasons to support a claim that are, in fact, restatements of one another. Sometimes they write reasons that are very unequal in weight, and sometimes they write reasons for which they actually have no evidence. The job, then, is to almost imagine how an essay would go, thinking through the predictable challenges and revising the essay plan on the go, based on that work.

As you model doing this work on your own claim, you might make a show of discovering that your initial claim, while fine, doesn't get at a statement that is more precisely true for you. Perhaps you'll begin with the claim that gossip is bad because it passes around untruths, and then move to arguing, "Gossip is the most hurtful thing you can do to a friend. It erodes trust, it makes people feel badly about themselves, and it creates insiders and outsiders."

## BEND II: DRAFTING AND REVISING A PERSUASIVE ESSAY

Students will spend Bend II drafting and revising their essays. You'll teach them several ways they can make their writing stronger and more persuasive. At the end of the bend, they'll have the chance to self-assess their writing with the Argument Writing Checklists.

### Bend II, Session 1: Getting In and Out of Illustrative Stories

It will only take students a day or two to draft their essays, and then they'll begin revising their drafts. As they write and revise, you can continue to teach them ways to make their drafts stronger, and they can apply this new knowledge to new body paragraphs or use it to revise paragraphs they have already drafted.

You might teach that at this stage of the writing process, writers often identify the need to shift from making a claim to including vignettes or Small Moment stories that illustrate a reason. One workable way to do this is simply to say, "For example . . ." and then begin providing evidence that might, for example, take the form of a mini-story. Here, you might share that it is helpful set up the context of the story first. While writing a paragraph about the harmful effects of gossip, for example, you might set up a story like this: "When I was in sixth grade I learned firsthand how devastating gossip could be. It all started with a lunch line and my hand-me-down sweater." Teach students that this context need be only a sentence or two at most.

During the mid-workshop teaching point or the share, you could point out that writers have ways to shift from telling an anecdote that illustrates their reason to analyzing the link between that anecdote and their reason. One way they unpack their information through this sort of analysis is by using a prompt. You might demonstrate how you do this with your essay, and then give students this list to try out in their own essays:

- This shows that . . . Therefore . . .
- This reveals . . . Consequently . . .
- This illuminates . . . which shows . . .
- This suggests . . . which means that . . .

### Bend II, Session 2: Angling Stories to Make Points

As students move through their first draft, you will want to teach them a few strategies that will help to improve the quality of their essays quickly. One important strategy is to study any instances when they told stories to make points and to ask, "Was the story angled to bring out the point?" Often this leads writers to rewrite sections, so that the parts of the stories related to the point are stretched out, so there is more internal thinking that highlights the point, and so the stories start and end in ways that also highlight the point. Students could work in partnerships to be sure the points they are making are clear to an audience, and if not, to help each other clarify these.

### Bend II, Session 3: Writing Introductions and Conclusions

Another way for students to revise in this first round of essays is to revisit and make more robust their introductions and conclusions. The Common Core Standards expect that students in sixth grade are able to introduce a topic clearly and to write concluding statements that follow from the rest of the essay. By seventh grade, they are expected to introduce counterargument in their introductions. Whether you are teaching this unit to sixth- or seventh-graders, chances are, the notion of counterargument has been raised, so take the opportunity to teach into it.

You might teach students that one way writers introduce and acknowledge counterarguments in an introduction is by suggesting that the issue under discussion is a complicated one. You might model this with your essay on gossip by acknowledging that it is a bit glib to simply say, "Don't gossip." Most people gossip. So your essay might begin this way: "Most people find themselves gossiping about their friends at one time or another. It is hard not to do. But all too often, gossip is used to be mean, to make ourselves feel better than others, or to exclude someone. We all should stop gossiping, because gossip is just one of the worst things you can do to a friend." Teach your students that by discussing what is complicated about the issue, you position yourself in a bigger conversation and position yourself to do thinking that has some complexity.

In your share, you might link the work students have learned to do in their introductions to their conclusions, by suggesting that writers know the importance of revisiting the content they raised in their introductions in their conclusions. Furthermore, you might convey that essayists often end with a conclusion that both names a counterargument and includes a call to action—a plea for what should change in the word based on the essay's assertions. This teaching addresses the Common Core's expectations for seventh-graders, while it is a step above what's expected of sixth-graders. However, if you teach sixth grade, you will probably find that your students are eager to tackle something more sophisticated in their endings. It's okay if they simply make gestures toward this but don't do it with finesse; they'll have time to practice this work again in later grades.

## Bend II, Session 4: Revising with Great Speeches in Mind

As another revision strategy, you might introduce the use of speeches as mentor texts, teaching students that essayists often try on some of the writerly moves that speech writers have made, to improve their own powers of persuasion. They might look at speeches by government leaders, by revolutionaries, or by ordinary people who have made extraordinary strides through oration. There are many powerful speeches in films, such as *The Great Debaters*. You might print out speeches made by significant, persuasive historical figures, such as President John F. Kennedy, Dr. Martin Luther King, Jr., Patrick Henry, and Sojourner Truth. By now, your students should know how to study a mentor text, annotate it, talk about it, name some of the writerly moves in it, and then try to duplicate some of them in their own work.

In small groups or conferences, you might either demonstrate how to mentor yourself to one of these authors, or you might do some guided writing with students, coauthoring some sections of their essays together, in the spirit of the mentor text you choose. This kind of guided writing is useful both for more reluctant writers and for strong writers, depending on the complexity of the mentor text.

For your share on this day, you might invite students to deliver their revised flash-drafts as speeches, in small groups, and give props to each other for particularly effective parts.

## Bend II, Session 5: Analyzing Essays against a Checklist

At the end of this bend, students should have time to assess their writing against some of the expectations you have for them. You'll teach them that to work toward making their best work even better, they can hold their writing up to the Argument Writing Checklist to identify areas of need and areas of success. Students can then look at their particular grade level expectations and assess the degree to which their essay has reached these, naming goals for themselves as they work.

### Argument Writing Checklist

| | Grade 6 | NOT YET | STARTING TO | YES! | Grade 7 | NOT YET | STARTING TO | YES! |
|---|---|---|---|---|---|---|---|---|
| | **Structure** | | | | **Structure** | | | |
| **Overall** | I explained the topic/text and staked out a position that can be supported by a variety of trustworthy sources. Each part of my text helped build my argument, and led to a conclusion. | ☐ | ☐ | ☐ | I laid out a well-supported argument and made it clear that this argument is part of a bigger conversation about a topic/text. I acknowledged positions on the topic or text that might disagree with my own position, but I still showed why my position makes sense. | ☐ | ☐ | ☐ |
| **Lead** | I wrote an introduction to interest readers and help them understand and care about a topic or text. I thought backwards between the piece and the introduction to make sure that the introduction fit with the whole. | ☐ | ☐ | ☐ | I interested the reader in my argument and helped them to understand the backstory behind it. I gave the backstory in a way that got the reader ready to see my point. | ☐ | ☐ | ☐ |
| | Not only did I clearly state my claim, I also told my readers how my text would unfold. | ☐ | ☐ | ☐ | I made it clear to readers what my piece will argue and forecasted the parts of my argument. | ☐ | ☐ | ☐ |
| **Transitions** | I used transitions to help readers understand how the different parts of my piece fit together to explain and support my argument. | ☐ | ☐ | ☐ | I used transitions to link the parts of my argument. The transitions help the reader follow from part to part and make it clear when I am stating a claim or counterclaim, giving a reason, or offering or analyzing evidence. These transitions include terms such as *as the text states, this means, another reason, some people may say, but, nevertheless,* and *on the other hand.* | ☐ | ☐ | ☐ |
| | I used transitions to help connect claim(s), reasons, and evidence, and to imply relationships such as when material exemplifies, adds on to, is similar to, explains, is a result of, or contrasts. I use transitions such as *for instance, in addition, one reason, furthermore, according to, this evidence suggests,* and *thus we can say that.* | ☐ | ☐ | ☐ | | | | |

# BEND III: TRY IT AGAIN, WITH A TWIST: RESEARCH AND PERSUASIVE ESSAYS

In this bend you have two goals. One is to set your students up to write another round of essays so they have a chance both to synthesize the skills they have learned and to add in some new moves. The other goal is to set students up to begin to incorporate some research into their writing and to discover the ways this evidence can change their course of thinking. To reach Standard W.1c, students should be able to support their claims using credible sources. Before you begin, retrieve those text sets you gathered at the start of the unit (see the Getting Ready section for more guidance), and then say something like, "Writers, you have grown as essayists. You have learned how to be more persuasive in your writing. Now you are going to have a chance to repeat the skills you have learned, but with a twist. This time when you are working on your claims, your structure, and your evidence, you are going to find some research to back these up."

## Bend III, Session 1: Using Past Learning to Get a Running Start on a New Piece

To begin, you might invite students to revisit the list of issues they generated at the beginning of the unit and choose a second issue that would make a good persuasive topic. Then, they could write entries off of that issue, drawing on all they've learned about writing arguments. As your teaching point, you could remind students that once essayists understand how to get started in their writing, they carry that knowledge with them forever, putting it to use whenever they start a new piece.

Don't be surprised if a great many of your students begin to draft little mini flash-draft essays. However, if very few or no students are adopting any of the moves of the previous two bends, be sure to stop them immediately and challenge them to think through their plan for writing that day, using the instructional charts, checklists, and notes to help them focus their goals. This work fits into Norman Webb's Depth of Knowledge chart level three, which outlines the task of applying what one has learned previously to a new project.

## Bend III, Session 2: Using Texts to Shape Ideas about Topics

Once your students have selected their new topic, you'll be ready to introduce text sets to them, which they will use to push their thinking and writing about a topic. Today your teaching point might be that essayists use their reading and rereading of informational texts to shape their ideas.

You will want to give students options of the text sets you have available—leadership, friendship, kindness, conflict, community, and so on—and the chance to choose which text set/idea best fits their thinking so far. After students have spent time reading the texts, you might model how to connect what you read to the topic/issue you are thinking about.

The point of this research is not necessarily for students to find an article about the specific topic they are writing about, but instead to factor what they've learned in the article into their own thoughts and ideas. You might find it helpful to prompt students with "How do the texts you're reading inform the thinking in your writing?" "How does this idea connect to that one?" "How does the idea of [leadership] in this article inform your thinking about [bullying] in your writing?" This will challenge students to do more than just lift a quote from an article to support a fact they are making. It will instead spur deeper, more critical thinking.

## Bend III, Session 3: Developing and Organizing Essays

Once students have generated some writing, you'll want to set them up to think through the structure for their essays, either by jotting down a quick outline or by holding their structure in their heads, if they're able, as they get started writing. You might say, "Today I want to teach you that as essayists get ready to write, they spend a little time quickly organizing their information, either through a written or mental outline, so that it can make best use of the facts, thoughts, and stories they want to include, and then they get started writing." It's important that you channel students to collect some of the angled stories they intend to tell, in addition to their own ideas and the research they will add along the way.

Many teachers charge their students with the task of developing a system—using note cards or sections of their notebooks or folders—for collecting and logically organizing this information (CCSS W.6.1a, 7.1a). You could instead choose a system for your class, but eventually you will want your students to think through the purpose for a research system and to consider their own preferences.

As your mid-workshop teaching you might remind students that writers think about which evidence best supports their thinking and then make decisions about how and where they will include this in their writing. You might have students rank their evidence, from most to least compelling. Evaluating evidence in this way positions students to reach Standard W.1b, which describes the work of supporting claims "with clear reasons and relevant evidence, using credible sources and demonstrating an understanding of the topic or text."

## Bend III, Session 4: Drafting and Revising for Greater Sophistication

In this session you'll shine a spotlight on the craft moves that mentor authors make, teaching your students to study these and incorporate similar moves into their own writing. You might say something like, "Today I want to teach you that essayists study and read other (often more seasoned) essayists to get inspiration and ideas for their own writing. In particular, they focus on the craft moves these other authors make, thinking how they, too, might incorporate these moves into their own writing."

Since your class has had multiple opportunities to write essays by this point, your goal is to push students to use what they already know makes for powerful writing. Therefore, your lesson should be less concerned with "how to draft" or "how to revise" and more with "What makes a beautifully written essay?" Students will study the mentor texts they read in Bend II, looking for what each author has done in her writing to make it beautiful, powerful, and persuasive. Among other things, students might notice the use of repetition or question and answer or anecdotes that have been selected with the particular intent to move an audience.

### Bend III, Session 5: Creating Convincing Writing by Knowing Your Audience

On this day you'll convey to students that in any persuasive writing, it is important to know your audience. Of course, to know their audience, students will first need to decide who this audience will be. By deciding this, they can then think about language and examples they can emphasize or tailor to fit their intended audience. Your teaching point might sound something like this: "Today I want to teach you something that seasoned essayists know well: knowing your audience is key to writing persuasively. Specifically, essayists ask themselves, 'Who am I trying to persuade?' and 'What piece of evidence will most convince this audience?' Then they think about particular language and examples they can emphasize or tailor to fit their intended audience." Students should then spend some time rethinking their overall argument and tailoring it to fit their intended audience (CCSS W.4).

You might foster some of this work through partnerships during the share on this day, encouraging students to role-play so that one partner takes up the position of the audience member, asking clarifying or interest-based questions and pondering the topic to help the writer consider new possible points, angles, or ways to convince the audience of the ideas in the essay.

### Bend III, Session 6: Concentrating on Word Choice and Tone to Lift the Level of an Essay

In this session, you will teach students that when essayists write, they aim to write with powerful and precise vocabulary. This focus on word choice will do wonders to lift the level of students' essays, which often lack efficacy due to vague and generic language. An emphasis on word choice also positions students to meet the CCSS expectation that they will use vocabulary to clarify the relationship among claims and reasons (W.1.c).

You might say to your students, "Today I want to teach you that essayists know that the words they use matter. Essayists make careful and precise word choices to convey their exact ideas and to be as convincing as possible. As they search for the perfect word, they try out a few and zero in on the one they think is the best choice." As students get started, you might reinforce their work with a tip: "As you write, remember to stop now and then to talk back to your word choices. When they feel too vague, try to find the best words from your vocabulary to use in your essay, even asking a partner to help if need be."

One of the things that makes persuasive writing so much fun to read is that it has a strong tone. During the share, you might stay to students, "In addition to word choice, persuasive writers consider the tone they are trying to strike in an essay, knowing they can engage readers this way and also convey meaning. Writers consider the various tones they have noticed in mentor texts—tones of humor, urgency, empathy—and try these out in sections of their essays."

You'll want to encourage students to experiment—to write a designated section of their essay in a few different tones, using a mentor text for help, to see which one works best to capture the argument and the audience's attention. Considering the effect of one's writing is an important aspect of the CCSS, which expects that students in sixth grade write texts in appropriate ways for different purposes and audiences. Meanwhile, you might also emphasize what it means to write in a formal tone, because the Standards also expect that students "establish and maintain a formal style" (W.1d) when they write persuasively.

As students start to finish their pieces, have them edit with a partner, using everything they know about conventions to make their writing as accurate as possible.

## Bend III, Session 7: Celebration and Publication

Of course, essays are not meant to be read only by the writer. They are meant to be out in the world, persuading people. To this end, you will want to end your unit on persuasive essays with a celebration in which you share your students' written texts with an audience. You might invite another class to your room to listen to students' essays, or you could welcome students' family members.

You might consider translating students' writing into a medium that can reach a wider audience, such as digital movie making. You can use video cameras if you have access to them, but digital movies can also be made using students' cell phone or tablet cameras. You may want to use a program such as iMovie, Final Cut Pro, or Voice Thread for students to produce their videos. If access to technology is limited, another option is to do an analog version by creating storyboards for an imagined movie (although, of course, creating an actual film would be much better).

If you opt for this technological route of celebration, you might invite your students to study a few iMovies, videos of persuasive speeches, and PSAs and name the moves they see—both in the written scripts and in the images and sounds used. Great examples include the "Pep Talk" video by Kid President and eleven-year-old Birke Baehr's TEDx video called "What's Wrong with Our Food System." There are also a multitude of "It Gets Better" videos, additional Kid President speeches, and other PSAs readily available online. You might spend a day or so letting students plan their movies, writing out a quick outline for how these will go, drafting a voiceover script for the narrator, collecting images and songs online to use, and so on. When students are ready to produce their clips, you will want them to work in groups or partnerships. At the very least they will need a camera person unless they are solely using images, and then they could produce their clip themselves.

This work may take a couple of class periods—and will go much faster if students work on their projects outside of school or in a technology class. As a celebration, perhaps invite parents and guardians in to see round table presentations of the class's videos, post them on a class or school website, make a YouTube channel for your class, or post them on your school's video display so that students walking into the school can hear these powerful ideas, and they can be seen by more than just the people in your classroom.

# SOME POSSIBLE TEXTS TO SUPPORT RESEARCH 🖫

## Community

- http://www.washington.edu/admin/hr/benefits/publications/carelink/tipsheets/community.pdf (short article on importance of community and how to be a part of it—aimed at adults)
- http://education.cu-portland.edu/blog/creating-a-bully-free-school-national-bullying-prevention-month/ (building a bullying-free community)
- http://www.wikihow.com/Help-Make-Your-School-Bully%E2%80%90Proof (another on how to build a bully-free community)
- http://www.youtube.com/watch?v=g-w6H2rs3FU (video on bully-free community)
- http://www.citizing.org/data/pdfs/sso/SSOIssueBrief_RoleOfCommunity.pdf (high Lexile, but it's a student commentary on the role of community in education)

## Leadership

- http://www.cafanet.com/LinkClick.aspx?fileticket=qwswE8roe74%3D&tabid=96 (chapter about the importance of leadership)
- http://www.aboutleaders.com/bid/169732/Kids-Leadership-and-a-Community-Experience (article for kids on components of leadership)
- http://www.life123.com/parenting/young-children/good-leadership-skills/ethical-leadership.shtml (article on the importance of teaching ethical leadership to students—short)
- http://money.cnn.com/2008/11/11/news/companies/secretsofsuccess_gladwell.fortune/ (Malcolm Gladwell interview—skewed toward a business angle, but an adept student could apply it to any situation)
- http://www.ted.com/talks/stanley_mcchrystal.html (TED talk video on how to lead)
- http://www.time.com/time/magazine/article/0,9171,1821659,00.html (high Lexile, but could be great for some; article on Nelson Mandela's eight principals of leadership)

## Kindness

- http://www.scholastic.com/parents/resources/article/social-emotional-skills/kindness-counts (low Lexile level)
- http://parenting.kaboose.com/behavior/kindness.html (article on how to teach kids kindness)
- http://everydaymiracles.hubpages.com/hub/Kindness-Can (importance of kindness article)
- http://www.livescience.com/25816-kindness-makes-kids-happier.html (article that may have some convincing evidence for kids to be kind)
- http://www.heartlight.org/articles/200808/20080802_humankindness.html (Cold War example of kindness making a difference)

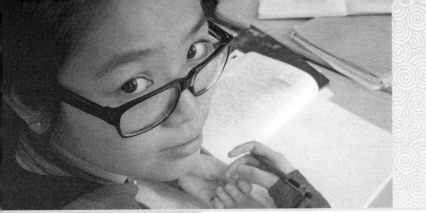

# Memoir

*Writing to Reflect on Experience and
Suggest Thematic Connections*

## RATIONALE/INTRODUCTION

At the Teachers College Reading and Writing Project we have discovered the power of this unit to dramatically alter the quality of students' writing, all the while tapping into their motivation to write about topics that are especially personal. Start by clarifying for yourself (so you can for your writers) the difference between personal narrative writing and memoir. In the former, writers write true stories and revise them as they bring out the story shape that is nascent in them, and as they think "What's this story really about?" they then bring that idea forward in the story. When working on memoir, writers are more apt to start with some big, important ideas that they want to explore and to communicate—something that says to the world, "This is who I am." The idea comes first, and then writers collect small moments around the idea, bringing out themes through a variety of narrative and expository techniques. You won't say to students, "This is how your memoir should be structured." Instead, you will ask them to draw on all they know about forwarding meaning through both storytelling and exposition and to weave these two together to craft a text that is utterly *them*. For this reason you do not say that memoir belongs to the narrative genre or the opinion/argument genre, but rather that it is a hybrid of the two.

Therefore, this unit, like its fifth-grade counterpart, brings together the art of narrative and expository writing and supports both the first and third Common Core State Standards in writing. Read memoirs by Joan Didion and David Sedaris, and you'll see the blending of ideas and vignettes that lead the writer and reader on a compelling journey of introspection and insight. Memoir demands much in the way of structure, expecting writers to skillfully move between conveying events and experiences and explication. This means that you will ask students to draw upon and extend their prior narrative skills to engage the reader, sequence events, and convey meaning through storytelling, and to draw on their expository work to skillfully unpack and couch those stories in idea-based writing. To do this, students must learn to analyze their life experiences to determine what it is they most want to convey about themselves and their lives and make purposeful craft and structure choices to do so. This is the same work they are asked to do in the Common Core Reading Standard 2—in particular, discerning central ideas, lessons, and themes (RL 7.2)—as well as Standards 7.4, 7.5, and 7.6, where students consider the effect of author's craft and structure on meaning.

This genre lays the groundwork for future high-stakes writing that students will be asked to do for application essays, job applications, and in writing prompts on exams, such as the SAT and the ACT. Beyond test scores, data, and standards, though, adolescents need opportunities to write to make sense of their lives. Seventh and eighth grade is a time of emotional roller coasters and shifting perspectives. Teachers who devote time each year to a study of memoir writing always report that they hear their students' voices like never before, and they find that the tone of their classroom—and often that of the school—shifts in dramatic ways. This kind of writing is not just an expectation within national standards, it is a tool that quite literally changes lives.

## A SUMMARY OF THE BENDS IN THE ROAD FOR THIS UNIT

**In Bend I (Collecting: Writing "Big" and "Small" to Discover Meaningful Topics, Patterns, and Questions to Explore in Memoir)**, students will collect entries and freewriting in their notebooks as they work toward developing a seed idea. They will learn that memoirists balance narrative and expository skills by writing both large and small about a topic. That is, students will learn to move between reliving small moments from their lives and writing to capture those experiences on the page and stepping back to analyze the themes and lessons those moments convey.

**In Bend II (Drawing on the Qualities of Good Writing to Write—and Revise—Shapely Memoir)**, you will challenge students to put together all they have learned in the unit thus far (and from prior narrative writing units) to turn their entries into memoirs. As part of this, students will learn strategies for conveying something important about themselves through the events they describe; they will learn how to examine mentor texts through the lens of structure, determining which structure(s) will best work to bring out their intended meaning; and they will go through the process of flash-drafting, revising, and editing, all the while aiming to do this with purpose.

**In Bend III (Writing a Second Memoir, with a Focus on Bringing Out Meaning)**, students will quickly select a second idea to turn into a memoir, forgoing the collecting strategies to instead launch into drafting, revising, and editing. They will focus especially on bringing out meaning, drawing on strategies they've already learned as well as new ones you'll teach them (or remind them of from prior years). This bend emphasizes revision in bigger ways; as part of this, students will revisit some of the work they did earlier in the unit, now with increased sophistication.

**In Bend IV (Publishing and Celebrating)**, students will join you in determining a plan for publication and celebration. They will then spend a day making final edits and revisions, paying particular attention to how their words sound when read aloud.

## GETTING READY

One of the hallmarks of this unit, and arguably one of the most exciting parts, is that you won't say to your students, "This is how a memoir goes. Now write one." Instead, you will open their eyes to the varied and complex structures that we refer to as memoir and ask students to make decisions, based on the stories they have to tell and the themes they want to convey, and to pick a structure that matches their intentions. This means that it will be unbelievably important for you to expose students to a variety of *different* structures— to show them that a memoir can look like a story with just a bit of exposition or like a five-paragraph essay.

The fifth-grade memoir unit (*Shaping Texts: From Essay and Narrative to Memoir*) uses "Quietly Struggling," an essay-like memoir by Kelly Boland Hohne as a mentor text. You might decide to show your students this piece or to go in search of another. Then too, you'll want pieces of writing that feel more story-like, more narrative, and yet clearly convey a message to readers with varied amounts of expository writing. Ralph Fletcher's memoir, *Marshfield Dreams*, is full of chapters worth studying, as is Jean Little's *Little by Little*. We also recommend the anthology *When I Was Your Age: Original Stories about Growing Up*, edited by Amy Ehrlich, passages from *Knots in My Yo-Yo String*, by Jerry Spinelli, *Going Where I'm Coming From*, edited by Anne Mazer, as well as excerpts (selected for appropriate content) from *Persepolis*, by Marjane Satrapi (a graphic novel), *Fist, Stick, Knife, Gun*, by Geoffrey Canada, and *Long Way Gone*, by Ishmael Beah. You might want to invite students to study pieces that illustrate how writers construct texts that defy easy labels. "Eleven," by Sandra Cisneros, from *Woman Hollering Creek and Other Stories* could be in that folder—and don't worry if students have studied it before. We also recommend "Not Enough Emilys," by Jean Little, from *Hey, World, Here I Am* and "My Grandmother's Hair," by Cynthia Rylant.

A note about difficulty: be sure that you include texts that are calibrated to the level at which each reader can read with over 96% fluency, accuracy, and comprehension. It is far more challenging to study a text as a *writer*, mining it for writerly craft moves worth trying ourselves. Therefore, while you want to ensure that students are surrounded by texts that are rich and worth studying, you might also consider whether or not they feel like the kinds of memoirs students can mentor themselves to. Some of these mentor lessons will be taught explicitly, in minilessons and conferences, and some of the lessons will be implicit, gleaned as children study texts that sound like the ones they will be writing. Even just one dearly loved and closely studied text can infuse a writing workshop with new energy and lots of opportunities for new learning. You will want to read a few memoirs aloud and to pull your students close to study one or two with tremendous detail.

## BEND I: COLLECTING: WRITING "BIG" AND "SMALL" TO DISCOVER MEANINGFUL TOPICS, PATTERNS, AND QUESTIONS TO EXPLORE IN MEMOIR

This first bend gives students the chance to reflect and write about their lives, bringing together all they know about narrative writing and expository writing, into a hybrid genre we call *memoir*.

### Bend I, Session 1: Drawing on Known Strategies to Collect and Develop Small-Moment Story Ideas

In the first bend of this unit, you will teach students to use their notebooks to research their lives, collecting both entries and idea-based writing. They will learn that writers write both "big" and "small," writing about large ideas and theories and then zooming in to write about one time when that idea was true. Then too, your emphasis will be on helping students to write a lot and to move through the writing process with a sense of independence and repertoire. If you began the year with *Personal Narrative: Crafting Powerful Life Stories*, then students' notebooks are likely already teeming with entries.

You'll begin by channeling students to write small moments again, this time emphasizing the importance of writing about moments that will yield larger insights. You might say, "Today I want to teach you that writers often begin by writing lots and lots of anecdotes—Small Moment stories—that capture the tensions in their lives, that show pivotal points and life themes. If they feel stuck for ideas, writers rely on what they already know. One way to do this is by listing out the strategies they've learned for collecting small moments (first times, last times, important people, places, things, issues) in a notebook and then using one of them to quickly develop new topics to write about." A lesson like this sends a clear message to students: "You know something about this kind of writing. Let's use it."

You'll also want to be clear about your expectations for volume. By seventh and eighth grade, students should easily fill several pages of a notebook in one sitting. You might consider using the mid-workshop teaching on this first day as an opportunity to support velocity. "Miranda is already onto page 2," you might say to the class. "Who else has come close to filling a page with writing?" Then a few minutes later, "Remember, collecting is a time to try out *different* Small Moment stories. If you're finding yourself drafting the entire story of one moment, force yourself to move on to a different entry. You can draw a line under what you've done or turn the page and start anew. You can always return to that first story, but you'll want to have lots and lots of material to choose from for your memoir."

### Bend I, Session 2: Writing to Find Depth in Already Uncovered Ideas: Exploring the Unknown in the Known

Once students have collected several anecdotes and vignettes, you'll want to teach them to look back over these to investigate patterns, or themes. During the connection, you might convey to them that as writers, they are ever on the lookout for emotions that keep recurring, as well as objects or relationships that preoccupy them. Then teach them that when collecting for a memoir, writers don't just write to come up with new story ideas. They write to find depth in the ideas they've already uncovered. Sometimes they do this by exploring the unknown in a topic or idea, writing to investigate questions like "What don't I know about what I know?" and "Where's the mystery in this topic or idea?"

As with all new strategies, it will be important for you to model what this looks like. You might begin by revisiting the entry you wrote yesterday and explaining to students that instead of writing about one small seed idea, this time you will try to write about the big topics of your life. Then do this by drawing on the day's strategy, asking, "Where's the mystery in this topic or idea?"

During this day's mid-workshop, you might want to draw students' attention to the fact that writing big often gives us ideas for writing small. That is, if I've written to explore the mystery in a small moment and realized that it is really about the pressure I put on myself, then I might ask myself, "What other times in my life fit with this same theme? Are there other moments where I've put a lot of pressure on myself?" Point out to students that writers can return to writing small by writing to capture the new, small moment ideas they generate. Model seesawing between storytelling and exposition—and encourage your students to do so as well.

As a share, or perhaps another session, you might teach students another generating strategy. You might refer to strategies that students have used before, such as gathering ideas around cogent issues that matter to them—issues relating to what's right and wrong, what's difficult, what's fair and unfair, or what people should or shouldn't do.

## Bend I, Session 3: Using Mentors to Inspire Stories Worth Telling

Perhaps the best way to show your writers what it looks like to address topics that matter in the form of a well-crafted memoir is by reading aloud a few published memoirs—ones you've selected because they tackle important topics, letting the reader in on truths that matter to—and reveal something about—their authors. First, invite your students to let the writing wash over them, and then in the silence afterward, to write what they need to write—not about the texts themselves, but about their own ideas and lives, letting the texts act as inspiration to lead them toward their own truths, their own voices. The importance of this can't be overemphasized. Of all the qualities of good writing, the one that matters the most may be that elusive quality writers refer to as *voice*. A person writes with voice when she allows the imprint of her personality to come through in her writing.

As writers kick off these first few days of inspired writing, it's important to note that the work directly supports the expectation of the third Common Core anchor standard, "Write narratives to develop real or imagined experiences or events using effective technique, relevant descriptive details, and well-structured event sequences." You may want to offer your writers reminders of what it means to write with elaboration and focus, and how to experiment with foreshadowing and recollection to bring out meaning. Point of view, too, will be key, here, because your writers are the "characters" in their texts and will want to orient the reader to their thoughts, beliefs, and experiences (CCSS W.3a).

By the end of the third or fourth session, students should have plenty of entries from which to choose a memoir topic, or seed idea. Teach them to reread their writing in search of a theme, issue, topic, or moment that stands out to them. The raw materials that comprise each of their seeds will be different, and you'll want to let students know that this is how it should be. Some of them will have chosen a single moment coupled with a larger idea to become their first memoir. Other writers may be working in the reverse order—having identified an issue or theme their memoir will be about (and perhaps some freewriting they did about that topic). In the end, their drafts will be a mixture of this large and small writing.

For homework on this night, you might ask students to box off all notebook entries that relate to their seed idea, reread these, and write long. Then you could quickly demonstrate in the share how you take your topic—the pressure you put on yourself—and use thought prompts to push your thinking further and to develop more concrete examples to support your idea. We recommend sending students home with a copy of prompts that they too can use to write long. For instance, consider the "Prompts to Push Our Thinking" chart in Session 1 of *Writing About Reading*:

## Prompts to Push Our Thinking

I used to think . . .
But now I am realizing . . .

My ideas about . . . are complicated.
On the one hand I think . . . On the other hand, I think . . .

Some people think . . .
But I believe . . .

When I first . . . , I thought . . .
But now when I . . . , I realize that really . . .

## BEND II: DRAWING ON THE QUALITIES OF GOOD WRITING TO WRITE—AND REVISE—SHAPELY MEMOIR

Now that students have had a chance to generate ideas and entries in their notebooks, you'll move them into the work of turning their raw materials into a first draft—and meanwhile, revising, goal-setting, and editing to make this first memoir as good as it can be. Throughout this bend, you will highlight the importance of structure and what it means to reveal something about yourself through the genre of memoir.

### Bend II, Session 1: Focusing a Story on You, Not the Events

As students develop their seed ideas, it will be crucial for them to ask themselves, "What is it I really want to say?" You'll want to remind them that because they are writing memoir, their draft will not be about events alone. Instead, it will be about the person who experienced the events; as such, it should convey something meaningful about that person. Your goal today will be to help students clarify the larger points they hope to convey in their memoirs. You might say, "Today I want to teach you that writers focus a memoir not on events, but on themselves, asking questions like, 'What am I trying to say about myself in this piece?' and 'What do I want my readers to know about me?' Once a writer has begun to determine what he is trying to say, he can aim to write in ways that highlight that meaning."

It will be important to show students what this looks like by revising one or more of your stories to show something about yourself. As you model, think aloud about what you hope to show, and voice over the narrative techniques you might draw on to do this. For instance, if you want your memoir that tells the story of a basketball game to illustrate the pressure you put on yourself to perform well, you might show students how you add a bit of internal thinking and detail to the moment you prepare for your foul shot. "Everyone's watching. You can't afford to miss this," you might whisper to yourself as you wipe your sweaty palm on your mesh shorts. Alternatively, you might seize the opportunity for reading–writing connections and ask students to study the ways other writers have revealed important things about themselves, mulling over how anything from description to figurative language can deepen a writer's understanding of the experiences she has chosen to record on the page.

## Bend II, Session 2: Using Mentor Texts to Adjust Structure

Because students have responsibility for imagining a way to structure their memoir (among other writing decisions), you will want to spend a day on the task of reading memoirs with a special attentiveness to structure. Suggest that students can use mentor texts, both student exemplars and published texts, to notice the kinds of decisions these authors made and to then imagine the structures their own texts might take. You might say, "Today I want to teach you that memoirists structure their texts in a variety of ways. One way to decide how your own piece will go is to study the structure choices other authors have made, paying attention to how those choices suit their topics, convey their intended meaning, and help them connect with their audience." Then show students how you note the differences in a few structures (perhaps boxing out the parts that resemble narratives versus those that resemble essays), decide which structure best suits your topic and intentions, and then make a writing plan for yourself. In this way, you position students to address the Common Core Anchor Standard 4, "Produce clear and coherent writing in which the development, organization, and style are appropriate to task, purpose, and audience."

You'll want to have a few carefully prepared pieces for today's lesson, spotlighting two to three different structures. We recommend showing students one that is written as expository, one that is a narrative with reflective sections, and perhaps another that goes back and forth between exposition and storytelling throughout. Students will need some time to study these memoirs and to annotate what they notice, so plan to give them the first half of the workshop to simply be memoir readers. Then, in the mid-workshop teaching, call for students' attention and channel them to switch gears by deciding on a structure that matches their writing intentions and then making a plan that realizes that vision. Consider letting students know that writers often have to grow into a structure. That is, just because a student has collected two stories about her father so far does not mean she is bound to writing a memoir with two stories embedded in it. Instead, she might gather more stories about her father in preparation for drafting a memoir that reads more like an essay, or expand on one particularly poignant story and cut another.

In your share you might extend the teaching, suggesting that a memoirist needs to ask questions like, "Will the piece contain one focused narrative? Two stories held together by reflection? Will there be a clearly stated idea, or will the story suggest a theme?" Sometimes young writers find it helpful to take a few minutes to make a storyboard before drafting the memoir—showing in each box which anecdote they'll tell and where the bits of reflective writing will be.

**Bend II, Session 3: Flash-Drafting**

Finally, the day to put it all together has arrived! Today students will draft their memoirs. We recommend you convey a clear vision for how the workshop will go today so that students are set up for success. For instance, you might say, "Writers, today is the day when I get out of the way and let you write. I am sending you off with pockets full of tips and strategies for writing long and strong, culled from years of doing this work. Yesterday you read published memoirs, thought deeply about how your own memoirs would go, and created plans. Today I'll give you a moment to reread those plans, remind yourself of what you plan to create, and then send you off to draft, using everything you know about narrative and argument writing. Your first draft might not be perfect (first drafts never are), but it will be a start. Tomorrow you'll take those drafts and begin revising." With that, you'll rally students to draft their memoirs from start to finish. This day is as much about supporting students' independence as it is about getting them to begin drafting, so give them the space to make their own decisions and find their own way (while offering less confident students the support they need to get going).

**Bend II, Sessions 4 and 5: Revising for Structure on the Run**

One of the reasons we ask students to flash-draft is so we can then ask them to revise in large-scale ways. We've found that students are far more willing to rework a piece of writing that was done in one sitting than one that was created painstakingly across several days. Today and tomorrow you will want to teach students to revise by redrafting—quite literally taking the piece that they wrote, setting it aside, and rewriting it from beginning to end. You'll want to study carefully what your students created and balance what you find with your own goals for this unit. Then, decide what you'll teach and go for it! Here are a few revision lessons we've found to be particularly effective for seventh- and eighth-graders:

- If your writers need coaching on getting started with their revisions, you might teach them to read with beginnings and endings in mind. Your teaching point might be, "Writers know that beginnings set the tone for their memoir, and endings leave readers with final thoughts. Today I want to teach you that writers reread these parts with questions in mind. When rereading their introductions, memoirists often ask, 'Did I create a context and point of view for my reader? Have I introduced a narrator and/or character?' When looking at endings, they often ask, 'Have I reflected on the experiences and events in this memoir for my reader?' After asking these questions, writers make a plan for how they'll do these things more effectively and redraft their memoirs from start to finish." Many writers will find that the first drafting process helped them clarify in their minds why an anecdote is so important and what idea it is really showing. Then they can go back and insert reflection at the beginning of the piece. Or they can try waiting until the end and putting reflection there.

- If students need support bringing forward a clear message, you might teach, "Writers know that details in a memoir can say something about the kind of person they are, the kind of life they lead. As writers, you can reread your pieces asking, 'What have I conveyed about myself and my experiences to my reader?' Oftentimes, you will find that you want to change that message slightly and use this opportunity to redraft."

- If your students are ready to consider the finer details of their memoirs, you might teach them to use symbolism to convey meaning. Writers can often take a tiny detail from their lives—often something very ordinary—and let that one detail represent the whole big message of their memoir. Teach students that "writers often find that an object becomes symbolic as they write about it. When this happens, they choose to give that object meaning and mention it more than once in the story. This lets readers know that the object has meaning, too." (This addresses CCSS L.5: "Demonstrate understanding of figurative language, word relationships, and nuances in word relationships.")

### Narrative Writing Checklist

| | Grade 7 | NOT YET | STARTING TO | YES! | Grade 8 | NOT YET | STARTING TO | YES! |
|---|---|---|---|---|---|---|---|---|
| | **Structure** | | | | **Structure** | | | |
| **Overall** | I created a narrative that has realistic characters, tension, and change; and that not only conveys, but also develops an idea, lesson, or theme. | ☐ | ☐ | ☐ | I not only created a narrative with well-developed characters who change, I used the story to comment on a social issue, teach a lesson, and/or develop a point of view. | ☐ | ☐ | ☐ |
| **Lead** | I wrote a beginning that not only sets the story in motion, it also grounds it in a place or situation. It included details that will later be important to the story. These details might point to the central issue or conflict, show how story elements connect, or hint at key character traits. | ☐ | ☐ | ☐ | In establishing the situation and place, I hinted at a bigger context for the story (revealing issues that have been brewing, showing how the setting affects the character, contextualizing a time in history, and/or developing one out of many points of view). | ☐ | ☐ | ☐ |
| **Transitions** | I used transitional phrases and clauses to connect what happened to why it happened (*If he hadn't . . . he might not have, because of, although, little did she know that*). | ☐ | ☐ | ☐ | I used transitional phrases and clauses, grammatical structures (for example, paragraphing, descriptive phrases, and clauses) and text structures (such as chapter divisions and extended italics) to alert my reader to changes in the setting, the mood, the point of view, or the time in the story. | ☐ | ☐ | ☐ |
| **Ending** | I gave the reader a sense of closure by showing clearly how the character or place has changed or the problem has been resolved. If there wasn't resolution, I gave details to leave the reader thinking about a central idea or theme. | ☐ | ☐ | ☐ | I gave the reader a sense of closure by revealing character change(s) that followed from events in the story, or perhaps a resolution. If there wasn't resolution, I wrote to convey how the events of the story affected the characters, and to circle back to a central idea, issue, or theme. | ☐ | ☐ | ☐ |
| **Organization** | I used a traditional—or slightly modified—story structure (rising action, conflict, falling action) to best bring out the meaning of my story and reach my audience. | ☐ | ☐ | ☐ | I modified a traditional story structure, dealing with time in purposeful ways, to best suit my genre, bring out the meaning of my story, and reach my audience. | ☐ | ☐ | ☐ |

## Bend II, Session 6: Setting Goals for Revision Using Checklists and Partners

During this bend, you'll want to teach students that writers set new goals, revisit old goals, and work on becoming more adept writers. To do this, you can refer students back to both the Narrative and Argument Writing Checklists. Students have used these checklists before and will simply need to be reminded to reread their pieces asking, "Which goals have I met? Which goals am I starting to meet? Which goals have I not yet worked toward?" Partners can also be helpful tools for reflection, especially when you teach students to talk to each other about their intentions: how they want to develop their memoir, what structure and craft they'll use, and the revision work they still have to do. This practice not only pushes students to defend and thereby reflect on their plan for the piece, but it also supports the first Common Core speaking and listening standard, to "engage effectively in a range of collaborative discussions (one-on-one, in groups, and teacher led) with diverse partners on grade 7[8] topics, texts, issues, building on others' ideas and expressing their own clearly."

If you are angling this unit to solidify your students' independence and commitment to the writing process, then today's minilesson might teach how good writing partners are actually good writing teachers. In other words, partners confer with one another. Teach students that a good writing teacher looks backward to look forward. He might ask questions about previous work and how it turned out, why a writer is trying certain things, and what plans the writer has for what she will do next. You might want to hold a conference with one student in front of the class, giving the rest of the class the opportunity to observe and take notes on the kinds of questions you pose. Help students to generate a chart and point out that they can ask themselves the same questions they ask other writers. For example, just as a writing teacher might ask them about the last thing they tried to do in their piece and how that worked out, they can ask themselves to reflect on the same question, studying a piece for insight into where they might go next.

### Bend II, Session 7: Editing

You will probably want to give students one final day to work on their first memoirs, though they will not publish these. In Bend III you will take

**Argument Writing Checklist**

|  | Grade 7 | NOT YET | STARTING TO | YES! | Grade 8 | NOT YET | STARTING TO | YES! |
|---|---|---|---|---|---|---|---|---|
|  | **Structure** | | | | **Structure** | | | |
| **Overall** | I laid out a well-supported argument and made it clear that this argument is part of a bigger conversation about a topic/text. I acknowledged positions on the topic or text that might disagree with my own position, but I still showed why my position makes sense. | ☐ | ☐ | ☐ | I laid out an argument about a topic/text and made it clear why my particular argument is important and valid. I stayed fair to those who might disagree with me by describing how my position is one of several and making it clear where my position stands in relation to others. | ☐ | ☐ | ☐ |
| **Lead** | I interested the reader in my argument and helped them to understand the backstory behind it. I gave the backstory in a way that got the reader ready to see my point. | ☐ | ☐ | ☐ | After hooking the reader, I provided specific context for my own as well as another position(s), introduced my position, and oriented readers to the overall line of argument I planned to develop. | ☐ | ☐ | ☐ |
|  | I made it clear to readers what my piece will argue and forecasted the parts of my argument. | ☐ | ☐ | ☐ | | | | |
| **Transitions** | I used transitions to link the parts of my argument. The transitions help the reader follow from part to part and make it clear when I am stating a claim or counterclaim, giving a reason, or offering or analyzing evidence. These transitions include terms such as *as the text states, this means, another reason, some people may say, but, nevertheless,* and *on the other hand.* | ☐ | ☐ | ☐ | I used transitions to lead the reader across parts of the text and to help the reader note how parts of the text relate back to earlier parts. I used phrases such as *now some argue, while this may be true, it is also the case that, despite this, as stated earlier, taken as a whole, this is significant because, the evidence points to,* and *by doing so . . .* | ☐ | ☐ | ☐ |
| **Ending** | In my conclusion, I reinforced and built on the main point(s) in a way that makes the entire text a cohesive whole. The conclusion may reiterate how the support for my claim outweighed the counterclaim(s), restate the main points, respond to them, or highlight their significance. | ☐ | ☐ | ☐ | In the conclusion, I described the significance of my argument for stakeholders, or offered additional insights, implications, questions, or challenges. | ☐ | ☐ | ☐ |

students through the writing process one more time, and to have the time to do that, we recommend that you do not ask your students to publish at the end of Bend II. Instead, let them know that you are preserving their energy for one more round of writing, after which they will have the opportunity to choose their best memoir (either the one written in Bends I and II or the one written in Bend III) for publication.

Today, give your students the opportunity to give their writing one last read-through. There are hundreds of editing strategies you might choose to teach; you will want to highlight ones that suit your class. You might say, "Today I want to teach you that writers spend time editing their work before considering it finished. There are many methods to choose from. It is up to each writer to decide for himself what the most effective strategy is. I will remind you of a few editing strategies you have learned before and then send you off to do as many of them as you see fit." On a chart, you can then list the editing strategies you've taught or ones you know students have learned in the past. These might include:

1. Reread looking for words that seem "off." When you find a word you think you've misspelled, you can try to spell it correctly in the margin of your paper, consult a dictionary or other resource, or ask a friend.

2. Writing partners can help you to spot mistakes you might otherwise pass by. Writers often ask a friend or partner to read over their piece, looking for mistakes.

3. When looking for spelling mistakes, many writers find it helpful to read their writing backward—starting from the end and looking at each word carefully until they reach the beginning. This helps them see each word the way they wrote it, not the way they <u>meant</u> to write it.

## BEND III: WRITING A SECOND MEMOIR, WITH A FOCUS ON BRINGING OUT MEANING

After celebrating the work students did in Bend I and Bend II, get ready to rally their energy for another round of writing. We don't recommend going back to the very beginning of the process—having students spend days collecting again—but instead count on the fact that they have plenty of raw material in their notebooks and need only the opportunity to do something with it. During this bend, you'll suggest that students draw on all they now know about writing memoir and that they apply their efforts to upping the ante, aiming see more, do more, and especially to bring out the meaning in this second piece of writing.

### Bend III, Session 1: Beginning a Second Memoir

Today you will invite students to return to their notebooks, look for a new topic to write about, plan, rehearse, and draft anew! Your teaching point might be, "Like any good writer, your notebooks are teeming with stories to be told! Before we end this unit, I want to give you the opportunity to try out one more memoir—one that is different than the one you just finished. Right now, will you open up your notebook and box out another idea for a memoir?"

Again and again, we've found that if we don't make a big deal of this process, students won't either! Assume they have idea upon idea to write about, and they'll live up to the challenge. For those that are stuck, you can plan to hold a small-group conference in the meeting area following the minilesson. For the others, continue on. "Take a moment and share your idea with your partner. Are you deciding between two? Have you decided the structure you might try this time?" As students talk to each other, make sure that you hang the list of memoir structures they uncovered in Bend II. Then call students back together and show them how to quickly rehearse for and then begin drafting their new memoirs. "Today I want to teach you that writing needn't be a big deal. Writers have thousands of ideas hiding in their notebooks and often reach in, select one that stirs them, spend a moment thinking about how the piece will be structured, and then get right to drafting! It's as easy as that!"

You'll want to make a big deal over students who are doing this work expeditiously. Praise them openly and often, calling on others to follow their lead. Remind your writers that first drafts needn't be perfect. They are called *first drafts* for good reason.

### Bend III, Session 2: Tinkering with Structure

On the second day of this bend, you'll want to move right on to the work of revision. Remind writers that there's a special sort of reading writers do when they read their own writing to plan for revision. Rather than skimming it as if they've seen the draft a hundred times, they examine the draft in all its particulars, allowing the page to teach them how to write. In addition, they read the draft noting the component sections, asking, "How is this draft almost but not quite structured?" Then they make revisions to bring forth the intended structures.

You may find that you need to confer with individuals or small groups of students who don't yet have a firm grasp on structure. What you'll want to convey to these kids is that they are, in fact, merely revisiting structures they have studied and written within in the past. You might even draw on old charts from narrative and essay writing units that students will recall, to serve as reminders.

### Bend III, Session 3: Elaborating to Bring Out the Most Important Part of a Memoir

At this point, you'll probably want to teach students how to revisit and elaborate on the most significant parts of their draft. There are any number of strategies and craft moves you could share with them today. You might, for example, teach them that memoirists include telling details to convey their thoughts and feelings. You'll certainly want to show students how to emphasize the parts of their story that illuminate the central idea or theme. One significant craft move writers use to illuminate theme is the use of refrains. You can teach your students to reread their writing for powerful lines that are worth highlighting and to then figure out where to repeat those lines throughout the piece to make the most essential ideas stand out. Using a metaphor or comparison also adds beauty to memoir and can provide a means of capturing an idea or feeling that is too big or complicated for words. A recurring image dropped with purpose throughout a narrative can reveal the implicit truth that lies within the piece. The repeated image of Great Grandmother planting teeth as a way of showing new beginnings in *Marshfield Dreams* supports Fletcher's message that it's important to move on, but to also hold on in our hearts to the meaningful things and people we sometimes leave behind. If you teach metaphor, you'll want to emphasize that the task isn't to tack on a comparison, but rather to find a strong metaphorical image that emerges from the writing that already exists. This work is highlighted in Common Core Language Standard 5, which calls on students to "demonstrate understanding of figurative language, word relationships, and nuances in word meanings."

Of course, you won't be able to teach all of this in one day. If many of these craft moves are familiar to your students (which they will be if they have grown up writing in the *Units of Study* series), then you might teach a repertoire lesson like you did for editing. In this instance, you'd say something like, "Writers know that revision is not one-size-fits-all. Not every writer's piece needs the same thing. Instead, writers think back over everything they've learned about revision and ask, 'Which strategy or technique will help to make my memoir the best it can be? What will I do first? Next?'" Then show students how to recall a list of revision strategies, identify a few things your writing needs, and then get started with your revision.

## Bend III, Session 4: Experimenting with Structure to Evoke Meaning

Now that your students have given some time and thought to structure, you might teach them that writers sometimes experiment with structure to illuminate their underlying theme. "Today I want to teach you that memoirists often play with structure, trying to find the one that best conveys their intended meaning." Then you could model thinking through several options and rehearsing a few out loud.

For example, you could introduce the notion of a journey structure that starts with an anecdote in which you, the writer, are on the cusp of learning something big, and then ends with an anecdote that shows the completion of an emotional journey or a journey of thought through a marked change.

Next, you might show students how to create a circular structure, which begins and ends with a repeated image, scene, or line. While you won't want to overwhelm students with too many structures, especially ones they have not identified and talked about before, you do want to model a willingness to play with your memoir in ways that attempt to highlight its true meaning.

During your share, you might spotlight the importance of revising for clear transitions: from moment to moment and from moment to reflection and back. The Common Core highlights the importance of students' use of words that help "to convey sequence and signal shifts from one time frame or setting to the other." Words such as *previously*, *prior*, and *earlier*, for example, might signal a flashback; *meanwhile, at the same time*, and *simultaneously* might help a writer transition to inner thinking in the moment; *later, after*, and *I now realize* indicate movement forward in time, perhaps even up to the present moment of writing. Paying attention to transitions will reinforce any temporal structure (journey, circular, or otherwise) that students attempt, while also adding a feeling of cohesion to their writing.

## Bend III, Session 5: Creating a Blend of Dialogue, Thinking, and Action to Revise for Meaning

Another way students can revise (and elaborate) is by incorporating more than one small moment into their piece or by angling the same small moment to show more than one idea or emotion—of one or more people. Memoirs tend to center on moments of complicated emotions. You might present this strategy in this way: "Today I want to remind you that memoirists often tackle complicated emotions in their pieces. One way they revise to bring these out is through careful weaving of dialogue, thinking, and actions."

To model this, you might say, "Listen to this last scene in *Marshfield Dreams* when friends share memories of Ralph as he lies in his makeshift grave."

"He was a good friend," Andy began, then stopped. I lay on the pine needles, eyes shut, smelling the mix of the piney smell and the gooey, rotting earth underneath. I waited for Andy to continue, but he didn't say anything. Then he whispered: "He was the brother I never had."

Then point out that in this passage, Ralph Fletcher doesn't have to tell the reader that his buddies are feeling sad about saying good-bye to their friend. He shows us through the small but heartrending actions and words of Andy suddenly stopping, mid-speech, only able to whisper his true feelings.

For today's share, you might continue this work by asking students to read their memoir drafts interpretively—to practice a kind of critical literacy on themselves. They might ask themselves, "Whose voices have I included in my storytelling? Whose have I not?" Of course, they do not have access to other people's inner thinking about these key moments, but in their own account they can include questions about others' reactions, or they can speculate about other people's feelings. For example, a student writing about the time a boy held her hand on a school trip when they were sitting on the bus together, might ask herself, "What was he thinking? Why was he doing this? Had he always liked me and never said anything? Was he just being mean and setting me up to be dumped?" Teach students that they can flesh out the other people in their memoir, if only through pausing to consider what these others *might* have been thinking or feeling.

### Bend III, Session 6: Revising Endings with Help from Mentor Texts

As you near the end of this bend, you might want to touch upon strategies for endings by inviting students to study mentor texts, noticing how writers reflect upon their experiences and provide closure. The Common Core State Standards highlight the importance for students to "provide a conclusion that follows from and reflects on the narrated experiences or events." To this end, you might suggest that memoirists try out several endings. "Today I want to teach you that writers look at the endings used by mentor authors and steal ideas for their own piece." Some of Jerry Spinelli's memoirs in *Knots in My Yo-Yo String*, for instance, end with reflection from a current perspective. Others hint at what happens next for the writer—which story will be next. Others end with a sort of cliffhanger, leaving it unclear whether the writer had learned his lesson or it would be repeated.

## BEND IV: PUBLISHING AND CELEBRATING

In this final bend, students will make plans for the celebration that completes this unit as writers share their memoirs with an audience. Before the celebration occurs, they will take time to make the final edits and revision to their work, making the effort to convey their ideas in just the right way.

### Bend IV, Session 1: Making Celebration Plans: Organizing Classroom Anthologies

Katherine Bomer has often called for more emphasis on celebration as a significant part of the writing process. For example, she has suggested that students might write their memoirs in large print and then wallpaper corridors and ceilings as installation pieces. In this way, their words become both enlarged (to symbolize their meaning) and pieces of art. This is an apt tribute to the soul-searching that students have done over the course of this unit, and is also an unusual way to celebrate. Many of our schools have chosen this as an option, with great success. Another option is to invite students to rehearse reading their pieces out loud, then record them for a kind of *This American Life* podcast. Students could sort their pieces by theme and publish them in a few anthologies. If you choose this option, you might say, "As we think forward, as a class, about our plans for publication, I want to teach you that classes of writers often decide to publish their memoirs in thematic anthologies. This means we may want to start imagining the themes of those anthologies and whose memoirs will go in which. We could also publish some anthologies by subject or by era. That is, we might have one anthology called 'Learning to Be Strong: Tough Girl Memoirs' and another called 'Pets and Our Lives' and another called 'Before We Were Six.'"

Students could then sort their memoirs by topic, deciding on which categories will best capture the themes they've touched on and the stories they've told. As part of this conversation—or perhaps later, during the share—they might consider where to feature their work. Perhaps they'll choose to hang it in different places around the school, so there are writing boards for pieces about families in one location, ones for pieces that include pets and animals in another location, and so forth. Invite your students into the celebration decisions!

## Bend IV, Session 2: Making Final Revisions before Publishing

Before your students publish, you will probably find it useful to teach final editing strategies. One that is especially helpful to any writer finalizing a piece is to listen to the sound of the words on the page. You might say, "Today I want to teach you that when writers prepare their writing for publication, it helps to read it out loud to hear the sound of each word and the rhythm of the sentences. Truman Capote, a writer known for his impeccable style of prose, wrote, 'To me, the greatest pleasure of writing is the inner music the words make.' The sound of our words is powerful. Writers communicate with readers by choosing words that convey not only the content but also the mood, the tone, and the feelings that they want to convey." You could then model for students how you read your own piece aloud, making changes in spelling, punctuation, and word choice to adjust the sound and rhythm of your writing.

## Bend IV, Session 3: Celebrating the Journey of Memoir Writing

Finally, you will invite students to publish! They have worked hard to dig deep, finding moments that matter, ones that reveal something essential about themselves to then craft into shapely memoirs. They have revised, edited, drafted anew, and pushed themselves through the process to think thematically, to bring out meaning. You will want to give them a celebration that recognizes this journey of thought. Whether you select Katherine Bomer's suggestion, choose to showcase a class anthology, or celebrate in a more performance-based way—perhaps with students' family members or with students from other classrooms—be sure that the celebration feels as significant as your students' writing.

# Historical Fiction
## *Weaving Together Fact and Fiction*

## RATIONALE/INTRODUCTION

This unit of study is not a beginner unit. It's highly engaging and challenging. If your students have experience with narrative writing, this unit will certainly help them hone and extend those skills. There are three possible ways to approach this unit. First, you might choose to teach this unit in collaboration with students' instruction in social studies or history. Students would first spend several weeks researching a time period in social studies and then would bring their knowledge to their work in this unit. Another option would be to teach this unit alongside a reading unit on historical fiction and informational reading about history. A third option is to teach this as an isolated writing unit, in which case you could either allow students to choose time periods about which they have some prior knowledge, or you could support their work by engaging them in a class study of a time period of your choosing.

This unit particularly addresses Common Core Writing Standard 3, the narrative writing standard, including its substandards. The standards for narrative writing are particularly high, and your students will need to draw upon and extend their prior narrative skills to engage the reader, provide an organizational structure that sequences events, develop characters, and provide closure. In this unit, we ask students to do even more: we ask them to focus on pivotal moments in the characters' lives and to apply the same close reading strategies to their own narratives that they do to reading literature (Reading Standard 2 in particular: discerning central ideas, lessons, and themes). In some sessions, students are channeled to compose snippets of informational writing, so this unit also supports work toward Writing Standard 2.

If possible, we encourage you to teach historical fiction as a collaborative social studies unit, one in which students are immersed in research about a time period for at least a week before they begin to develop their own stories. Doing so will further strengthen students' reading and writing skills, plus add an air of authenticity to their stories. In this scenario, students would ideally have access to a variety of research materials. In social studies, students might study photographs and pictures of artifacts from various time periods, and of course they will need access to books or online resources where they can research everything from the art to the clothing to the technology and weapons of the time period. Then too, they'll want to study the major historical conflicts, including the events and people who had an impact during the period.

For many teachers, this unit offers a nice parallel to a reading unit on historical fiction and information texts. If your students are reading historical fiction and informational texts as well as writing them, you can teach them to read with an awareness of the craft moves an author has made and to then try some of those craft moves in their own writing. For example, students might note that an author has inserted historical objects, clothing, and inventions into a historical fiction text, so some may decide to do the same in their writing. Then too, readers can be taught to notice moments when they have strong emotional responses to their books and to study what the author has done to make those moments matter. During writing, students can try to create their own such moments. By partnering this writing unit with the same genre in their reading work, you can provide students with many opportunities to carry strengths from one discipline to another, and you also provide an avenue for students to learn some of the historical details that will enrich their texts.

To write accurately about a time period, students of course need to know the time period—and they need to know it well, so they can bring to their stories not simply a knowledge of major events and historical figures, but of everyday life, including details about place, dress, food, jobs, and so forth. So if you decide to teach this as an isolated writing unit, it will be critical that students choose a time period they have studied in the past, either independently or as a group. We also urge you to give students at least a day to recall, review, and record details of that time period. If your students don't have a ton of knowledge about a time period, you could decide to channel the entire class toward a time period of your choosing. Then, you can immerse your students in the details of this time period to support their writing.

However you choose to approach the unit, we do suggest that students produce some informational writing while working on their pieces. It seems fitting, after all, that if they will be reading some informational texts to ground them in their time period, they take the opportunity to mentor themselves with these texts just as with the narratives you or they are reading. Many of your students, then, will compose historical fiction narratives that contain prefaces or endnotes that supply historical context to their stories. You may even have a few students that go further and choose to independently compose an essay or informational book to go alongside their narrative. Picture the nonfiction books that go with the American Girl series or the preface to a book like *Freedom Summer* by Deborah Wiles, and you'll have an idea of mentor texts for pairing information writing with historical fiction.

As you think about what your goals will be for the unit, think also about how you can help your students care about the unit. It is always important to launch a unit by rallying students around the big work that they'll be doing. Historical fiction films and television shows might engage your students quickly in this genre. You might say, "Think of some of the biggest blockbuster movies of the past few years: *300*, *Gladiator*, even *Titanic* was just rereleased. We love historical fiction because it describes the action, suspense, and even love stories that connect all of us across time and culture. In this unit, you will have a chance to author texts like these yourselves. You will walk in the footsteps of a redcoat just before the Boston Massacre or a young boy sold into slavery, and have the opportunity to tell their stories, through their eyes."

## A SUMMARY OF THE BENDS IN THE ROAD OF THIS UNIT

**In Bend I (Collecting Ideas for Historical Fiction: Finding Stories that Are Both Personal and Historical)**, you will teach students to generate possible story ideas while drawing upon students' past experience generating ideas for fiction stories. The important thing to keep in mind is that fiction writers don't begin by actually writing their stories. Far from it! They instead begin by rehearsing, which involves thinking about a lot of possible story ideas, generating possible stories, and then, once one has the gist of an idea, thinking deeply about the setting, the characters, and the various ways the story might spin out. When writing a story set in a historical era, the need for rehearsal is amplified. You will teach students that the question a historical fiction writer needs to ask is not just "What would make a great story?" but also "What might have occurred within that time and place that might make a great story?"

**In Bend II (Developing the Story: Shaping Historically True Characters and Plots)**, you will teach students how to develop their characters by placing them inside everyday scenes. As students put their characters at the dinner table or on their way to school, they will attend to the time period and historical setting, while also considering and revealing their characters' struggles and motivations. You will then teach students to draft multiple possible plans for their stories, checking and revising for historical accuracy before they settle upon the piece they will draft.

**In Bend III (Drafting and Revising: Crafting a Compelling Historical Fiction Story)**, you will teach students how to draft from inside the world of their stories. From there, you will teach them to revise with an eye on craft and historical accuracy. Among other things, students will attend to conclusions and historical settings and try their hand at symbolism and prefaces or endnotes.

**In Bend IV (Editing and Publishing: Preparing a Historical Fiction Story for Readers)**, you will help students put the finishing touches on their pieces. This bend—and the unit—will end with a culminating celebration of their stories and of your and their hard work!

## GETTING READY

To write convincing historical fiction, the writer must know about the historical period in which her story will be set. However, the extent to which you prioritize historical research in this unit will be your choice entirely. If you wish to focus more exclusively on narrative writing, you can ask students to write about time periods with which they are already familiar, or you can teach students enough information about a particular time period to enable them to write successfully in this genre.

If you decide that you want to use the invitation to write historical fiction as a way to lure students into an active, invested study of a particular time and place in history, you might structure your social studies curriculum work (or collaborate with a social studies teacher who is willing to do so) so that your class focuses on one particular historical era, and then ask that your students set their historical fiction stories within that era. Students will be more engaged and alert learners of history if they know they'll be synthesizing and applying their knowledge of history to their own historical fiction stories. The work also addresses the Common Core State Standards' expectation that by seventh grade, students are able to "compare and contrast a fictional portrayal . . . and a historical account of the same period as a means of understanding how authors of fiction use or alter history." Be sure, too, that you allow students to learn about the historical era through film, photographs, museum collections, and stories as well as through expository texts, since it will be important for them to develop images of the time and place that they can then draw upon as they create stories set in that historical context.

If you decide to teach this unit alongside a historical fiction reading unit, students won't necessarily be reading about the same time period they are studying in social studies or writing about in writing workshop. More critical is that there are enough historical fiction books to sustain students for the month, which would mean a minimum of four per student with, ideally, some choice involved when picking those four texts. And if students are in book clubs, you will, of course, need multiple copies of each text.

However you choose to approach the unit, you'll want to gather some historical fiction and information texts on the same time period that you can read aloud to the class and then rely upon in writing minilessons and conferences. Our website (readingandwritingproject.com) has lists compiled by teachers throughout the country of much-loved genre-specific titles. For example, if you've decided to focus on the American civil rights movement, you might put together a read-aloud collection including *Goin' Someplace Special*, by Patricia C. McKissack, *The Other Side*, by Jacqueline Woodson, *Freedom on the Menu: The Greensboro Sit-Ins*, by Carole Boston Weatherford, and *The Bat Boy and His Violin*, by Gavin Curtis. You'll want not only to situate all your read-aloud work within the one selected era, but also to read aloud some relevant nonfiction material related in content and theme to the time period, perhaps selecting informational texts such as chapters out of *A History of US*, by Joy Hakim, *Through My Eyes*, by Ruby Bridges, *Dream of Freedom*, by Diane McWhorter, and primary sources such as Martin Luther King, Jr.'s "Letter From Birmingham City Jail." If nonfiction materials are slim, you can rely more heavily on the articles and photos from the time period, as mentioned earlier, or you could create short "fact sheets" on important people, issues, places, and events during various periods for students to use as supplemental materials.

Of course, this unit will not be the first time your students write narratives or informational paragraphs, so we highly recommend beginning with some on-demand assessment. Perhaps take a portion of a class period to ask your students to write a quick fiction story, even just the start of one or a key scene, so you can see what they already bring to this study. You might find that you need to weave more work on focus or character development into the unit. Or perhaps you'll realize your students are ready to study more complex ways to structure their writing, such as with flashbacks and flash-forwards or shifting narrators.

## BEND I: COLLECTING IDEAS FOR HISTORICAL FICTION: FINDING STORIES THAT ARE BOTH PERSONAL AND HISTORICAL

Note that if you choose to teach this writing unit alongside a reading or social studies unit, the initial research will probably last a few days, during which time you can draw upon strategies from prior reading and writing units to remind students how to gather and organize information. Over the course of several days, students might collect writing in their writing or social studies notebooks about daily life and personal issues, timelines of actual events, and ideas based on photographs and images from that period. You can use mid-workshop teaching and shares, along with your minilessons, to teach students not only what and how to research, but how to explore possible fictional characters or plots that *could* exist in the context of what they are learning.

If you instead decide to have students write historical fiction about a time period they already know well, we encourage you to give students at least a day to revisit that time period, now with a new focus on story creation. If possible, you can help students bring their historical knowledge to the forefront by revisiting texts they have already read; you might also or instead have them freewrite or talk briefly with peers about all they know, jotting key information. Whatever approach you take (researching or recalling a historical time period), you will teach students to look for fictional stories hidden in history—and, over the course of this first bend, additional strategies for generating possible story ideas and creating characters.

### Bend I, Session 1: Finding Fictional Stories Hidden in History

Whatever approach you take to the unit—one that starts with research or with topics students already know well—you can teach students, "Historical fiction writers become researchers and learn as much as they can about a time period that interests them, all the while asking themselves, 'What stories are hidden here?'" You will want to show the class how you jot what you know ("Sometimes even young boys had to sell things like newspapers during the Depression to help their families") and then use what you know about fiction to gather some ideas for characters and/or plots. ("Maybe a boy, Zachary, who steals his friend's newspapers . . .") You might highlight for students how story ideas often emerge from the smaller details in history, and you might encourage them to conjure up everything they know not just about central issues and major events, but also about daily life.

Expect your students to use their writer's notebooks in a variety of ways on this day, from making webs of information about a time period, to listing possible story ideas, to sketching details about setting. End this session with a share in which students work in small groups, discussing some of their learning and thinking about the time period. If you have decided to allow students to choose any time period, aim to group students who have chosen similar time periods for this share.

## Bend I, Session 2: Calling On Past Knowledge to Collect Ideas

As with any genre, you'll want to offer students at least a couple of different ways to gather ideas, knowing that different strategies will resonate with different writers—and knowing that to truly internalize a skill, your students need to develop a repertoire of strategies to practice that skill. Whenever possible, you'll also want to build transference and independence by reminding students to draw on everything they already know as writers. Toward both of those ends, you might say to students, "Today I want to teach you that another way historical fiction writers collect possible story ideas is by using strategies that already work well for them as fiction writers. Writers often look back through their notebooks and at charts and use strategies they know for writing any kind of fiction, such as starting with character or plot."

Keep in mind that when you send your students off to write, some of them will be able to generate story ideas and write possible plot summaries in a historical fiction vein. Others may benefit from collecting a realistic fiction–like blurb and then going back and revising it to match the time period.

You might use a mid-workshop teaching point to teach your historical fiction writers not only to collect ideas for stories, but also to test out those ideas by drawing on all they know about the era and about the genre. To test a story idea against knowledge of the era, a writer might reread his entries and ask, "Does this make sense for the time period? Does it ring true? What is a different way it could go?" For example, a student may have jotted in her notebook that she could write a story about a boy in the Civil War who wants to spend time with his older brother but he is working all the time, so they drive together to Florida on vacation. After asking herself if the story makes sense for the period and rings true, the writer could revise the story blurb to say, "I could write a story about a boy in the Civil War who wants to spend time with his older brother but their family is divided and he is on the Confederate side, so . . . " Help students to consider details right at the start, such as naming the character with a time-appropriate name and thinking about period-based motivations.

Some writers will seem more wedded to historical facts than to story ideas. You might use your conferring and small-group work to remind students that they are, first and foremost, story writers. You could say, "Writers, when I collect ideas for historical fiction writing, I want to make sure that I am still writing about people and issues that feel true to me. Remember that when we wrote realistic fiction, we learned that we can take the real struggles of our own lives and give those struggles to a character. You can still do that when writing historical fiction." You could then show your students that for you, one of the biggest challenges to this day is, say, getting along with your older brother. You could teach students that people in history struggled with the same issues, and we can think about how those struggles may have looked if set in another time and place: "Okay, so now let me see . . . I want to set my story in the Revolutionary War—and I want to make it a story about a boy who gets into an argument with his brother. Oh, I know,

I learned that young boys weren't supposed to go to war but some lied about their age and got in anyway, so maybe this boy wants to fight, but his older brother knows the boy is too young. Maybe they have an argument and . . ."

### Bend I, Session 3: Developing Character Traits that Intersect with the Time Period and Plot

As historical fiction writers develop characters for their stories, they consider how the time period and plot intersect with the character's internal and external traits. In this session, teach your writers, "Historical fiction writers often craft their characters by considering what issues existed during the time period and then asking themselves, 'What kinds of traits could add tension during this time period?' For example, during the Great Depression many people felt nervous and uncertain about the future. Maybe a character who is almost always positive and hopeful would run into challenges. Maybe on the inside that character feels optimistic, at least initially, and on the outside he keeps looking for but failing to find work until he begins to feel more downtrodden."

As you send students off to write, remind them to call on strategies they know for developing characters. They might, for example, create character T-charts, with a list of the main character's traits on one side and a list of traits common to those living in the time period on the other side. Then, students might do some jotting to explore the ways the main character's traits fit in with or are in conflict with the prevailing characteristics of the time. Of course, students can also flesh out storylines in addition to exploring characters. In a mid-workshop teaching point, you may want to suggest to students that as they jot, they should mark things that they need to go back to later and fact-check.

During the conferring and small-group work, you may want to teach some students ways to make their protagonists more real. As they develop internal and external traits for their characters, you can remind them that characters, like people, are complex. If someone seems too good to be true, for example, you might encourage students to make their characters more multidimensional by balancing them out with other traits.

For homework, you might direct students to settle upon an idea for their stories, one that includes a central character and a developing plotline that involves something the character wants as well as the obstacles he faces when trying to attain that want.

## BEND II: DEVELOPING THE STORY: SHAPING HISTORICALLY TRUE CHARACTERS AND PLOTS

As your students come to this bend, they should be honing in on a central character and plotline for their stories. If some of your students are still waffling over characters or plots, gather them in a small group to help them to settle on plans so that they get the most benefit from the series of lessons in this bend. Over the next several days, they will draft isolated scenes in their notebooks to develop their characters and plots, as well as their settings. From there, students will draft more thorough story plans and will check them for historical accuracy.

## Bend II, Session 1: Crafting Scenes that Show Characters' Struggles and Motivations

With your students settling upon their story ideas, you can teach them to write in their notebooks everyday scenes that bring their characters and their storylines to life—and that begin to develop their characters' struggles and motivations. Your teaching point might be, "Historical fiction writers develop their characters' struggles and motivations, considering both those that are personal and those that come from the historical period. Writers put their characters into everyday scenes—having supper with family or traveling to school in the morning—that *show* these struggles and motivations. As they do so, they may revise traits they had been developing, to make sure their characters are realistic and true to the time period."

As your students write scenes, you will be able to assess whether they are remembering the instruction about writing in a scene from previous narrative units—the importance of dialogue and small actions, of writing the external and the internal story, of making movies in one's mind and storytelling rather than summarizing. You can look across your students' trial scenes and make some choices about the whole-class minilessons you need to teach and about your conferring and small-group work, as well.

## Bend II, Session 2: Developing Historically Accurate Settings

Over the course of a couple of days, you can spotlight your teaching on what you would like your students to consider and fine-tune as they continue to put their characters into isolated scenes. Because setting is a defining feature of historical fiction, you will want to devote some of your teaching to this story element. Your teaching point might be, "Historical fiction writers take great care to develop clear and historically accurate settings for their stories. They consider how locations affect characters and plot points. They try out their characters in many different places as they think about how their stories might go differently in each. They can look back to illustrations or photographs from the time period and imagine how their characters might act within them." This teaching supports the Common Core expectation that by eighth grade students use "precise and relevant words and phrases to convey experiences and events (W.8.3d)."

## Bend II, Session 3: Drafting Multiple Plans

Now that students have drafted several everyday scenes, they should have a fully developed central character and an emerging sense of how their stories might go. Today you can guide them to choose a story idea that they will want to take all the way through the writing process toward publication. Your teaching point might be, "Historical fiction writers can draw from a variety of familiar techniques to plot out their stories. They often draft multiple plans, perhaps using story mountains, booklets (made from folded copy paper or loose leaf, onto which they sketch or jot each part of the story), or storyboards."

During independent writing and conferring, students might benefit from learning other sophisticated ways to add to their plans. For example, writers may create two timelines, one personal and one historical, to notice ways the two intersect. You could explain that in some historical fiction, the big problem a character faces is, in fact, the historical struggle, such as slavery in *Roll of Thunder Hear My Cry*, by Mildred Taylor, or enlistment in the army in *My Brother Sam Is Dead*, by James Lincoln Collier. In others, the struggle is a more personal one, such as learning to love someone or adjusting to a family change in *Sarah Plain and Tall*, by Patricia McLachlan, with the historical setting functioning really as a backdrop.

Yet another way you could teach students to add to their plans is to develop secondary characters' internal thinking and actions. You could also teach students to develop mini-story mountains for each scene, thus leading them to consider rising and falling tensions throughout the story.

As students finalize their plans, this will be an important time for lots of quick, on-the-run assessment on your part. Many students will be planning to attempt novel-sized stories, which will almost inevitably lead to a lot of summarizing and not a lot of small moment development. Use what you need of the workshop time—mid-workshop teaching, conferring and small-group work—to help them realize that their stories will inevitably be more focused, and therefore better written, if they revolve around two or, at most, three small moments.

## Bend II, Session 4: Checking Plans for Historical Accuracy

Before students move from planning to drafting, you might give them the opportunity to revise those plans for historical accuracy. You might teach them, "Historical fiction writers aim to keep their drafting well within the time period they are studying. One way to keep this information fresh in their minds is to compose summaries of the time period—quick paragraphs, using information writing structures—to hold onto the key events, people, and ideas one needs to know. Then, before committing to draft a plan, they are careful to check for historical accuracy. They look at both their entire draft plan and the specific details they have been developing and ask questions like, "Does this feel true to the time period? Do I know a more specific way to describe this (piece of clothing, item in the house, person's name, etc.)?"

To check their understanding of the time period, students can draw on what they know about information writing to write mini–informational texts comprised of a few paragraphs. Students could organize these according to parts of the time period, for example, choosing the most essential events or concepts and treating each as a section or topic sentence ("The Boston Massacre was an altercation that fueled tensions between the colonists and the British"). Or each section or paragraph could be an idea the writer has about the time period ("One truth about the colonial period is that the genders were not equally valued"). Or, like the preface to the picture book *Freedom Summer*, by Deborah Wiles, students could try a chronological structure. These texts need not take long to write, and later in the unit they can be revised to become a preface or end note to students' narratives.

Today students can use these write-ups to fine-tune their plans for accuracy. While they are drafting, students can have them accessible to keep the facts of the period at the forefront of their minds.

# BEND III: DRAFTING AND REVISING: CRAFTING A COMPELLING HISTORICAL FICTION STORY

Ideally, your students will come to this bend with a solid plan in hand. Over the next several days, they will quickly draft and then thoroughly revise their stories, often turning to published texts for guidance and inspiration.

## Bend III, Session 1: Drafting from Inside the World of the Story

You'll want to encourage students to use their revised draft plan and all they know about their time period as a guide for their drafting, but you'll also want them to enter the world of their story from the first sentence, so that each scene emerges from their pen almost (though, because of all their hard work, of course not quite) like magic. You might say to the class, "Historical fiction writers look back over artifacts they collected and notes they took, trying to live the time period in their minds and experience the events of each scene, and then draft while walking in the character's shoes. As they write, they consider ways to use period language to describe small, unique details." Keep in mind that although historical accuracy will be important in the long run, when your students are starting their stories, by far the most important thing for you to stress will be the importance of storytelling rather than summarizing.

In your minilesson, you may model how you read your plan, filling your mind with how you want the story to unfold, before closing your eyes to take yourself back in time. You may think aloud about where you are, what you are wearing, feeling, doing in this exact moment, before picking up your pen and letting the first few sentences pour out. When you pause, it will likely be to think aloud again about how to slow down the moment or how to bring in more of those small, historical details. You need not write more than a few sentences before inviting students to envision how their drafts will unfold before you send them back to their writing spots to embark on their drafts.

This is one of those magic sessions in which all of the groundwork and planning you led your students to do will come to fruition. Volume (and spirits) should be high on this day, and you should do your best to spur your students' energy while giving them plenty of time to write. Keep your conferences short and light, perhaps moving from table to table offering encouragement and compliments. Keep in mind that students will have several days to revise their work, so what is less important is that their writing is perfect, and what is more important is that their drafts are substantial enough to take through a revision process. Send your students home with the assignment of finishing their drafts tonight.

## Bend III, Session 2: Inserting Back Stories and Flashbacks to Provide Extra Information

One challenge with historical fiction is that stories often require more background information than what can be told in sequential order. You might therefore teach students to use back stories and flashbacks to convey events that have already happened. You can explain to students that in a back story, the character often describes something that already happened: "I had a brother once, named John, but he fell down a well, and my parents were never the same after that." However, a flashback brings the reader right to the earlier time: "When my mother handed baby Thomas to me and I had him in my arms, I remembered the night, six months earlier, when I had been trying to get to sleep, and I suddenly heard a sharp cry. I knew right away it was baby Thomas and I knew something was wrong."

After providing these examples, you might say to students, "Today I want to teach you that when you want to refer to historical events that happened before the central moments of your story, you don't have to write a long novel! Writers insert a flashback or back story, often by having one character ask a question and another character tell a little story or give a little history that will help your reader understand more of the background of your story." Even if your students don't master this craft, studying and trying it will expand their writing terrain.

Students will spend this writing session adding to their drafts, looking for places to add flashbacks, and also looking for any places that need clarification or fixing up. During today's share, you might give students the opportunity to study their drafts through the lens of the Narrative Writing Checklist. Encourage students to reflect honestly, setting for themselves clear goals to reach toward in the days ahead.

## Narrative Writing Checklist

| | Grade 7 | NOT YET | STARTING TO | YES! | Grade 8 | NOT YET | STARTING TO | YES! |
|---|---|---|---|---|---|---|---|---|
| **Structure** | | | | | **Structure** | | | |
| **Overall** | I created a narrative that has realistic characters, tension, and change; and that not only conveys, but also develops an idea, lesson, or theme. | ☐ | ☐ | ☐ | I not only created a narrative with well-developed characters who change, I used the story to comment on a social issue, teach a lesson, and/or develop a point of view. | ☐ | ☐ | ☐ |
| **Lead** | I wrote a beginning that not only sets the story in motion, it also grounds it in a place or situation. It included details that will later be important to the story. These details might point to the central issue or conflict, show how story elements connect, or hint at key character traits. | ☐ | ☐ | ☐ | In establishing the situation and place, I hinted at a bigger context for the story (revealing issues that have been brewing, showing how the setting affects the character, contextualizing a time in history, and/or developing one out of many points of view). | ☐ | ☐ | ☐ |
| **Transitions** | I used transitional phrases and clauses to connect what happened to why it happened (*If he hadn't . . . he might not have, because of, although, little did she know that*). | ☐ | ☐ | ☐ | I used transitional phrases and clauses, grammatical structures (for example, paragraphs, descriptive phrases, and clauses) and text structures (such as chapter divisions and extended italics) to alert my reader to changes in the setting, the mood, the point of view, or the time in the story. | ☐ | ☐ | ☐ |
| **Ending** | I gave the reader a sense of closure by showing clearly how the character or place has changed or the problem has been resolved. If there wasn't resolution, I gave details to leave the reader thinking about a central idea or theme. | ☐ | ☐ | ☐ | I gave the reader a sense of closure by revealing character change(s) that followed from events in the story, or perhaps a resolution. If there wasn't resolution, I wrote to convey how the events of the story affected the characters, and to circle back to a central idea, issue, or theme. | ☐ | ☐ | ☐ |
| **Organization** | I used a traditional—or slightly modified—story structure (rising action, conflict, falling action) to best bring out the meaning of my story and reach my audience. | ☐ | ☐ | ☐ | I modified a traditional story structure, dealing with time in purposeful ways, to best suit my genre, bring out the meaning of my story, and reach my audience. | ☐ | ☐ | ☐ |

## Bend III, Session 3: Crafting Meaningful Endings

As your students roll up their sleeves and dig into the challenging work of revision, you'll want to remind them that any work they do should be in the service of deepening and conveying meaning, including historical accuracy. With that end goal in mind, you might teach them ways to rethink and rewrite their endings. Historical fiction often has more of a sense of being unsettled or lacking resolution than other types of fiction, perhaps because it so closely resembles true historical events. True, one character could potentially work to overcome and might even have great influence within a particular struggle, but usually one character, especially a fictitious character, will most likely not defeat the entire British army, give women the right to vote, or solve the stock market crisis. Often historical fiction, such as *Number the Stars*, by Lois Lowry, or *Rose Blanche*, by Christophe Gallaz and Roberto Innocenti, is less about resolving the historical struggle and more about bearing witness. Further, the teaching in this section moves students toward the Common Core recommendation for all middle school narrative writers to "provide a conclusion that follows from and reflects on the narrated experiences or events" (W.7.3e, W.8.3e).

Your teaching point might sound like, "Historical fiction writers are careful to revise their endings, making certain they write the kinds of endings their stories deserve. There are different ways a character's story can end, but the historical context needs to remain true—meaning that usually the historical issue is not fully resolved. Sometimes at the end of a historical fiction story we see how characters are affected, or affect, the struggle. They might be a silent witness—or perhaps they take some sort of small action. Or they might be a victim and learn something about themselves through their struggle."

To exemplify your teaching, you might show your students how, as you think hard about revising your final scene, you decide whether your story will be one that celebrates overcoming adversity or one in which the character bravely bears witness to suffering to call humanity to learn from the past and take action in the future. When you send students off to write, you'll probably want to encourage them to try several different endings before settling upon the one that best conveys what they want to get across to readers.

During the conferring and small-group work, you might teach certain students to be wary of Superman-type endings. For example, you might coach a student who is considering an ending like this, "So maybe in the end Jason can be so worried about his brother that he tells Abraham Lincoln that he needs to free the slaves," and suggest that he instead consider something the character discovers about himself or about his brother that was hiding there all along. He might try out something like, "Maybe Jason learns that while he cannot change what happens to his brother, Jason will still always remember his brother as the one who believed in him. Or maybe . . ."

Invite students to share their possible endings with each other at the end of the session and to offer each other thoughts on which ending works best.

### Bend III, Session 4: Using Symbolism to Convey Meaning

Especially if your students are reading historical fiction, you might spend the next few days emphasizing the reading–writing connection as you teach students to try out writers' techniques you have previously studied together as readers. However, even if students are not reading historical fiction alongside this writing unit, you might encourage students to gather inspiration for revision from mentor texts.

Today you might remind students about the symbolism you've discussed in a class read-aloud, and if relevant, any that they've noticed in their independent novels. Using a read-aloud or mentor text, you might quickly revisit a few places where a symbol appears (such as the Star of David in *Number the Stars*, by Lois Lowry), theorize what it means, and notice how the author inserts and builds meaning around that symbol. Or you might do similar work in your own writing, showing the class how you created and wove a symbol into a couple of parts of your story.

Send students off, encouraging them to consider similar work in their own drafts and to draw on their increasing repertoire of revision moves. For the mid-workshop teaching point, you might encourage students to consider their titles and try out some that may have symbolic meanings for their readers.

### Bend III, Session 5: Layering Essential Details about Time and Place in Opening Scenes

In today's lesson, you might encourage students to revisit their opening scenes, making sure they orient their readers to the setting of their stories. This is particularly important in historical fiction, where setting is so central to the story. You might say, "Today I want to teach you that writers look closely at how other writers give clues about when and where their stories take place. Some writers, for instance, give headings: 'Boston, 1776.' Others include details that help the reader picture the place. Details about transportation, housing, technology, food, clothes, help the reader locate the setting. Sometimes the writer has the narrator tell the setting; the narrator might simply say, for example, that she lives in a small town in France and the war is on." Then, send your writers off to work saying, "Writers, you can try several different opening scenes for your story, and then choose the one that works best, perhaps even with some feedback from your writing partner."

### Bend III, Session 6: Creating Settings with Emotional Atmospheres, or Moods

In this session, you might teach readers that they can use setting details not simply to convey time and place, but to convey mood, as well—and that the mood will likely change across the story to reflect the changing emotions of the characters. To deliver your teaching, you might say, "Today I want to teach you that story writers often use physical setting details to create an emotional atmosphere, so that even when scenes occur in the same location, they might convey a very different mood. One of the easiest ways to alter an emotional atmosphere is to use the weather—the sun shines and the birds chirp when you want the mood to be happy and carefree. The sky darkens, the clouds get gloomy, the wind whistles when you want it to feel ominous."

During independent writing time, encourage your writers to try multiple ways particular scenes could go. Even though they will be drafting on loose-leaf paper or on a computer, suggest that they return to their writer's notebooks to try several versions of a scene before settling on the version that feels exactly right. During the share, you might gather your writers and encourage them to share out some of the words and phrases that they used to convey mood through setting (a heavy gray fog clung to the mountainside, dark clouds loomed in the distance, threatening to drench the village). You might even ask students to guess the mood others were trying to convey through their setting details.

### Bend III, Session 7: Contextualizing Stories with Prefaces and Endnotes

As students near the final stages of their revision work, you might invite them to look back to the informational sections they wrote before drafting and decide if an informational preface or endnote is appropriate for their story. In some instances, authors choose to supply their readers with key information up front, so readers enter the world of the story fully aware of the major events to come. In other cases, authors prefer to have their readers experience events as if for the first time right alongside the protagonists, and then they supply an endnote that contextualizes the events in the story. You might say to students, "Historical fiction writers sometimes supply their readers with a preface or endnote. They decide the *purpose* they would like these to fulfill. Will they help readers understand what is true and what is fabricated in the narrative? Will they emphasize a human struggle? Will they provide the back story or after-events that the narrative did not? It helps to study how other authors have used prefaces and endnotes and then to try out a few forms ourselves, perhaps even revising entries we've already written about the time period."

During independent writing time, you could invite your students to study examples, such as the preface to *Freedom Summer*, by Deborah Wiles, or the endnote to *The Yellow Star*, by Carmen Deedy.

## BEND IV: EDITING AND PUBLISHING: PREPARING A HISTORICAL FICTION STORY FOR READERS

Over the next couple of days, your writers will put the finishing touches on their stories before sharing and celebrating their final products. To prepare for this work, you'll want to get a sense of students' editing needs, so you can plan accordingly for your whole-class and differentiated instruction. Though we offer suggestions below, as always, we encourage you to emphasize instruction that matches the needs of your class, this time in regard to syntax, punctuation, and spelling. Whatever their knowledge base, this is a time to remind students that they already know a great deal about ways to edit their pieces, and it's important that they bring all that knowledge to the forefront as they take their final steps toward publication.

As writers work independently to edit their pieces, you could suggest they pay particular attention to the craft or language section of the Narrative Writing Checklist. Suggest that your students use the checklist to edit their own work, carefully checking off sections as they go, and then trade pieces with a partner.

## Narrative Writing Checklist (continued)

| | Grade 7 | NOT YET | STARTING TO | YES! | Grade 8 | NOT YET | STARTING TO | YES! |
|---|---|---|---|---|---|---|---|---|
| | **Development** | | | | **Development** | | | |
| **Elaboration** | I developed the action, dialogue, details, and inner thinking to convey an issue, idea, or lesson. I showed what is specific about the central character. I developed the setting and the character's relationship to the setting. | ☐ | ☐ | ☐ | I developed complicated story elements; I may have contrasted the character's thinking with his or her actions or dialogue. | ☐ | ☐ | ☐ |
| | | | | | I developed the central character's relationship to other characters. I showed character flaws as well as strengths to add complexity. | ☐ | ☐ | ☐ |
| | | | | | My details conveyed meaning and related to or developed a lesson or theme. | ☐ | ☐ | ☐ |
| **Craft or Language** | I developed contradictions and change in characters and situations. | ☐ | ☐ | ☐ | I conveyed the pressures characters feel and the dreams they hold. I related those to their actions. I developed complicated characters who change and/or who change others. | ☐ | ☐ | ☐ |
| | I used specific details and figurative language to help the reader understand the place and the mood (such as making an object or place symbolic, using the weather, using repetition). | ☐ | ☐ | ☐ | I created a mood as well as a physical setting, and showed how the place changed, or its relationships to the characters changed. I used symbolism to connect with a theme. | ☐ | ☐ | ☐ |
| | I varied my tone to match the variety of emotions experienced by the characters across the story. | ☐ | ☐ | ☐ | I varied my tone to bring out different perspectives within the story, or to show a gap between the narrator's point of view and that of other characters. | ☐ | ☐ | ☐ |
| | **Conventions** | | | | **Conventions** | | | |
| **Spelling** | I used the internet and other sources at hand to check spelling of literary and high-frequency words. | ☐ | ☐ | ☐ | I used the internet and other sources to check the spelling of literary, historical, and geographical words. | ☐ | ☐ | ☐ |

## Bend IV, Session 1: Editing for Voice: Giving Characters Their Own Sound

Historical fiction, and really any sort of narrative writing, is a perfect opportunity to study how the way the narrator speaks can often be different than how the characters speak; each character might even use language in a slightly different way. Students might also consider how punctuation changes the sound of characters' voices—short and choppy, long-winded, excitable. *Catching Up on Conventions* (2009), by Chantal Francois and Elisa Zonana, has a powerful section about teaching students code-switching—how different contexts require different forms of grammar or punctuation.

Your teaching point today might be, "Historical fiction writers often read their writing aloud, noting how words, punctuation, and other structures help to set the mood, tone, and content of their pieces. One way to do this is to pay close attention to the ways characters talk, giving each their own rhythm and style, and using punctuation to help create this sound."

You might use today's share to revisit the Narrative Writing Checklist once again, this time with a focus on conventions, as well as any other editing checklists or charts you may have gathered across the year. You can remind your writers that they can reread their pieces slowly, looking through one lens at a time (more sophisticated writers could probably hold on to several), stopping at each sentence to ask themselves, "Did I ___ correctly in this sentence?"

### Bend IV, Session 2: Scrutinizing Word Choice for Historical Accuracy

You might use today to teach students to use more domain-specific (in this case, more historically accurate and specific) vocabulary. You might say to students, "Historical fiction writers carefully reread their writing, looking for the words they chose to describe objects, places, or people, and then looking back to their research to see if there are more historically specific ways to name them."

Or you might instead (or in addition, during the mid-workshop teaching) encourage students to check their verb tense for consistency. They might choose to use past tense throughout to indicate the historical nature of the events they are describing, or perhaps present tense to help readers feel as if they are running right alongside the protagonist.

### Bend IV, Session 3: Bringing Stories to Life: A Final Celebration

At the end of the unit you will be amazed how far your students (and you) have come in this study! Historical fiction is not a simple genre, yet through your support and guidance your students will have learned not only to write within this genre, but also to have better control and understanding of narrative craft and structure in general. You will no doubt want to celebrate their accomplishments in grand, public ways—or at the very least, among yourselves. One choice is to have students dress up for the celebration as a character from their story, perhaps even talking as if they are in the time period as they interact with one another. Or you might channel groups to work together to act out brief moments from a few student stories.

In some classrooms, students also pair their narratives with some historical artifacts. If you chose to open this unit with research, your students will likely already have artifacts from the first week of the study. Otherwise, they might collect a few relevant graphics or photographs as they put the finishing touches on their stories, so they can present their fictional work alongside visuals of the time period that inspired their creation.

# Poetry
*Immersion and Innovation*

## RATIONALE/INTRODUCTION

"Well, write poetry, for God's sake, it's the only thing that matters." This invitation from e e cummings speaks to a deep-seated belief that even if poetry writing does not appear as a separate writing standard, it is well worth teaching, practicing, and celebrating. Poetry, and its sibling, songwriting, are genres that matter to human beings at a core level—and they matter to seventh-graders. Nowhere will young writers more authentically waver over choosing just the right word. As rapper and producer Jay-Z writes in his writing-life memoir (2011), *Decoded*, "A poet's mission is to make words do more work than they normally do, to make them work on more than one level." This work of writing "on more than one level" will support students' understanding of how figurative language and symbolism work—which is crucial for an academic appreciation of literature, whether it takes the form of fiction or nonfiction, poetry or prose. The Common Core State Standards call on readers to be able not just to name, but also to analyze the effects of author's craft and structure. In poetry, craft and structure get center stage more explicitly than in other genres, making it an ideal venue for practicing this kind of work. But poetry—the reading and writing of it—also serves a very adolescent need to speak from the heart, to exaggerate and elaborate emotions that already feel bigger than life. Let's give the kids a chance to break out of essay structure—to find other modes of making meaning and to share them in multiple formats.

The unit will end with students collecting a bundle of their best work to share—they may create a chapbook (a small collection of poetry, usually about one topic or theme) or personal or class anthology and put it on display or invite family in for a gallery walk. We also recommend an opportunity for poetry performance—whether in the form of an in-class slam or an evening open-mike poetry cafe. Poems are meant to be read out loud, and some of your students for whom writing is not always an avenue for personal bests may come out of their shells when live performance is an option for publishing their work.

# A SUMMARY OF THE BENDS IN THE ROAD OF THIS UNIT

**In Bend I (Trying Out Narrative and Lyric Poetry)**, you'll suggest that poems can have origins in old writing, and you will set students up to mine their notebooks for pieces that can be turned into poems through new word choice and line breaks. This bend depends on an immediate, intense immersion in poetry, in particular, narrative and lyric poetry, so that students will have the rhythms, sounds, and format of these genres in their heads as they begin writing. You'll teach students to look at the details of their lives and to the world around them for inspiration and to focus on meaning first as they begin writing.

**In Bend II (Revising so that Every Syllable Counts (Even if I'm Not Counting Syllables!))**, you'll teach students the ins and outs of revision as they work to make their poems more exact representations of their observations, feelings, and insights. Specifically, students will learn to pay close attention to word choice and to the shape and length of a poem, as well as to other techniques that poets use, such as metaphor, simile, alliteration, and onomatopoeia. Students will learn to experiment with literary devices and meaning and with conventions, too, as they aim to revise in meaningful ways.

**In Bend III (Chapbooks and Slams: Publishing Poems with Flair)**, you'll decide on a way to publish your students' work and to celebrate the end of this unit, perhaps through a poetry performance (or slam) or through thematically based chapbooks. Students will work with partners, choosing poems they would like to showcase, giving attention specifically to the groupings their poems fall into—and to any themes that emerge as they examine their writing. They will work on introductions that may take the form of an essay or an informational piece to establish the context for the theme they select. Students will leave the unit with a reminder from you that from this day forward, they can respond to the world as poets do, finding the words to make sense of big questions and to give voice to whatever moves them.

## GETTING READY

The beginning of this unit depends on students having access to loads of poetry to read while they are starting to write. If you are not teaching a parallel unit of study in reading workshop where you are introducing students to different kinds of poems and giving them time to read, study, and talk about them, you will need to add some days here at the beginning for that crucial work.

Narrative and lyric poetry are arguably the two most practiced styles of poetry today; epic poetry is just not as popular these days. Narrative poems are characterized by storytelling. They employ a narrative, or sequential structure, and include other story elements as well, such as a recognizable setting and a character or characters. Lyric poetry is told from the point of view of a speaker and sometimes includes some storytelling; other times it is more essayistic. The key element in lyric poetry is the voice of the speaker—hence the connection to the term *lyrics* in songs. The speaker may or may not represent the views of the poet, but instead is a kind of first-person narrator or persona that the poet adopts to explore a point of view or emotion.

In this first bend you'll teach students ways to collect first drafts of poems that fall into both these broad categories. The point is not to test them on these terms, but to use these two different entry points into poetry as a place to get started. You won't want to care, in other words, whether students actually produce *x* number of narrative and *y* number of lyric poems. You will just want them writing poems, right away. And some of your young poets may take to storytelling through poetry, whereas others may prefer the more philosophical, reflective path of the lyric poem.

A few texts will help you imagine many ways to teach students to write poetry. You may want *A Note Slipped under the Door: Teaching from Poems We Love*, by Nick Flynn and Shirley McPhillips (2000); *Awakening the Heart: Exploring Poetry in Elementary and Middle School*, by Georgia Heard (1998); *Getting the Knack: 20 Poetry Writing Exercises*, by Stephen Dunning and William Stafford (1992); *Knock at a Star: A Child's Introduction to Poetry*, by X. J. Kennedy, Dorothy M. Kennedy, and Karen Lee Baker (1999); *Looking to Write: Students Writing through the Visual Arts*, by Mary Ehrenworth (2003); and Paul Janeczko's (2011) *Reading Poetry in the Middle Grades: 20 Poems and Activities that Meet the Common Core Standards and Cultivate a Passion for Poetry*.

You'll also want some good collections of poetry written by adolescents to inspire your students. Some teachers have valued *You Hear Me?* (2011) (this book has graphic content, so please check with your administrator) and *Things I Have to Tell You* (2001) (again, please check), both edited by Betsy Franco, and *Paint Me Like I Am*, (2003) edited by WritersCorps. You'll want collections of contemporary poems as well, including, perhaps, *Poetry 180*, a collection of poems for high school students, edited by Billy Collins (2003); *Honey I Love*, by Eloise Greenfield (1986); *This Place I Know: Poems of Comfort*, edited by Georgia Heard (2006); and Walter Dean Myers' (2004) *Here in Harlem: Poems in Many Voices*. You also will want collections by Langston Hughes, Nikki Giovanni, Billy Collins, Lucille Clifton, and Mary Oliver and canonical poets such as Robert Frost and Walt Whitman. If you are seeking other poetry resources, you may want to explore the website for The Poetry Foundation, an independent literary organization, which includes a students' poetry section. Again, we have a more extensive list of poetry resources on our website, and we welcome your suggestions for additional must-read titles.

We have also seen incredible results from introducing poetry collections that are actually collections of lyrics from popular singer/songwriters. Tupac Shakur's (2009) *The Rose that Grew from Concrete* and Alicia Keys' (2004) *Tears for Water: Songbook of Poems and Lyrics* are two examples. You will definitely want to excerpt passages from Jay-Z's recently published memoir (2011), *Decoded*; although many parts may be too adult for middle school, there are long sections that detail Jay-Z's passion for writing and his obsession with rhyming and language. Another appealing feature of this book is that his song lyrics are included and footnoted to explain their references—a great way to show students the multilayered meanings of poems and songs. It helps when Jay-Z is your spokesperson!

# BEND I: TRYING OUT NARRATIVE AND LYRIC POETRY

As this unit begins, you will immerse your students in narrative and lyric poetry and teach them how to draw inspiration from their lives and the world around them as they begin writing poetry of their own.

## Bend I, Session 1: Finding Poems in Old Writing Projects

This unit begins with an invitation to students to mine their notebooks for old writing that can become poems. Maybe they've written a narrative about a moment that especially mattered to them that could now become the bones of a poem, through some structural revision. Or perhaps they've posed a question about people in a literary essay or about a life process in an informational piece that can now become the seed for a poem. This should be an exciting discovery for your seventh-graders! "Poets take note of what matters to them," is what you'll convey, "and what matters pops up again and again, across different genres of writing." Your teaching point might sound something like this: "Today I want to teach you that poets find poems in writing they've done already. Poets reimagine a story or an entry they've written, and by adding line breaks and revising for just the right words, they make a new poem out of old writing." It will be fun for your students to go on a "treasure hunt" through their notebooks, recalling old writing that they especially loved and that they can now revise to take new shape.

You'll want to remind students, too, that life itself can be a source of poetry. The writing homework you assign on the first day of this unit may be to not just *read* poems but to *live* poems, to see that poems hide in the corners of one's everyday life.

## Bend I, Session 2: Looking Inward and Outward to Find Inspiration in the Details of Life

You might pick up on the homework assignment that students will have completed the night before with a reminder that poets find significance in the details of ordinary life, gathering entries, images, and lists that might later be turned into publishable texts. Poets, you'll convey, look carefully at everyday objects and note their surprising beauty. You may want to suggest that as poets, students can look inward—the place in their heart that is filled by their family dog—as well as outward—the worm on the sidewalk, the vibration of their cell phone. As students write, you may emphasize free verse poetry as an easy way to get started. Teach students to aim first for meaning and for finding a way to describe what matters with words that will get their reader to see the world in a new way.

In a mid-workshop or share, you might continue to teach students ways to unpack their own lives for poetic potential. You might say that poets look for moments of trouble or surprising beauty, thoughts that seem urgent and universal, images that are surprising or particularly clear, language that is vivid and engaging. You won't want to overwhelm students with too many options, so select some examples from this list (or find similar descriptors of your own!), perhaps using some for other teaching moments. You may want to begin a chart today (or soon hereafter) that captures the sorts of things poets do when writing a poem. The chart might be titled, "Poets Sometimes . . ." or "Places Poets Search for Inspiration."

## Bend I, Session 3: Looking to the World for Inspiration

By now, students have likely written a handful of poems or more, mostly of a personal nature. Today you might open up the range of possible poetry topics by inviting students to take on issues or debates in the world in the form of a poem. You might want to convey that poets can reflect on a problem that is universal or shared by many. They write to try out different points of view: either in a two-voice form or writing to present a single view, then another, then another. They remember that details matter—just as in argument writing—but the details in a poem will be less research-based and more observational. As students head off to write, invite them to move from poem to poem, drawing on any of the strategies they have learned thus far. Encourage them to consider moving out of their comfort zones, perhaps trying poems on topics that previously have been uncharted territory.

During a share, you might build on today's teaching by shifting the focus from what *poets* do to what a *poem* does. Here, you'll want to draw on a few powerful mentor poems or on the poems your kids have written to highlight the message that poems often convey feelings. You could then encourage writers to begin writing with moments and memories of a strong feeling, such as pride, regret, joy, or loss. You might point out that many poems are the study of an individual; these kinds of poems are designed to help readers understand something about people. Some students may feel inspired to write a poem about a specific person who instills certain feelings in them. You could also point out that some poems are written to inspire feelings about social issues and the injustices of the world. Adolescents can write poems about issues of fairness, bullying, and belonging. Of course, the loftier the idea of a poem, the more the poem needs to be grounded in something tangible, such as an image, a moment, or a person.

## Bend I, Session 4: Asking Unanswerable Questions

Often students learn that when they pose questions, their next job is to try to answer them—certainly during math and science, and even in many reading and writing workshops. So it may come as a surprise both to you and them that in a unit on poetry, it is permissible to ask and not answer questions. In fact, it is a literary device. You can phrase it this way: "Today I want to teach you that poets aren't afraid to ask unanswerable questions in their writing. Poets know that to dig deep often means raising questions about big, unknowable things. Poets can think about the really big questions they have about the world: What do I wonder about? What mystifies me?"

As part of their entry into this world of question posing, you might invite your poets to make a list poem of their questions before you send them off to write. During writing time, they might take one of the questions they raised and write a whole poem that shows how they try to make sense of that question, both in their lives and in their hearts. In a mid-workshop teaching point or share, you might draw on a mentor text, such as Mary Oliver's "Roses, Late Summer" or "The Summer Day" in *House of Light* or Langston Hughes's "Harlem." Invite students to study and draw inspiration from how these poets used questions to evoke images, instill feelings, and promote ideas. You might also channel students to analyze the impact of certain word choices or poetic devices such as repetition and rhyme, thus supporting students in reaching for the work called for by Standards RL.6.4, RL.7.4, and RL.8.4.

### Bend I, Session 5: Offering Feedback to Writing Partners during Revision

Toward the end of this first bend, a session on the use of partners will set up your students for the work that is to come, particularly in revision. Here, you'll want be careful how you word your teaching. It is important to teach partners to work carefully with each other; your young poets are putting their private, innermost feelings onto the page and can be vulnerable and therefore defensive about their work. By setting up protocols and prompts for partner work, you make it clear that even poetry is open for feedback and critique—when provided in a respectful, thoughtful manner. You'll want to convey that just as other writers revise again and again to get their writing just right, poets take their work through hundreds of revisions— all to get the exact right imagery, sound, and feel. You might want to share a list of partner talk prompts:

- Partners compliment each other as a first step in responding to new work.

- Partners talk about *how* they are writing, as well as *what* they are writing about. They can ask each other, "Which strategies have worked for you in your poetry writing?" "Which ones are you having trouble with?"

- Partners work on one piece of writing at a time, so that they can read the poem line by line and talk about what is and isn't yet working.

- Partners decide on specific next steps for their writing, and they write these down as assignments, either in a planner or in their notebooks.

As you finish this bend with your students, here are some predictable mid-workshop teaching points, small groups, and conferences:

| For writers who need more support | For writers who are ready for an extension |
|---|---|
| Writers learn new vocabulary from other writers and use these new words to create poems with beautiful and specific language. (Here the cocreation of a word wall with strong verbs and other descriptive language will help.) | Poets develop comparisons that are extremely surprising but supportable. They may focus on one rich comparison and extend it through an entire poem (see Langston Hughes's "Harlem") or write a poem in which they develop many, many metaphors or similes (see Langston Hughes's "Dreams" or Pablo Neruda's "Ode to My Socks"). Poets push to find comparisons that are not cliché—ones that startle, delight, or sometimes disturb. |

| For writers who need more support | For writers who are ready for an extension |
|---|---|
| Poets use their reading to create copy-change poems or found poems. Poets look closely at a short poem and use its structure to create a copy-change poem, changing the subject of the poem, but copying exactly the number of syllables in each word, the number of words in a line, the number of lines in a stanza. Poets create found poems by choosing words or lines from other kinds of text (newspaper articles, advertisements, fiction) and rearranging these to make a poem. *Note: Both of these kinds of writing require a citation: poets must write the author and title of the original text as part of their title.* | Poets use traditional forms as a way to structure their writing through purposeful repetition, rhyme, and/or meter. Poets look closely at a mentor poem in that form, write to approximate the form, and then revise to perfect it. |

## BEND II: REVISING SO THAT EVERY SYLLABLE COUNTS (EVEN IF I'M NOT COUNTING SYLLABLES!)

Now that students have been exposed to various strategies for generating and writing meaningful poems, you will want to teach into that writing, lifting the quality of their drafts and inviting them to revise, revise, revise. There is no particular sequence to the various things you'll highlight. What's important is that your students collect a repertoire of things to think about as they write poems and that they draw on all of these, repeatedly, as they draft and revise poem after poem. Doing intense revision and cycling through the writing process many times in poetry helps students to build revision muscles and to take greater revision risks, which will strengthen their revision in other genres and support the process work outlined in Standards W.6.5, W.7.5, and W.8.5.

### Bend II, Session 1: Paying Attention to the Sounds and Meanings of Words

One thing you might teach your students is that a powerful revision move is to read drafts of poems out loud. There is a difference in sound and meaning between *rock* and *stone*, *shine* and *sparkle*, *cry* and *weep*. Students should be able to hear how the right choice of words can make a poem funny or wistful or sad—and also how a word can convey a lesser or greater intensity of emotion or action. You'll want to encourage students to play around with their own word choices, to have fun with reciting lines aloud, trying out new words or phrases to be sure they've conveyed the exact feeling and impact they are aiming to convey.

During independent writing time, expect a cacophony of voices, words, and sounds. But be sure to channel your students to focus their efforts on writing and revising, not just on reading their poems.

For your share, you might revisit one of your own mentor texts that you read aloud and invite students to examine with you how long vowel sounds can have a very different effect than short, choppy, hard consonant sounds. In this way, they'll learn that poems are crafted with consideration for the smallest details, including the very sounds of parts of words. Students might revise for the sounds of their poems also by weighing the choices they are making with repetition and punctuation, both of which can change the way lines and stanzas sound.

### Bend II, Session 2: Relating the Physical Appearance of a Poem to Its Meaning

As your students create sounds in their poems that further express their thoughts and feelings, you can teach them that sounds in a poem are created not only by word choice but also by layout on the paper. Although it may seem odd to focus on this so early, you may want to seize the moment to make students aware of the fact that poems, unlike most genres of writing, can take on many different forms on the page—that in fact, poets play around with the physical shape of a poem as much as they do with the words and sounds that make up the poem.

You might word your teaching point like this: "Today I want to teach you that poets think about how the length of the poem and the size and style of the font connect to the ideas, images, or stories in the text. For example, if you write a long poem about a small object, you let the reader know that you think there's more to this object than meets the eye." You might show your young poets how you carefully consider where to break a line so that the sound, rhythm, and look of each line achieve the overall tone and meaning that you wish to convey. When you send students off to write, you might also invite them to explore ways that poets use the white space around the words to pause, take a breath, and make a line or two stand out from all the others.

All of this, of course, can be captured in the "Poets Sometimes . . ." chart in your room from Bend I, Session 2. Now is a good time to start layering in more academic vocabulary for reading, writing, and thinking about poetry. For example, if on the chart one of your points reads, "Poets sometimes create a pattern with rhyming words," you might explain to the class how poets have a word for that technique; they call it creating a *rhyme scheme*. You might then add the words *rhyme scheme* next to the kid-friendly phrase on the chart.

Some terms you might introduce into your discussions, either in this session or another, include:

- *Line breaks:* Poets can use line breaks to create a visual and rhythmic pause or place a slight emphasis on the last word in a line. Poets may try breaking the lines in different places, reading poems out loud or to a partner, and deciding where pauses would be appropriate and which words are worth emphasizing as the ends of lines.

- *Stanza breaks:* These are the chapters, section markers, or paragraph breaks of poems; they signal that some kind of change has taken place. Poets may try out different stanza breaks, always thinking about the purpose the break is serving. Different kinds of changes to consider: a shift in an idea, a new voice speaking, time passing, or a new image.

- *Form/rhyme scheme:* After poets have tried a formal structure, they might push themselves to use the form in ways that support what they are really trying to say. For example, in poems with patterns of repetition, writers make sure that the words or lines they choose to repeat are significant to the core images and ideas in the poem. As a revision, poets can try different words or lines until the most appropriate ones are discovered. Similarly, rhyming words catch attention. So if young writers are working on rhyme scheme, you may teach them to try out many possible rhymes until they are sure the words they've chosen are worth the extra attention they will get.

- *Shape:* Poets can write poems whose shape matches either an idea or an image that they are conveying. "Concrete poems" literally take the shape of their subjects; other poems take on a metaphorical shape by moving down the page in ways that suggest a kind of movement, a form in nature, or a physical structure.

- *White space:* Poets may use the blank space on the page to support ideas or images in the poem; the space on the page can be a metaphorical setting for the poem. If there is a lot of white space left on the page, it might suggest a setting of emptiness or silence; if the words are crowded onto the page, the poem might suggest a setting of chaos or noise.

- *Alliteration:* Poets can write phrases or whole lines that use the same starting sound as a way to call attention to that phrase or line. Poets think about the tone of the poem in the relevant section and choose starting sounds that match that tone. Hard sounds might indicate a harsh or unforgiving setting ("The car crashed, careening in crazy curlicues"); soft sounds might indicate a soothing or comforting feeling ("The sea sighed, sifting across the sand").

- *Onomatopoeia:* Poets choose words that sound like what they mean. Poets search for the perfect word for an action or description by trying out many verbs and adjectives and by searching for words that have a double-edged meaning ("The roach scuttled across the floor"). As a community, the class might publicly display onomatopoeic words that they discovered when reading, and students might try them in their work.

- *Simile, metaphor, imagery:* Poets choose simile and metaphor when they want to compare two things in surprising, unconventional ways. Poets can write images the same way they created the images in other units of study—through envisioning. In poetry, however, often an image or metaphor undergirds a poem and is central to its implicit meaning or the residue that lingers when the poem is finished.

## Bend II, Session 3: Revising for Craft Again and Again

As students revise their poems, you'll help them realize that writing is more like playing in clay than inscribing in marble. It is important for writers to try out many different versions of their poems to find the version that conveys their ideas in the strongest way. The act of revision brings new and more powerful ideas—and often a departure from old ones. You might teach your students that what poets want to say may change or evolve as they experiment with the way they are saying it.

Say to your students, "Today I want to teach you that poets use craft to make changes that best express what they most want to convey to the reader. They try out many different versions of their poems, asking themselves, 'What effect does *this* craft move make? *That* one? Is this what I really want to say?'" This comes at the perfect time, because your students will now be learning—and trying out—one craft move after another. Especially once they know the official names for the craft moves they are trying out, they'll feel extra "poet-like" by experimenting with alliteration or the fun-to-pronounce onomatopoeia.

### Bend II, Session 4: Using Craft in Fresh, Interesting Ways

As your students revise, as they try different ways to say something, they can draw upon strategies poets through the ages have used. For example, poets often aim to convey meaning through metaphor and simile. Here, you'll want to emphasize that craft has been around for ages, but that poets aim to use it in fresh, innovative ways. You might demonstrate this through a mentor poem such as "Mother to Son," by Langston Hughes. This poem is a terrific illustration of the fact that poets don't just compare things that most people think of as similar; poets often try out really surprising comparisons. Examine this line: "Life for me ain't been no crystal stair. It's had tacks in it, and splinters, and boards torn up, and places with no carpet on the floor—Bare." Here, you may need to help your students create "mind pictures" by placing an ordinary thing next to something they've never before compared it to (*life* and *crystal stair*): "The sky is big and limitless, like the first day of school."

During independent writing time, your students will continue to revise, armed with this new teaching. Of course, students can also draft new poems should they feel inspired.

You may want to use a mid-workshop teaching point or share to suggest that any part of a poem can be reconsidered and given a more innovative twist—the title, for instance. A writer can often enhance the meaning of a poem by setting up readers to expect one thing and then taking the poem in an entirely new direction. A poem titled "Family" that is an observation of a pile of worms, adds an interesting layer to the word *family*! What if it were instead called "Rainy Days," "Garden Helpers," or "Before the Flowers"?

### Bend II, Session 5: Giving Special Attention to Endings

Because poems—and certainly the ones your students write—are often short, each word and image matters enormously, and perhaps none more than the final one. You might consider, then, devoting a day to poetry endings. You could word your teaching point like this: "Today I want to teach you that the last moments of a poem are like a gift to your reader: they usually leave a last special image or often contain the poet's big idea or comment about everything else she wrote about."

In this way, you teach your writers to explore with care the possible endings for their poems. Just like in narrative and essay writing, young poets will want to try out multiple ways that their endings could go, until they find the one that feels the most evocative, powerful, and right.

**Bend II, Session 6: Experimenting with Voice and Word Choice**

One very important consideration for poets is to connect with readers, to help readers feel invited to share in the feelings and ideas expressed in the poem. To teach this, you might say, "Today I want to teach you that one important consideration for poets is to help the reader connect with the ideas of the speaker. One way poets do this is to experiment with other voices, like the second-person and first-person plural, as a way to pull in readers—to *universalize* their ideas."

Students can practice experimenting with word choice and voice by changing pronouns. For example: "I love New York for its brash, brawling sprawl" might become "Don't you love New York for its brash, brawling sprawl?" or "We love New York for its brash, brawling sprawl." Point out to students how the intimacy of these pronouns invites the reader to share the speaker's idea by including him in the sentiment.

As a share, you might demonstrate another part of speech with which poets can experiment to create a more powerful poem: verbs, verbs, verbs. In some ways, nothing matters other than verbs. Especially in poetry, verb choice is crucial, because the right verb often eliminates the need for adjectives, adverbs, and sometimes even nouns. Model for students how poets search for the perfect verb. Teach children that poets often make efforts to cut adjectives, instead using strong, image-oriented verbs as a way to move their verse forward. Once students are focused on finding the right verb for each part of their poem, remind them to reread their writing for correct grammar use—to make sure they have selected the right form of the verb: one that agrees with the subject of the phrase.

# BEND III: CHAPBOOKS AND SLAMS: PUBLISHING POEMS WITH FLAIR

As the unit approaches celebration, you may invite your poets to make choices about how they will share their poems with others. In some classrooms, this takes the form of posting poems in public places, throughout the school and the neighborhood. In others, it takes the form of creating chapbooks, or self-published books of poems. You might also create opportunities for students to read and perform poems, both student-written and published mentor poems. These performances can occur not only in the classroom but also in the larger community. Or you might mail individual poems to people who would benefit from hearing them or be grateful for receiving them.

**Bend III, Session 1: Selecting Poems that "Go Together" to Publish in a Chapbook**

On the first day of this bend, you may want to teach your writers that poets look over their drafts and decide which poems go together and how they should be arranged. Convey to them that sometimes new poems are drafted to go with the theme or concept of a chapbook. Some poets look across common themes. Your students might notice, for example, that many of their poems are about family or about feeling proud or about an important place. Partnerships will be very helpful during this phase of the writing process. You might steer partners to ask each other the following questions (or ones along these lines) to help each other choose poems to publish:

- Which of your poems do you like the best? Why?
- What are some different ways you could group your poems together?
- What kind of poetry writing did you enjoy the most?
- Which images do you love?

Of course, you will want to make sure your students continue to write and revise their poems during independent writing time as well as consider themes and presentation. In a mid-workshop teaching point, you might suggest that students shift into doing some thoughtful revision of the poems that are likely contenders for final publication.

## Bend III, Session 2: Creating Introductions to Poetry Collections

As your soon-to-be-published poets assemble their anthologies, they might also decide to include the mentor poems they studied or other published poems that fit within the same theme—so be sure to offer them this option. Doing so may get them to think more meaningfully about the theme that they have selected, which will set up for today's teaching point: "Today I want to teach you that poets create introductions for their anthologies, setting the context for the theme that the poems explore and giving them another opportunity to practice either essay writing (if they take up an idea and explore it) or informational writing (if they write to explain what their anthology is about)."

In addition to students publishing chapbooks, you may want to consider a performance in the form of an in-class slam, with poets lining up and performing their own memorized works or mentor poems.

If students are preparing to perform, the following tips will help them perform poetry in such a way that listeners will be able to engage with and understand their poems:

- When readers read a poem out loud, they use line breaks, sentence punctuation, and stanza breaks as cues for when to pause in their reading. Line breaks are indications of slight pauses; ending punctuation indicates a longer pause; stanza breaks may indicate either a slight or long pause, depending on the context.

- Readers use the meaning of the text to correct themselves and put pauses in places that make it easy for a listener to understand what's happening in the poem.

- Readers emphasize certain words when they read out loud. They are careful not to speak in a monotone and to use their voices to show the listener what's important in the text. They practice emphasizing different words until they're sure of how they want the poem to sound.

- Readers understand that they can use their voice to show the emotion or mood of the poem. When rehearsing, they can try on different tones of voice until it feels like they have the right sound as they read.

- When performing a poem, readers try to read at a pace that's appropriate to the poem. The listener should be able to hear every word, so we're careful not to rush or blur words together. Speeding up can add intensity to the poem, and slowing down can bring emphasis to a passage. Use these techniques purposefully to support the different parts of the poem. Use clues from the text like punctuation, spacing, and white space as indications of how fast or slowly to read.

## Bend III, Session 3: Celebration and a Final Reminder

Regardless of how you choose for your students to publish, remember that the secret of poetry is the heart. Poets write from the heart. They teach us to look at the world differently. They help us to celebrate small beauties. They inspire us to be outraged over injustices great and small. And so, as you reach the end of this unit, convey that sentiment to your budding poets. Remind them to hold a focus on the work that they do as poets in the world, not just today, as they celebrate the writing they've done over the course of this unit, but on every day going forward—that they interpret and respond to the world through words and use poems to capture something that moves them or makes them wonder, or to sustain others in hard times, or to express outrage and grief, excitement, and joy.

# Documentaries
*Bringing History to Life*

## RATIONALE/INTRODUCTION

Historical documentaries are filled with drama. And it's no surprise that even mentioning the word *drama* to a class full of seventh- or eighth-graders is typically enough to grab their attention. Just as drama and conflict permeate the entertainment and social life of most adolescents, drama and conflict are interwoven throughout America's history. Award-winning documentarian Ken Burns has spent more than twenty-five years capturing that drama, controversy, and tragedy in his historical documentaries. When speaking about what sparked his fascination with documentary films, he said, "I began to feel that the drama of the truth that is in the moment and in the past is richer and more interesting than the drama of Hollywood movies. So I began looking at documentary films." Just as Burns has made his mark on the documentary world, teachers from across the country have invited students into the world of writing documentaries as a way to bring history to life and engage in real-world informational writing opportunities.

In this unit, students will lean on what they know about informational writing and parlay those skills into writing a historical documentary. Writing historical documentaries integrates many of the important literacy skills your students have practiced across the year, including using primary and secondary sources, pairing research with analysis, and communicating with clear and specific language. This unit most obviously meets the Common Core State Standards for informational writing (W.7.2, W.8.2), yet it also leans on both multimodal research, where students gather information from both print and digital sources (W.7.8, W.8.8), and the use of technology to publish writing (W.7.6, W.8.6).

This unit is designed for students who have previous experience in writing workshop classrooms and have some expertise with information writing. If your students are completely new to this genre, you might first choose the unit "Writing Information Books on Topics of Personal Expertise." To build on students' expertise, this documentaries unit channels them to consider ways to organize their writing using a variety of structures such as compare/contrast and pro/con as called for by the seventh-grade Common Core

Standards (W.7.2a). Students are also invited to explore ways to incorporate other text types in addition to the standard "all-about" type typically associated with information writing. Students might include essays or narratives; one section might be an interview with an expert presenting an argument about the causes of the American Revolution based on her years of research; another might be the story of Paul Revere and William Dawes risking their lives to alert the countryside of the imminent arrival of British troops.

This unit channels students to write a digital information book in which they take on a historical topic—say, the Salem witch trials—and draft a script containing segments (like chapters) that explore different parts of the topic and present it in documentary form. One possible final vision is for students to collaboratively create a short historical documentary about a topic using video-editing software, such as iMovie. Another option is to have students publish an analog historical documentary in the form of a physical informational book. Whether you decide to publish digitally or in print, students will still receive the rich opportunity to write about historical topics in compelling ways.

A note on publishing digitally: this method may feel a bit daunting, but it not need to be so. While you may not feel that you're the savviest with digital publishing programs, your students will likely bring plenty of know-how to this unit. Don't be afraid to position yourself as a learner and explore the technology alongside your students. If this is your first go at this type of a unit, start small. Instead of tackling a full-length documentary, aim your students toward short, four- to five-minute presentations.

## A SUMMARY OF THE BENDS IN THE ROAD FOR THIS UNIT

**In Bend I (Building Your Vision as a Documentarian: Finding an Angle on a Historical Event or Era)**, students will begin by studying a mentor text in the form of a documentary. After immersing themselves in the genre, they will then move on to studying a historical event or era about which to research, write, and produce a documentary. The bend closes as students plan for the structure of their initial scripts.

**In Bend II (Drafting and Revising Scripts: Writing to Tell a Compelling Historical Story)**, students will write a rough draft of a script that incorporates research and then revise that script in a variety of ways. They will learn to reconsider structure, to build cohesion within and across the text, and to ensure that their research is both accurate and compelling.

**In Bend III (Digital Storytelling: Weaving Together Images, Sound, and Script through Storyboards and Digital Publishing)**, students will take their rough-draft scripts and develop storyboards to plan for the audio, visual, and text-based portions of the documentaries. The bend ends with the production and presentation of the documentaries.

## GETTING READY

For this unit to be as successful as possible, you'll want your students to be semi-familiar with the historical topic they choose, because they'll call on background knowledge right away. Consider having students write about a topic they have studied in social studies or historical fiction reading. Students will need text sets and research materials to guide the work they do in this unit. If you are channeling students toward a topic related to social studies, these may well be the materials students used during that unit of study. We also have a large and varied selection of text sets on our website (www.readingandwritingproject.com) about many different time periods. Rely on these, the Internet, and materials in your classroom to create these sets.

We also recommend gathering a few mentor texts, examples of historical documentaries, for your students to view in the beginning of the unit and use as mentors throughout their writing process. You might visit websites like the History Channel, PBS, or the Discovery Channel to find clips of documentaries. Or you could rent or purchase a handful of full-length documentaries from the likes of Ken Burns to show students. In addition, there are subscriptions to online video libraries that your school or district can purchase, such as Discovery Education Streaming Plus, that are helpful digital resources. Lastly, a quick search of YouTube or Google can render student-created documentaries that might serve as the perfect mentor texts for this writing project.

Equipment needs will vary from classroom to classroom and school to school. At the bare minimum, you'll need a few computers that groups of students can use and software like iMovie or Adobe Premier. Again, you do not need to be an expert in this software; many of these programs are intuitive, and your students will bring their digital literacy skills to these programs. Of course, you may decide to take things a bit further and even rent digital video cameras or recording devices and microphones if students will be taking part in interviews or filming shots. You'll want to think about storage for these projects. Can you store directly onto the hard drive of the computers? Would you prefer USB drives or other external (or portable) storage devices? Is your building wired to save onto a shared drive, perhaps an online storage site, such as Dropbox?

We also recommend doing a bit of thinking about places to find digital images and music, because students will be using both in the making of their historical documentaries. Of course, copyright and fair use is something you'll want to keep in mind, but there are many options for acquiring these in legitimate ways. The Library of Congress is a good place to start, where there are many digital collections of photographs and artifacts with open access. Or visit the LIFE photo archive and search millions of photographs and other images, stretching from the 1750s to today. Teach students how to search for public domain music and images. This is knowledge that will serve them well throughout their academic years. Some teachers prefer to purchase royalty-free music CDs and public domain image CDs for students to use.

For further support on guiding students through this project, to you might read "Stories Worth Telling," Mary Palmer and Perry Lee's guide for student-created documentaries (published on www.apple.com/education), which was an inspiration for this unit. Here you'll find a plethora of information regarding specific programs, design specifics of the unit, and planning templates.

## Management and Other Logistics

This unit is designed to be collaborative. Students will spend a good bit of time working in groups. We recommend having each student research, write, and produce her own historical documentary, though some teachers will opt to form small groups of three or four students, where the group researches, writes, and produces the documentary together. The reason we tend to shy away from the latter option is that when producing one piece collaboratively, each student is often charged with writing far less. This doesn't mean this option can't be successful; you'll simply want to keep an eye on volume and ensure that *all* students are writing, and writing a lot. If students do work in groups, we recommend ensuring that each member of the group is responsible for a part of their own. For example, a group of students might publish a historical documentary on the Puritans and the Salem witch trials, and each student takes on a "chapter" or segment. For example, one student publishes a segment on the Puritan way of life in Salem, and another publishes a segment on the "bewitched" girls. That way, each student experiences the research, writing, and production of a small segment.

Alternatively, if your research materials are limited to one or two topics, you might organize this unit so that the whole class writes on the same topic, with each group of students choosing an angle (and then individual chapters within that angle) for which they'll be responsible. For instance, the class might be examining the historical, social, and economic issues of the Great Depression, and groups of students would take on different angles to examine, such as the impact on children, the role of women, or the economic factors of the Great Depression. Or you might suggest four to six general historical topics, events, or eras—ones that students have studied before or are currently studying and for which there are accessible research materials—and allow students to select a topic from those choices.

This unit allows for a variety of access points for students. The medium in which students are writing and publishing is multimodal; students will have access to a variety of tools to express their understanding and knowledge, such as images, short texts, music, and narration. As you launch this unit, some students might be drawn to the way images tell the historical story, while other students will pick up on how the music expresses the tone of a historical era. The goal is a unit that engages students with a range of learning styles, interests, and abilities.

**If You're Feeling Lost at Sea: Creating a Mentor Text**

Your students will benefit greatly from seeing an example and gaining inspiration at the beginning of the unit. You might scour the Internet for examples and still feel a bit lost at sea as you prepare your own demonstration writing for this unit. If that is the case, here is a quick guide to making a short documentary, from Mary Palmer and Perry Lee's unit on student-led documentaries (http://images.apple.com/education/docs/Documentary_Guide_10-09.pdf):

Think of any subject or activity students participate in at school. Recruit a few students to help create your mentor. Perhaps students in gym class could film setting up and following through a free-throw shot in basketball. Next, you and your students write up a quick script that teaches the steps of a successful free-throw shot. Then, import the video clips into iMovie or another software. You can add narration and match it up with the stages of setting up and following through on a free throw. You can add music where needed as a way to introduce the short movie or build tension. You can add additional images or text to explain or illustrate important parts of the topic. Yes, it might only be a two- to three-minute short movie, and yes, it doesn't have much to do with history, but you've just created your first short documentary. Many teachers have vouched for the ease they felt after creating a film like this, thus allowing them to be more confident coaching students through the process.

## BEND I: BUILDING YOUR VISION AS A DOCUMENTARIAN: FINDING AN ANGLE ON A HISTORICAL EVENT OR ERA

In Bend I, students begin the unit by studying a mentor text in the form of a documentary. As students immerse themselves in the genre, they'll identify and name qualities of documentary writing and production that they'll bring to their work in this unit. Students will then choose their own historical event or era to study—finding a particular aspect about which to research, write, and produce a documentary. There is an emphasis on coaching students to find one compelling story they want to capture through documentary, rather than attempting to capture a wide swath of information about a topic. Students will be writing from the get-go, drafting possible segments (or chapters) of their documentary after experimenting with different ways to structure the piece.

The bend closes as students incorporate research that supports the points they are making about their topic.

### Bend I, Session 1: Studying Mentors: Becoming Familiar with Documentaries as a Genre

We suggest you launch this unit by studying a mentor text—in this case, a documentary. Channel students to study the opening of a historical documentary in the same way they would any mentor text. First, you might give them the opportunity to simply watch the clip, taking in the subject. Then, you might ask students to watch the clip a second time, studying it as a documentary filmmaker. You may want to prepare a chart so that as a class you can list the "Qualities of Excellent Documentaries" that students notice.

Help them to see some of what you hope they'll notice, too. You might watch the clip several times, asking students to watch for the craft moves a documentary maker uses, such as the inclusion of narration, transitions between images, the use of music to open a scene, or particular ways that quotes or other sound bites are introduced by the narrator.

You could also launch this session with small groups of students studying the different storytelling tools documentary makers use. Teach students that documentary makers have multiple tools for telling a story: words, images, and sound. They use each tool to express different aspects of the topic, such as the most important parts or the tone of the topic. To make this work a bit easier, you might set students up in groups of three, where each student uses one lens to study the impact of the storytelling tool. For instance you might say, "Documentary makers use many tools when capturing a historical moment. They use images and sound to tell the story, as well as words in the form of narration or testimonies. You'll be working in groups to investigate these tools. One of you should study the impact of the words, the actual writing, while someone else studies how the images show a part of the historical story. Another should study the sound—what music is used? What other audio is used? How does the sound tell a part of the historical story? Then, we'll come together as a class and chart what each of you noticed."

You might demonstrate by showing a clip such as the opening scene from Ken Burns' 2012 documentary film *The Dust Bowl*. The film begins with the sounds of a dust storm, excerpts of firsthand accounts, and images of dust storms. Students analyzing the images might notice how the author uses strong, shocking images from the very beginning as a way to show the severity of the situation. Students who are analyzing the documentary's sound might notice that the sound of the actual dust storm startles the audience and takes them back in time. Then, the words or narration, begins. Here the documentarian colorfully sets the historical stage, describing the disaster with plenty of strong, descriptive words.

After the minilesson, send students off to continue studying mentor texts in small groups, assuming you have the technology for groups of students to watch different clips simultaneously. If not, you could continue to study the same clip together, keeping students longer than usual in the meeting area.

After students have had some time to analyze the visual, audio, and language tools used in a documentary, you might deliver a mid-workshop teaching point in which you support students in considering the point of view of the documentarian as well. Each documentarian has a point of view and conveys specific ideas or angles of his subject. For example, Ken Burns begins his documentary *The West* with stories about the original native peoples of the West, instead of the settlement of the West by Europeans. His choice about which story to tell first reveals his point of view—that the stories of the first inhabitants of the West are valuable and worth telling. You might quickly show students the mentor documentary again, asking them to consider the ideas being conveyed and the angle being shown. When studying the mentor documentary, students might write entries in their notebooks about the ideas being conveyed or the point of view presented in the documentary. Some thought prompts teachers have found helpful to support this analysis are:

- An idea or lesson the author teaches the audience is . . .
- The author's main message about the topic is . . .

- The author's point of view on this topic might be . . .
- If the author were to take a side in this debate, he or she would argue . . .

Students might share some of their analysis in an end-of-workshop share. Homework on this night could be to search online for clips of documentaries (be sure to provide a list of appropriate sites) and to analyze them in ways they learned about in this session.

## Bend I, Session 2: Collecting Entries on Possible Topics and Experimenting with Structure

In this session, students will search for historical stories they want to document and tell. Writers will try on several possible topics, generating entries that capture all that they know about several historical topics to settle on one that feels just right. You might say to your class, "Today I want to teach you that historical documentarians use strategies to generate ideas for topics that are similar to generating ideas for any kind of writing. One thing they do is collect entries in their writer's notebooks, writing long to capture all they know about several topics. Then, they choose the topic that feels the best." You might show them how you write everything that comes to your mind about your own topic, writing an entry such as the following about the Salem witch trials:

I know that witch trials weren't a new idea in 1692, because for several centuries in Europe, people were already executing women whom they suspected of witchcraft. Most of the people who settled in Massachusetts were Puritans, and they had left England because they desired religious freedom. Salem Village was overcrowded, and there was a lot of rivalry between wealthy merchant families and farming families. Reverend Samuel Parris was an important figure in Salem Village; he was the first ordained minister, but many people thought he was cruel and greedy. The Puritans believed that weak people were targeted by the Devil and then worked for him by practicing witchcraft.

After the minilesson, you'll send students off to begin gathering entries in their notebooks. If you have a sense that some students might struggle with this, you might gather them in a small group, coaching to help them elaborate on their thinking and get down what they know on paper. Teaching the students a few thought prompts can be especially effective:

- Another thing I know is . . .
- Another important idea is . . .
- For example . . .
- Readers need to know this because . . .

For students accelerating through this process and in need of an extra challenge, we suggest pulling a small group in which you teach them to imagine more focused angles they might explore about their topic. For instance, when thinking about the Salem witch trials, you might model narrowing the topic in the following ways:

- Causes and effects of the different events that made the Puritans suspect the Devil was at work in their community
- Comparing and contrasting the witch trials in Europe with the witch trials in Salem
- Why the Puritans were fearful of Satan

At the midway point of the workshop, students will most likely have a few entries drafted in their notebooks. Before they commit to a topic, you'll want to ask them to consider the potential segments they'll write. This is groundwork for developing a table of contents and will ensure that students are taking on a topic that they can write long about. If they can see multiple ways to break down a topic, it is an indicator that this may be just the right topic for them. You might teach your students that writers think about different ways that topics can be divided, such as parts, kinds, time periods, or famous examples. You'll want to make sure you have your own topic of personal expertise at the ready to demonstrate how this might go. For example, the demonstration topic, the Salem witch trials, might look like this when divided into parts:

### Overall Topic: The History of the Salem Witch Trial

**Parts**
- The Puritans and their religious beliefs
- The young Puritan girls who were "bewitched"
- The men and women in Salem who were accused of witchcraft
- The Puritans who participated in the witch hunt
- The Puritans who spoke out against the witch hunt

What is important is that kids are trying out different ways their topic could be divided, even if some ways lack finesse. Encourage students individually to practice breaking down their topic into parts, kinds, time periods, or famous examples for the remaining time in the workshop.

During a share, you might highlight examples of students who have tried various ways to divide a topic into parts. The work below, done by a student on the colonial heritage of the thirteen colonies, is an example of the kind of work you might spotlight:

### Daily Life of Colonies
- School
- Art and culture
- Religion
- Economy

## Important People of Colonial America

- John Winthrop
- Anne Hutchinson
- Thomas Hooker

## Original Colonies

- Jamestown
- Plymouth
- New England

For homework, consider asking students to choose one of the ways they divided the topic of interest into parts and flash-draft several of those parts. This way, they can see how much information they know about each part (and how much information they still need to gain). At the beginning of Session 3, students will hone in on one topic.

### Bend I, Session 3: Selecting a Historical Topic and Using a Variety of Structures to Plan Chapters or Segments

Students will enter this session having explored a few possible topics for their documentaries. You might begin this session having students meet with a partner to look back over their entries and lists, deciding on a topic that feels most compelling. You'll coach students to select the topic—the seed idea—they want to commit to during this unit of study. While this might feel like hefty work, we recommend ushering students through it quickly (relegating it to a three- to four-minute connection during the minilesson), choosing instead to focus this day's teaching on the writing work students will do once they've decided on a topic.

Today you will help students move from focusing on their larger topic to the parts, or segments, into which they will divide their topic. They will try on a few different organizational structures for size, using these structures as ways to possibly organize their tables of contents. Your teaching point for the day will likely sound something like this: "Writers explore different structures for the segments or chapters of their historical documentaries. Some of these might include boxes (a broad category of information) and bullets (details that fit), cause and effect, pros and cons, and similarities and differences. Doing this work helps writers to consider the most effective way of delivering information to their audience."

We recommend modeling how you do this with your own topic. You might start with boxes and bullets. With a topic such as the Puritans, you could model how your documentary might go were you to use a boxes (a broad category) and bullets (details) structure:

| The Puritans and Their Strict Religious Beliefs |
|---|

- Required church attendance
- Dress and moral codes
- Punishments
- Fear of magic and witchcraft

Then, you might model how your documentary might go were you to choose a pro/con organizational structure:

| Pros of the Puritans' Punishment System |
|---|

- People obeyed the laws, and life was orderly.
- If people did break a law, they were unlikely to be repeat offenders.
- Puritans raised very obedient children.

| Cons of the Puritans' Punishment System |
|---|

- People lived in fear.
- The punishments were often inhumane.
- People were not able to express themselves.

You might demonstrate one final structure, such as compare/contrast, for example, comparing and contrasting the various dress and moral codes that governed Puritan life.

Send students off to work, and encourage them to try several ways their documentary could go before settling on the plan that seems to be the best fit. Once students have begun to settle on plans, you might channel them to start collecting some of the information that will go into each segment. Beginning to collect information will help your students to try on their plan for size, making sure they will be able to collect enough information to make each section viable. In a mid-workshop teaching point, you might suggest that writers use organizational structures not only as a way to make plans for how their pieces will go, but as a way to elaborate and collect information that might go into their documentaries.

Through experimenting with structure, it is likely that students will revise their overall plan from Session 2, and this will be a great focus for the share. The Common Core highlights the importance of "selection, organization, and analysis of relevant content," and thus, you will want your writers to work to continually consider what material to include and how best to organize it. You might model revising your own plan for your documentary, charging your writers with going back to revise the plans they have drafted for their own work for homework.

If you find that students struggle and/or need more time with this work, you might choose to create two sessions out of the one we've just outlined. For instance, you might notice that students would benefit from learning that two chapters or segments often need to be combined into one as they redefine the structure of their documentaries. Other times, one broad chapter needs to be broken apart. So, for example, if a student was planning for a documentary about Lewis and Clark's 1804–1806 expedition, she might have the following categories:

- The Promise of the West
- The Louisiana Purchase
- Captain Meriwether Lewis
- William Clark
- President Thomas Jefferson
- The Problems and Hardships the Explorers Faced
- The Explorers' Achievements
- The Perspectives of the Native Americans

You might then show the class how the student created a more balanced plan in which each segment felt like it would teach a good amount of information, rather than some segments teaching a lot and some teaching more or less, combining the first two categories under the heading: "The West as a Land of Opportunity and Adventure" and combining the next three categories of Lewis, Clark, and Jefferson to make a chapter titled "The Ambitious Leaders."

This first bend ends as students settle upon a plan for their documentary so that they are ready to launch into script writing in Bend II.

## BEND II: DRAFTING AND REVISING SCRIPTS: WRITING TO TELL A COMPELLING HISTORICAL STORY

During this bend, you will channel your students to write a rough draft of a script that incorporates research, as well as revise that script before moving on to creating a storyboard for their documentary. It's important to note here that if your students are working in groups, you'll need to help them decide how to divvy up the writing. If you decide that each student should write her own script during this bend, they will be in a good position to produce high writing volume and will have plenty of opportunities to practice the informational writing lessons you'll teach. However, when it comes to Bend III (where students create a storyboard), they might coproduce the documentary, meaning each student takes on one section to produce.

### Bend II, Session 1: Creating a Rough Draft of a Script with Sections or Chapters

Documentaries have segments or chapters similar to informational books; therefore it makes sense to channel students to draft one segment or chapter at a time. On the first day of this bend, you might remind writers that just as an overall text has a logical organization, so does a single segment, and that writers draft with that structure in mind. You might say, "Planning for segments in historical documentaries is very similar to planning chapters in an information book. Writers consider how to organize the segment to best teach readers, perhaps considering dividing the segment into parts or kinds or chronological order or perhaps a combination of those."

You might model how you rehearse for drafting one of your chapters. For example, you might demonstrate how you rehearse for the segment about the "bewitched" girls, thinking through how to structure the section logically to best present the information to viewers. Think aloud to demonstrate how you plan to start with some background information on the everyday life of young girls in Salem's Puritan society, so that readers have some context. Then, you might plan to divide the segment into parts, first discussing Betty Parris, the first of a group of friends who made the accusations that led to the Salem witch trials. You might show that you could tell Betty's story, especially how she began showing signs of a strange illness and accused others of witchcraft. And then you might show that you could discuss the other girls, such as Ann Putman and Abigail Williams, who seemed to follow Betty's lead and soon began to behave quite erratically as well. Then, model how you would wrap up the chapter by discussing the way the girls went about identifying their witch tormentors in a conclusion of sorts. You might debrief, explaining that you used a combination of parts (the various girls who made accusations) and chronological (giving background information first, and ending with the aftermath).

Your model plan might go:

1. What was day-to-day life like for Puritan children, and especially for young girls, in Salem?

2. What did Puritan society expect and demand of girls?

3. Who was Betty Parris?

4. Who was Ann Putman?

5. Who was Abigail Williams?

6. How did the girls identify their tormentors?

Next, you might model how you would use your plan to start quickly drafting a segment, jotting a line or two out loud or on chart paper in front of your students.

Your writers will likely launch themselves into drafting with exhilaration and great energy. After all, they have been rehearsing and planning and have focused ideas for how their writing will go. On this day, encourage your writers to really push themselves toward high volume and stamina, aiming to finish at least one segment and start another before the end of the workshop.

You might interrupt students for a mid-workshop teaching point in which you ask them to set a volume goal for themselves—say a page and a half by the end of the session.

## Bend II, Session 2: Incorporating Research into Historical Documentary Scripts

In this session, help your writers make plans for the additional information they need to gather for their drafts. Teach students that writers make decisions about what kind of research to gather, which sources to use to find it, and where in their pieces the information will go. You might want to start a chart about purposes for different information, helping writers to see the value of including varied information. You might start your chart with the types of information listed in the Common Core grade-specific standards—"relevant facts, definitions, concrete details, quotations, or other information and examples"—and add to this list, explaining to students that conducting interviews or finding quotes can help make the writing feel more personal, while finding facts can help the writing to feel more authoritative (W.7.2, W.8.2).

At this point, your writers will no longer be moving lockstep through the writing process. On any given day, they will be proceeding through cycles of planning segments, drafting, and revising, and you will want to encourage them to move at their own pace. Students might use the teaching in this session as a revision strategy, conducting research as a way to add to sections they have already written, or they might use it as a way to write more comprehensive drafts, researching before they write new segments. Encourage your students to make choices about how to use your teaching going forward as they draft better and better new segments and return to previously written segments to make them even better.

You might interrupt your students' work for a mid-workshop teaching point on summarizing or para-phrasing, as well as to encourage your writers to keep a list of the sources they have used. Quoting, listing, and taking notes from sources is emphasized throughout the Common Core's standards for middle school. Christopher Lehman, in his book *Energize Research Reading and Writing* (2012), suggests that to improve note-taking (and avoid plagiarism), students should to take a mental pause from their reading to think before jotting. One way students might do this is to read, then cover up the text while they jot their notes. After jotting, they should reread the text, looking for any key information that they may have missed. You might model the last part of this strategy by showing how you return to a text to look for information that an expert on your topic may know but that you had missed. The key here is not just to rewrite every nuance, but to determine information that is central to understanding the concept.

One thing you will certainly want to teach your writers is to carefully consider the *selection* of their material, a key expectation of the Common Core. In a share session at the end of this workshop, you might teach your writers that they need to carefully consider what information should go within each segment as well as what might be excluded. Partnerships can help each other with this work as they rehearse segments with each other and share the work they've been doing.

## Bend II, Session 3: Revising Scripts for Structure, Accuracy, and Cohesion

At this point in the writing process, your students will have a variety of revision needs, and you will want to tailor your teaching accordingly. Rather than conducting a whole-class lesson, you might decide to teach several small groups today, each geared to address the specific needs of a set of students. Then too, you might find that the large majority of your class is in need of a specific kind of help, in which case a whole-class lesson is the way to go. Regardless of your choice, you'll find a variety of possible teaching points below. Keep in mind that this revision "session" might actually become two or three days of teaching. As long as students are writing and revising, keep teaching! When volume and stamina wane, you'll know it is time to move on.

If you notice your students need support with cohesion or flow, consider teaching a lesson on ways to make sure chapters fit or flow together. Remind your students that writers make connections within and across the categories of information in their texts, making sure it is clear how one section connects to the next (and to the overall text). It will be helpful for you to know that there is, in fact, a key shift that occurs between sixth and seventh grade in the Common Core State Standards. In sixth grade, the Common Core expects students to use "transitions to clarify relationships among ideas and concepts" (W.6.2). By seventh grade, they are expected to use "appropriate transitions to create cohesion and clarify the relationships among ideas and concepts" (W.7.2). This difference is subtle but critical. The Common Core expects that each part, section, and chapter of the informational writing of students from seventh grade onward is connected, seamlessly conveying important ideas and concepts. An important part of this teaching will be reminding students that writers don't just connect parts of a text; they do so logically. That is, there is a logical organization to the text, and the transitions they use convey this organization to the reader. You might create a class chart of some common transition phrases, including those highlighted by the Common Core for your grade level as well as others you deem useful. Be sure to identify which phrases can be used for which purposes, and encourage your students to add other phrases to the chart as they use them in their writing.

Your chart might look like:

### Common Transition Words and Phrases

| Giving an Example | Cause/Effect | Conflicting Information |
|---|---|---|
| • For instance | • Because of | • Unlike |
| • Such as | • As a result | • Despite |
| | | • On the other hand |
| | | • In contrast to |

You might also teach students that a common structure that documentary makers use is *Segment 1: news, news, reaction to news; Segment 2: news, news, reaction to news*; and so on. This helps segment chapters into small bursts of information, paired with the analysis of experts. In other words, some documentarians draft chapters or segments covering *This is what happened, this is what also happened, this is the reaction of others*, and then repeat that structure for following segments. This pattern-like structure provides a helpful, repetitive scaffold when students' drafts feel structurally challenged.

If you notice that the language students use could be more specific, accurate, or embellished, you might teach students that documentarians incorporate the language of the topic—in other words, the words and terms that experts on the topic would use. The more domain-specific words are used in context in the writing, the more expertise the writer establishes. Students' writing should be filled with precise, concrete nouns and action verbs as ways to teach the reader as much as possible about the topic. You might also teach your students that historical documentarians don't just use important terms once and move on. Important terms are often incorporated over and over because they represent concepts central to the topic.

A final revision possibility is to support students in revising the opening or closing scenes of their documentaries. Professional documentaries can serve as wonderful mentors and can be just the exemplars your writers need to write powerful and poignant openings and closings. You might refer to the chart you created in Session 1 where you analyzed and recorded qualities of successful documentaries with your students. Or you might encourage writers to draw on all they know about beginnings and endings in other kinds of writing. For example, they might choose a narrative style of beginning and ending, beginning by drawing viewers into the world of the documentary by introducing characters and naming a problem, and concluding with some kind of a resolution.

## BEND III: DIGITAL STORYTELLING: WEAVING TOGETHER IMAGES, SOUND, AND SCRIPT THROUGH STORYBOARD AND DIGITAL PUBLISHING

In this final bend, students take their rough-draft scripts and develop a storyboard that maps out the audio, images, and text for their documentaries. Whether your students are each working on their own documentaries or are working with a group to produce a shared documentary, make sure that each student takes ownership for at least one segment, so that all students have the opportunity to experience storyboarding and digital publishing. The bend ends with students producing their pieces and with a celebration of all that they have accomplished.

### Bend III, Session 1: Storyboarding to Incorporate Digital Elements

Once students have finished their drafts, they'll be ready to build a storyboard. Documentarians use storyboards to plan how a script will be paired with images and sound to create an overall meaning or message about a topic. Palmer and Lee suggest students use a simple yet effective storyboard, with one column for audio, one for images, and another for notes:

| Audio/Excerpts of Script | Video/Images | Notes |
|---|---|---|
| Beethoven's Fifth Symphony | Black screen fades to image of Salem witch trial | |
| Narration begins: "It was a time of extreme faith and extreme accusations." | New picture of witch trial | |

Some documentarians create separate columns for the audio and music. The audio column includes not only narration, but also the voices of interview subjects or dialogue from video clips. For example:

| Audio/Excerpts of Script | Video/Images | Music |
| --- | --- | --- |
| | Black screen fades to image of Salem witch trial | Beethoven's Fifth Symphony |
| Narration begins: "It was a time of extreme faith and extreme accusations." | New picture of witch trial | Fade out Beethoven's Fifth Symphony |

After showing students some options for how storyboards could be organized, model for them how you fill out a storyboard, inputting the script first, then matching the images and music to it. During the storyboarding process, students may realize that not all parts of their scripts will make it into the final documentary. In a mid-workshop teaching point, you might say, "Documentary makers know that all parts of their writing won't make the final cut. They use storyboards to plan for the text, images, and sounds they'll incorporate in each part of the documentary. They consider each of these separately, thinking about which quotes and portions of text will tell the story best, which images will best convey the events and tone of the time period, and what music matches the images and text they've selected. The parts that don't fit end up on the cutting room floor."

You might have some of the following questions posted on a chart for students as they work.

### When Building a Storyboard, Documentarians Consider . . .

- Which quotes help to highlight key information in the script?
- Which images strongly convey the information and tone of the event, time period, or topic?
- Do the images and music support the text in telling the story?
- Does the storyboard include enough expert analysis to accompany the text?
- What quotes, examples, or narration might be edited out?

Students may need a great deal of small-group coaching as they plan their storyboards, particularly for support with cohesion. You might channel students to consider questions such as "Do the images match the excerpts of the script? Does the mood of the music support or clash with the images presented?" If your students are working in groups, expect some lively debates as they consider what to keep and what to abandon from their scripts during this preproduction process.

In a mid-workshop teaching point, channel your writers to do some editing to ready their scripts for digital publication. You might suggest that students divide and conquer the editing responsibilities, nominating captains to be responsible for different kinds of editing. A few possibilities for editing captain jobs might include:

- Punctuation Captain: checks all on-screen text for variety of punctuation, if the type of punctuation matches the tone of the piece, sloppy misuse of capitals, and so on

- Sentence Captain: checks narration script for fragments, run-on sentences, redundant sentences, clichés, and so on

- Spelling Captain: checks all on-screen text for correct spelling of domain-specific language, high-frequency words, proper nouns specific to the topic, and so on

- Language Captain: checks narration script for informal language use, correct use of domain-specific language, balance of precise and accurate language and so on

You might suggest that students switch roles and take their work through a second round of editing, both to encourage deeper editing and to ensure your students get plenty of practice editing with different lenses.

In a share session at the end of the workshop, invite students to study their work with the Information Writing Checklist in hand. Encourage them to make final changes as they study the checklist and remember all of the ways information writers write well to teach readers. You may want to encourage students to review their storyboards one last time as homework tonight, editing and fixing up their writing according to the checklist to be ready for tomorrow's production session.

## Bend III, Session 2: Putting It All Together: Digital Production and the Editing Room

In this session, you'll teach students how to turn their vision into a reality by using video-editing software, such as iMovie, to create their historical documentary. This session will feel a bit like editing-on-the-go as students huddle together to transition their storyboards into actual segments. "Documentarians are artists," you might begin. "They take rough-draft scripts and storyboards and turn them into documentaries that they share with a larger audience. This means taking a storyboard plan and using technology to bring that vision to life."

### Information Writing Checklist

| | Grade 7 | NOT YET | STARTING TO | YES! | Grade 8 | NOT YET | STARTING TO | YES! |
|---|---|---|---|---|---|---|---|---|
| | **Structure** | | | | **Structure** | | | |
| **Overall** | I brought together ideas and information about a subject in a text that develops a sub-topic and/or an idea. I incorporated a variety of text structures as needed, including argument, explanation, narrative, and procedural passages. | ☐ | ☐ | ☐ | I discussed key concepts within a topic and made it clear why these concepts are important. I provided examples with relevant information, using a variety of text structures and formatting as needed to make concepts and information compelling and accessible. | ☐ | ☐ | ☐ |
| **Lead** | I interested the reader in the topic by explaining its significance, or providing a compelling fact, statistic, or anecdote. I made it clear what parts of the topic this text would tackle, and how the ideas and information in the text would unfold. | ☐ | ☐ | ☐ | After hooking the reader, I provided context, introduced a focus/main idea and oriented readers to the overall structure of the text (compare/contrast, cause and effect, claims and support, classification, etc.) | ☐ | ☐ | ☐ |
| **Transitions** | I used transitions to link concepts with related information. The transitions help the reader follow from part to part and make it clear when information is an example of a bigger idea, follows from an earlier point, introduces a new idea, or suggests a contrast. I used such transitions as: *specifically, for instance, related to, just as, turning to, on the other hand,* and *however.* | ☐ | ☐ | ☐ | I used transitions to lead the reader across parts of the text and to help the reader note how parts of the text relate back to earlier parts, using phrases such as *just as, returning to, as we saw earlier, similarly to, unlike,* and *and yet.* | ☐ | ☐ | ☐ |
| **Ending** | In my conclusion, I reinforced and built on the main point(s) in a way that made the entire piece a cohesive whole. The conclusion may have restated the main points, responded to them, or highlighted their significance. | ☐ | ☐ | ☐ | In the conclusion, I suggested implications, built up the significance of the main points, and/or alluded to potential challenges. | ☐ | ☐ | ☐ |

Today students will be recording narration, adding images and music, adjusting the pace of the slides and transitions between them, adding titles and subtitles, adjusting volume, and experimenting with effects. Of course, the best way to learn what to teach regarding these areas is by trying it out yourself, before asking your students to use it. Many teachers report that the software is often intuitive to use and that many of their students have prior experience with it and step forward to teach those that do not.

It may take more than one workshop for students to compile their final versions, depending on the availability of computers and your students' ease in using the software. But this is the moment when all of their hard work will come together. Students will delight in seeing their efforts in thinking, researching, writing, and editing finally come together as they make a piece of history come alive in digital form.

### Bend III, Session 3: Celebration: Screening Documentaries, Tribeca Film Festival Style

This session brings this unit to a close as students share their hard work and historical documentaries. You might transform your classroom into a mini–film festival, where groups of students take turns screening their documentaries to an audience of their peers. You might invite parents, guardians, other classes, or friends of the community to the festival, where students can indulge in a light concession fare of popcorn and bubbly soft drinks or juice. To fully embrace the festival spirit, students might give reviews afterward, or you might create a mock red carpet where filmmakers are interviewed by their classmates or peers. You'll determine the audience (you might invite older or younger grades) as well as the venue (you might celebrate in the classroom, library, or auditorium).

To further celebrate and capture students' work, you might encourage them to save their documentaries to a class website. Alternatively, you might opt to copy documentaries onto a DVD and share with students. Whichever way you choose to celebrate and share your students' work, create a celebration where the full range of your students' work—with its music, text, and images—can shine.

# Literary Essays
## *A Mini-Unit on Analyzing Complex Texts for Meaning, Craft, and Tone*

## RATIONALE/INTRODUCTION

Writers need to write about something they know and care a lot about, and they need to write for real reasons, such as to persuade others or discover something about themselves. To this end, a main goal of this unit is to help students deepen their relationship with books through writing as they grow insights and sharpen their analytical writing skills, including their ability to incorporate text evidence. Teaching students to write well about reading is a crucial part of any literacy curriculum. The unit described here is designed to round out the seventh-grade curriculum, because *The Literary Essay* is a full-length book in both the sixth- and eighth-grade *Units of Study* curricula. For seventh-grade teachers, this unit will provide a great opportunity to continue writing about reading across the year. It will challenge students beyond the work done in *Writing Realistic Fiction: Symbolism, Syntax, and Truth* and will prepare them for *The Art of Argument: Research-Based Essays*.

To ensure full engagement in this unit, encourage your students to write about a character or theme in a story that has been particularly meaningful to them. By asking students to write about a character or theme that is meaningful to *you*, they are more likely to write from a place of compliance, not compassion, and you will see the difference this makes in their analyses and writing.

It is also important to consider writing fluency—the ability of students to express their ideas clearly and support them with lots of detail, with high volume, and at an efficient rate. This unit aims to teach writers to get a quick draft of an essay going and then to further develop their argument and deepen their analysis of the text—and ultimately, to repeat this process until they become more expert at this kind of writing. In each bend of this unit, therefore, students move through the process of planning, drafting, and revising a literary essay. Considering the amount of writing that students do in high school and college, at the time of high-stakes tests such as the SAT and AP exams, and it makes good sense to support them now with expressing their ideas and supporting ideas with evidence quickly and efficiently.

The Common Core State Standards call for text-based analysis and response, not only in the standards for opinion and information writing, but also in the standards for speaking and listening and research. In short, it can be argued that this skill—writing about reading—is one of the most essential skills emphasized in the CCSS, in no small way because the ability to reflect on ideas garnered from reading (both fiction and nonfiction) is essential to college and career achievement.

We've focused the unit on developing compelling arguments about characters; supporting ideas with carefully chosen evidence; and exploring themes, issues, and lessons relevant to the books students read and the lives they live. This unit tends to be the most successful when students have a lot of support developing clear, evidence-based claims and when they are given a great deal of agency to develop ideas that feel relevant to them. As students learn to develop their own claims, they will see big, important ideas lurking in the books they read, and they will learn that writing about these ideas can lead to new insights about their own lives as well.

## A SUMMARY OF THE BENDS IN THE ROAD FOR THIS UNIT

**In Bend I (Writing Literary Essays that Explore a Theme or a Character in a Single Text)**, you will invite your students to develop and draft a literary essay about one text. You will begin by teaching ways to study and write about texts that yield fruitful ideas for essays. Then, you will channel your writers to collect evidence and, finally, to organize their evidence into cohesive drafts in support of their claims.

**In Bend II (Writing across Texts to Explore the Different Treatment of Similar Themes)**, students will work to build an argument that cuts across more than one text. This exercise will match up with instruction and club talk in reading workshop, because students will be engaged in thinking, jotting, and talking about more than one book—finding places where texts are similar and also digging deeper to think about how two books that ostensibly advance the same theme actually do so in different ways. In a challenging close to the unit, students will be introduced to ways to incorporate secondary criticism and other source material outside of the text itself.

## GETTING READY

For some lovely examples of essays that can serve as mentors for the essays students will create, see the contest winners from the Library of Congress Letters about Literature project (www.lettersaboutliterature .org). We also encourage you to read reviews in the *The New York Review of Books* or the *London Review of Books*, where you'll note a highly personal tone to some of the essays. One of our favorite examples of writing about reading is *The Child that Books Built*, in which Francis Spufford (2003) explains why *Narnia* was the most important literature of his childhood. We also recommend using student-written literary essays—from either other classes or other years—and to let these serve as guideposts for students. Even if they are not perfect, students can study them for the moves they will replicate as literary essayists.

Of course, perhaps the most important model of this sort of writing will be your own. Throughout this unit we'll reference the demonstration piece of writing that you will compose alongside the students, showing them how to craft an essay each step of the way. Because this is a text that you are creating, you can ensure that your writing is sophisticated and yet feels achievable to the students in your class. That is, aim to write one notch above the writing they are doing so that you can show them new moves without conveying a sense that literary essay is "too hard" or "confusing."

## BEND I: WRITING LITERARY ESSAYS THAT EXPLORE A THEME OR A CHARACTER IN A SINGLE TEXT

There are reasons to read critically that cut deeper than the current standards movement. We must teach our students to be the kind of thinkers and questioners who don't take what others say at face value. Instead, they examine and weigh evidence and develop their own ideas, based on their core beliefs. Writing is one of the best ways that your students can deepen their thinking about texts. They can study the ideas they capture on paper and analyze their own arguments in ways that only writing can support.

It will be crucial that you find ways to bring the energy kids have for reading into writing workshop this month. You will want to draw on the passion, the commitment, the obsession that your young readers develop for the characters and worlds of their reading lives as the fuel to jump-start literary essays. During a transition to writing from reading workshop you might even say something like, "Don't even put your books away. We're going to need them today and this whole month for our writing work."

### Bend I, Session 1: Exploring Ideas about Texts through Writing

By this time in the year, and in their reading lives, your students have likely learned that literature can lead them to think about important truths in the world. Whether you're teaching a reading unit that supports interpretation and text analysis concurrently or not, you will want to remind students that most texts contain ideas that take more than a casual read to unlock and that one way to unlock these ideas is through writing.

"We want to be the kind of people," you might say to your students, "who don't just see the surface of things. We don't want to always take what others say at face value; we don't want to believe everything that advertisers or even reporters tell us. But thinking critically in this way takes practice. Writing is one of the best ways we have to push our thinking to new levels. And when we write about reading, when we push ourselves to articulate an idea from a text and to be precise about it, when we map out how that idea begins and grows throughout a book, that's often when we come to new thinking. In this unit, we're going to practice using writing to think clearly and deeply about reading."

You might demonstrate this teaching using a short text that your class knows well, preferably something you have read and discussed earlier in the year. Show your students how you revisit the text, this time thinking as a writer aiming to grow ideas. You might demonstrate how you write a free-form entry in your writer's notebook, aiming to write as much as you can about an idea that is cropping up for you as you read the text anew.

Send students off to work, channeling them to look back at books or short texts they've read, trying out ideas they've had by writing that idea in a number of ways, writing long to find new truths. In a mid-workshop teaching point, you might remind students of prompts they can use to uncover new thinking as they write, such as "This makes me realize . . ." or "I'm still wondering . . ." or "On the other hand . . ."

## Bend I, Session 2: Revisiting Pivotal Moments in Texts

You will want to focus two to three days of your teaching on close rereading and developing ideas about literature. Therefore, you'll want to be sure you are offering students some ways to come up with fruitful ideas. The pivotal moments in stories are places to revisit and search for deeper meaning. You might say to your students, "One place that essayists know is particularly fruitful when searching for big ideas in a text are pivotal moments. Writers can zoom in on turning points or moments that a character faces a big decision or overcomes an obstacle and ask, 'What does this moment really mean? What is it teaching the character or me?'"

On this day, as you send students off to work, encourage them to be as industrious as possible and to be not afraid to explore ideas in writing, even if those ideas seem disconnected or far-fetched. Now is the time for students to venture outside the confines of their texts and to take risks with the ideas they try out. Later, when students are collecting evidence, you'll support them in making sure their ideas are connected and grounded in their texts.

In a mid-workshop teaching point, you can teach students that when they are writing about reading, they might think about themes that they've encountered before and ask, "What does this text have to say about this theme?" Some likely themes in adolescent literature include growing up, the individual versus the group, and trying to be good in a flawed world.

## Bend I, Session 3: Analyzing Characters to Uncover Big Ideas

We have found that character-based ideas tend to be more accessible and more easily supported, so if your class, or a small group of students, is in need of extra support in interpretation or in finding accountable text evidence, you may choose to angle the work toward character-based ideas, such as "Percy, in *The Lightning Thief*, values his friendships over his family."

Teach students ways to study characters that tend to have a big payoff when searching for ideas. To teach that studying characters can lead to powerful thinking, you might unveil a chart made especially for this day:

## Studying Characters to Grow Powerful Ideas about Texts

As essayists, we can study:

- Moments of strong emotion
- Turning points for characters
- Places where characters make choices
- Places where characters learn lessons or change

You will also want to point out, perhaps in a mid-workshop teaching point, that some ideas emerge only at the end of the story (this is especially true in shorter texts). In that case, it will be impossible to provide evidence from across the text to support that claim. The strongest ideas for essays are ones for which the writer can provide evidence from all parts of the text.

### Bend I, Session 4: Crafting Thesis Statements

After a few sessions in which students have been writing long to develop ideas, move them toward crafting concise thesis statements—thesis statements that will lead to well-structured, clear essays. This work is more challenging than it may at first appear, because the thesis sets up all the rest of the essay work.

You might give your students examples of different ways that essays based on a single text might go, because doing so may help them to learn how to write their own thesis statements. Once they see possible templates, it's more likely that they can craft a thesis that will adhere to one of these structures. Your teaching point on this day will likely sound something like this: "Today I want to teach you that literary essayists develop a thesis by zooming in on the topic and text they hope to write about, picking a rough idea, and then trying that idea out several different ways until they find a thesis they can support." You'll want to show students how you try several drafts of the same thesis, imagining different ways of saying something similar, and then rehearsing that thesis by checking to see if there is enough evidence from the text to support it.

There are a few templates that seem to especially work for literary essays. Help writers to use these with elasticity, so they are still able to write about the ideas that matter most to them. Some writers will have a claim about a character or a text and then give reasons for that claim, as they do in other types of essays. "So and so is a complex character because A, because B, and above all because C." Or "So and so is able to face challenges because of A, B, and C."

As students work on crafting their own thesis statements, we recommend being somewhat heavy-handed in your conferring and making an effort to get to as many students as possible. You don't want any students to leave the starting block with a thesis that is bound to fail because they are unable to support it.

You might interrupt students for a mid-workshop teaching point to introduce them to another kind of essay structure—one in which the writer advances a theme and then supports it with one paragraph of text evidence and one paragraph that shows how the writer, too, has experienced this theme. This structure might help those who are struggling to craft a thesis statement that encapsulates the whole of a text.

During an end-of-workshop share, you might ask writers to share their burgeoning thesis statements with a partner and then talk through some of the possible evidence they will use to support their thesis statements. Talking through evidence right at the start will help your writers to identify potentially problematic thesis statements and will demonstrate how writers often have to revise a thesis statement to make it really work with the evidence they have in mind.

## Bend I, Session 5: Collecting and Testing Evidence

In this session, you and your students will begin the most critical work of this unit. You will want to shorten your whole-class teaching as much as possible during these next days, because the most important instruction will be the more personalized, targeted work of conferences and small groups as students write independently. Your students will have very different kinds of thesis statements and will likely be drawing from different texts to find support. The big goal now is to support them in identifying evidence from their texts in the form of angled retellings of select scenes, paraphrased sections, and direct citations.

Before beginning this work, you'll want to think about how you will teach students to physically collect and store evidence for their essays. If students have experience with writing workshop, it is likely they already know a few methods for organizing evidence and will simply need to be reminded of those options and then given some choice. If not, model a few options and allow writers to make decisions about the organization style that is the best fit for them. We've found a few to be incredibly successful. For students who benefit from tactile experiences, you might show them how they can create actual, physical folders for each of their bullets (for instance, a folder in which they will collect evidence to support point A, another for point B, and yet another for point C), in which they can place evidence gathered on sheets of paper. Alternatively, students might set up their notebooks or a small booklet so that there is section of paper for each body paragraph, onto which they put evidence as they collect it.

On this day, begin by teaching students that writers try out different pieces of textual evidence by asking themselves, "Does this really support the idea that I'm writing about?" If the evidence will take too much defending, if it doesn't pop out as truly connected, it's best not to use it. Partner work can take a bigger role here, because partners can try out their ideas and evidence on each other, regardless of whether they are writing about or reading the same text. In some ways, a partner new to a text is a perfect audience for this exercise. As students write independently, the key will be to move quickly from talk back to writing as partners jot down the words they used to justify their evidence or go back to the drawing board to find a more fitting example.

In a mid-workshop teaching point, you might lift the level of partner work by empowering students to push each other's thinking if need be. Teach students to be not afraid to say, "I'm not sure I see how this fits. Can you say more about why this scene shows how Percy puts his family's needs aside?"

If your students are writing about novels, especially longer ones, a likely small-group lesson will be prioritization. There will be hundreds of pages of text to choose from, and students may get overwhelmed looking for appropriate quotes or passages. Teach these students to search for a few key places where they stuck Post-its® or lingered while discussing the book with others. Those are the scenes that are going to yield the richest material. Remind your students that they don't need pages and pages of evidence; they just need enough evidence that their essays feel rich and varied.

### Bend I, Session 6: Using a Variety of Evidence to Support Ideas

Plan to focus some teaching on the kinds of evidence literary essayists collect and the ways they angle this evidence to best support the points they are trying to make. Assuming students have already learned a bit about paraphrasing and quoting in years past, we recommend teaching a repertoire lesson today.

You might say, "Essayists know that it is important to collect a variety of evidence to support a thesis. When writing about literature, essayists tend to rely on retelling parts of a story that support their idea or quoting directly from those parts. In both instances, they make sure to include only the part of the story that supports what they are really trying to say." Then, model for students how you can go back to a text and look for parts that support each of your body paragraphs and either paraphrase or quote from those parts.

When students go off to work independently, encourage them to collect as much evidence as they can find. We recommend using today's mid-workshop teaching time to introduce another kind of evidence—lists—in which students list several examples in support of a topic sentence. Tomorrow, when they begin drafting, they can decide which of all the evidence they collected will make the final cut.

You will want to set the expectation that students develop at least two supporting body paragraphs, which may incorporate one extended text example in the form of an angled retelling or a citation with explanation or which may include several examples in a listed, paraphrased format. Encourage students to try for a variety of kinds of evidence to practice the different methods. If you notice students lagging, having written just one text example on a half-sheet of paper and now feeling "done," quickly intervene: "I know you're capable of writing a whole page in five or six minutes. Check your work and set a goal for how many half pages of evidence you're going to have in the last fifteen minutes of writing workshop time."

Since some students may be working on essays that point to the text and their own lives, you will want to model how to collect evidence to support that structure. The search for evidence in this case is one that crosses the text and the essayist's own experience. This actually previews the compare-contrast work of the next part, because the writer must find parallel evidence from two separate sources. Which story from this character's life best demonstrates this idea? And which moment from my own life also shows this? The writer will then devote one paragraph to an anecdote from the story or book and one paragraph to an anecdote from his life. In each case, you will remind them of all they know about narrative writing to write small stories in a zoomed-in way, bringing out details that go with the thesis of the essay.

### Bend I, Session 7: Drafting a Cohesive Essay

On this day you will support students as they take the evidence they've collected and put it together to form the rough draft of their first essay. First, teach students the component parts of a body paragraph and then send them off to draft. We recommend teaching students that a strong body paragraph has a topic sentence, one to two pieces of evidence, and a final sentence or two in which the writer connects the evidence back to the topic sentence. You might even chart some productive ways to analyze or elaborate on evidence, moving beyond "This shows that . . ." Other possible transitions include "This demonstrates . . . ," "From this scene, we can infer that . . . ," and "The reader of this scene understands that . . ."

Students will be writing up a storm during independent writing time, drafting on loose-leaf paper or on a computer, putting together all of the evidence and ideas they have been collecting in notebooks or folders. Encourage your students to be discerning about which evidence to include in their drafts and to only use evidence that best supports the points they are aiming to make.

You might interrupt students with a mid-workshop teaching point in which you remind them to create cohesion in their drafts with some carefully placed transition words and phrases. Some important phrases to consider are "One reason . . . is true is . . . ," "For example . . ." and "This shows that . . ."

In an end of workshop share session, ask students to draw on all they know about introductions and conclusions to draft the beginning and ending of their essays. Your students might study the argument writing checklist to remind themselves of how to craft high-quality introductions and conclusions (see page 121), as well as how to do quick revision on the bodies of their essays.

You could choose to spend longer in this bend, asking students to revise their first drafts by moving now to the deeper revision lessons that come later in this unit. But it might prove helpful to move ahead now so that you are sure to get to this next essay structure. Additionally, students will have at least two essay drafts to work from during revision.

## BEND II: WRITING ACROSS TEXTS TO EXPLORE THE DIFFERENT TREATMENT OF SIMILAR THEMES

Now that your students have experience writing literary essays about a single text, in this bend, you will challenge them to read, analyze, and write about more than one text in a comparative essay. To set your students up to do this work, you might want to gather sets of texts that loosely address similar themes or issues, such as growing up, loneliness, or being an outsider. Or, you might encourage students to create these texts sets with you, allowing them to identify themes or issues that resonate with them.

### Bend II, Session 1: Identifying Ways Essayists Compare and Contrast Two Texts

By seventh grade, your students will likely have experience in analyzing different ways that texts treat a similar theme. In this session, you will channel students to bring that experience to writing a comparative essay. Your teaching point might be, "Today I want to teach you that when writers write a comparative essay, they take on a theme that emerges from more than one text, and they write about how that theme is treated differently by different authors or in different stories." You might tell students that these differences may include differences in tone (one is darker than another), differences in implications (one advocates for change, whereas another seems resigned to things as they are), and differences in intended audience (one might seem geared to a younger age group).

You're aiming for students to say more than "These books are both about growing up," because practically every instance of young adult literature will incorporate that theme. To demonstrate your teaching, offer an example of the kind of thinking you are hoping your students will aim for: "*The Hunger Games* and *Thirteen Reasons Why* offer different interpretations of what it means to grow up. Suzanne Collins, in *The Hunger Games*, suggests that to grow up, we must learn to sometimes sacrifice our own wishes. Jay Asher, in *Thirteen Reasons Why*, leaves us with the idea that growing up means realizing how much our actions affect others."

During independent writing time, channel students to work with the text sets that you or they created. Encourage them to draw on the methods for writing about reading that they learned in the previous bend. You might set them up to do some partner work in a mid-workshop teaching point. Each partner could choose one entry to share, and then partners could support each other in elaborating by assigning each other a few thought prompts to incorporate into the entry, such as "Another thought I have about this is . . . ," "On the other hand . . . ," "What I'm starting to realize is . . . ," and "For example . . .".

To engage students and deepen their understanding, you might decide to introduce cross-medium work as a homework assignment. As students watch television, listen to music, or visit websites, they should be on the lookout for some of the themes they are noticing in texts. The Common Core Standards expect students to be able to discuss the differences in the presentation of a text, such as a print version versus a film or televised version. Students will need to pay attention as readers and audience members, noticing where editing decisions have been made (which scenes are stretched and which are shrunk or even cut). Remind students to think about how the form of presentation makes an impact—how a particular scene, for example, plays out differently on a silent page than on film, with colorful images accompanied by an emotion-laden soundtrack. You might demonstrate this by reading aloud a scene from a novel, such as *Harry Potter and the Sorcerer's Stone*, and then showing the film version of the same scene. You might ask students, "What is similar in these two versions of the same scene? What is different? What is more effective in one version—and why?"

## Bend II, Session 2: Planning Essay Structure and Collecting Evidence

Because your writers have already practiced their skills in thematic thinking in the earlier part of this unit, you might not need to spend much time on generating ideas. You might instead move quickly to helping students plan for essays that compare and contrast, introducing some new structures.

Following are some possible bare-bones structures for a thesis-driven essay drawing on more than one text, as well as examples of these structures.

| Structure | Example |
|---|---|
| Thesis (or Big Idea or Theme)<br>• How one text approaches this thesis, idea, or theme<br>• How a different text approaches this same idea in a different way | "Carrots" and "My Side of the Story" by Adam Bagdasarian both teach us that children have a hard time understanding adults.<br>• "Carrots" teaches us . . . by . . .<br>• But "My Side of the Story" teaches us . . . by . . . |
| Thesis (or Big Idea or Theme)<br>• How two texts treat this idea in similar ways<br>• How the same two texts treat this idea in different ways | "Carrots" and "My Side of the Story" by Adam Bagdasarian both teach us that children have a hard time understanding adults.<br>• These two stories teach a similar lesson.<br>• But these two stories differ in important ways. |
| Thesis (or Big Idea or Theme)<br>• Support from more than one text<br>• How the writer's experience supports this same idea, in similar and/or different ways | "Carrots" and "My Side of the Story" by Adam Bagdasarian both teach us that children have a hard time understanding adults.<br>• Adam Bagdasarian's stories teach us that it's hard for children to understand adults.<br>• I can remember having a hard time understanding the adults in my life. |

You might start with a connection in which you ask students to look over their work from the previous session and box out an idea that has some heft and could be a possible thesis. In this session, they will begin collecting evidence to support this idea, and then they will finalize their thesis at the end of the session.

Next, you might unveil a chart with the possible structures for comparative essays outlined above. Explain that now that they have gone through the literary essay writing process once, they should be able to quickly identify the structure that would best support the possible thesis they just identified. From here, you can move to the heart of your teaching, in which you will set up your writers to search for supporting evidence from more than one text.

As students work, you'll want to reserve a great deal of workshop time for coaching on a small-scale or individual basis. You will want to teach writers that it's important, just as they were considering how relevant the evidence was in their one-text essay, to now consider just how well the evidence they're finding fits not just with the overarching thesis but with the evidence from the other text.

Elaboration will be even more important here, if that's possible, because writers might be navigating more than one text in a single paragraph. Simple strategies for clear citation, transitions between texts, and reminders of how to elaborate on evidence will be key.

At the end of the session, you may want to gather your writers to teach them that they may want to reexamine their thesis statements now that they have spent some time collecting evidence. The process of finding evidence should be a reflective one, and upon more close analysis of two texts, an essayist's understanding of how those texts connect and differ will likely change. For example, a first-draft thesis statement might be, "*Feed* by M. T. Anderson and *Mockingjay* by Suzanne Collins both teach us that it's hard to be yourself in a world of media." Upon studying these books more carefully, an essayist might decide that one or the other of these books has a more hopeful tone and revise the thesis accordingly.

Homework tonight will be hefty. Send your students home with the goal of writing bare-bones rough drafts of their essays, because the focus of the remaining sessions is revision.

## Bend II, Session 3: Revising with an Eye for Coherence, Flow, and Effect

The following sessions are revision lessons that aim to support students in crafting essays that make sense, that read smoothly, and that make an impact on the reader.

Teach your students that once writers have a first draft, which is likely a bare-bones thesis introduction followed by body paragraphs that are still mostly stitched-together examples and explanations, they know their work has just begun. Now is the time to reread and to ask, "What's missing? Where is there a hole in my argument? Where is there a piece of evidence that just doesn't fit?" Based on these reflections, writers rewrite to fill holes and to get rid of irrelevant passages.

On this day, it makes sense to keep your minilesson short and to gather students for small groups and conferences as needed. You might also want to deliver several mid-workshop teaching points if you find yourself teaching the same things over and over.

Be sure that you support not just your struggling writers, but advanced writers as well. For example, you might show students how essayists comment not just on the story itself, but also on how the author has told the story. This lifts the level of cognitive work significantly and propels students toward some of the higher-level analysis work called for by the Common Core. Angled retelling can still remain the focus of a body paragraph, but instead of merely referring to the thesis statement with "This shows that Katniss does what's right, even when it means sacrificing herself," the writer might take another sentence to discuss the author's craft in this same scene.

Some craft considerations include the author's use of a narrator's point of view to draw the reader in, the author's pacing of a scene to build suspense, or the words an author uses to pack a punch. So after an angled retelling, such as the one above, the essayist might add, "Suzanne Collins stretches out this scene, which takes no more than a few seconds, by letting us see Prim through Katniss's eyes. As Collins describes Prim 'walking with stiff, small steps up toward the stage,' we feel the pain of a sister. And Katniss's bold, self-sacrificing move makes sense."

In an end-of-workshop share, you might channel writers toward revision of tense and voice. You also might teach students that writers, instead of using the singular first-person pronoun *I* in academic writing, might use the more inclusive *we* to refer to any reader of the text. You might also do small-group work around the use of tense in essay. Present tense is often a good choice, because it can then remain consistent across the discussion of author's moves and the claims of the essayist: "Suzanne Collins stretches out this scene . . . Katniss's move makes sense."

## Bend II, Session 4: Presenting and Refuting Counterarguments

You can also teach your writers that essayists present and refute counterarguments as a way to strengthen their essays. This approach will be more successful with some claims than others, but if a writer is unable to develop any counterargument whatsoever, it might be that the thesis is not, in fact, a claim, but rather is a statement. Attempting to develop a counterargument may reveal weaknesses in the thesis statement that may encourage writers to do some quick revision.

You might deliver a teaching point in which you say, "One way that essayists strengthen their writing is by presenting and refuting a counterargument. Writers might develop this alternative argument in a separate paragraph, or briefly as part of a conclusion in a sentence, before turning back to their thesis idea." Then, teach your writers some sentence starters that pop out a counterargument: "Others might claim that . . ." or "Some people might argue that . . ." or "Another possible interpretation is . . ."

During independent writing time, your writers might be working on developing counterarguments and adding these to their drafts. You might encourage them to find evidence that specifically refutes the counterargument in order to strengthen these sections. If this counterargument work feels out of reach for some students, it isn't necessary to require them to do it. Instead, they might spend this session continuing to collect evidence and explanations to round out their drafts.

Just as presenting and refuting a counterargument has a great impact on swaying readers to agree with the ideas in an essay, introductions and conclusions hook and convince readers. In the share at the end of the workshop, invite your writers to try ways to introduce and conclude essays that are different from what they tried in the previous bend. You might demonstrate how an essay might start with a particularly vivid retelling from the story to set the scene. In conclusions, writers sometimes reflect on why the theme of the story or book is important and the ways people could live differently because of it.

## Bend II, Session 5: Revising with an Eye for Literary Elements

In this session, you will channel your writers to consider how to incorporate discussions of literary elements into their essays. The books that they are reading, if they are reading near or at grade-level texts, feature literary elements such as symbolism, foreshadowing, repetition, and multiple perspectives. Teach your students that, as commentators on this literature, they can note these moves and describe how they contribute to the themes and character development that make the books so powerful. Remind them that, as with all evidence, they must also consider how to unpack the author's language with their own explanations and ideas.

In a mid-workshop teaching point, you might remind your students how important it is to provide adequate context and background information for their evidence. You might say to your writers, "It's not enough to say, in a body paragraph, 'Suzanne Collins uses the mockingjay as a symbol of rebellion. This shows that *The Hunger Games* is a story of rebellion.' That kind of statement does none of the important

## Argument Writing Checklist

| | **Grade 7** | NOT YET | STARTING TO | YES! | **Grade 8** | NOT YET | STARTING TO | YES! |
|---|---|---|---|---|---|---|---|---|
| | **Structure** | | | | **Structure** | | | |
| **Overall** | I laid out a well-supported argument and made it clear that this argument is part of a bigger conversation about a topic/text. I acknowledged positions on the topic or text that might disagree with my own position, but I still showed why my position makes sense. | ☐ | ☐ | ☐ | I laid out an argument about a topic/text and made it clear why my particular argument is important and valid. I stayed fair to those who might disagree with me by describing how my position is one of several and making it clear where my position stands in relation to others. | ☐ | ☐ | ☐ |
| **Lead** | I interested the reader in my argument and helped them to understand the backstory behind it. I gave the backstory in a way that got the reader ready to see my point. | ☐ | ☐ | ☐ | After hooking the reader, I provided specific context for my own as well as another position(s), introduced my position, and oriented readers to the overall line of argument I planned to develop. | ☐ | ☐ | ☐ |
| | I made it clear to readers what my piece will argue and forecasted the parts of my argument. | ☐ | ☐ | ☐ | | | | |
| **Transitions** | I used transitions to link the parts of my argument. The transitions help the reader follow from part to part and make it clear when I am stating a claim or counterclaim, giving a reason, or offering or analyzing evidence. These transitions include terms such as *as the text states, this means, another reason, some people may say, but, nevertheless,* and *on the other hand.* | ☐ | ☐ | ☐ | I used transitions to lead the reader across parts of the text and to help the reader note how parts of the text relate back to earlier parts. I used phrases such as *now some argue, while this may be true, it is also the case that, despite this, as stated earlier, the evidence points to,* and *by doing so . . .* | ☐ | ☐ | ☐ |
| **Ending** | In my conclusion, I reinforced and built on the main point(s) in a way that makes the entire text a cohesive whole. The conclusion may reiterate how the support for my claim outweighed the counterclaim(s), restate the main points, respond to them, or highlight their significance. | ☐ | ☐ | ☐ | In the conclusion, I described the significance of my argument for stakeholders, or offered additional insights, implications, questions, or challenges. | ☐ | ☐ | ☐ |

work of connecting the image of a mockingjay to a concept like rebellion. Remember that someone new to *The Hunger Games* will have no idea what a mockingjay is without help from the essayist. Your point will be greatly strengthened if you explain this term and how important it is to the text."

You might want to end this bend with students using the Argument Writing Checklist to study their work and make final revisions to ready their pieces for publication.

## Bend II, Session 6: Using Outside Sources to Support a Literary Essay

For this final part, you might wish to teach your students how to incorporate outside information into their essays. Common Core descriptions of argument writing at late middle school and high school levels call for an increased inclusion of outside evidence. Additionally, as students get older and enter more academic and professional environments, they will need to base their arguments not merely on their own authority but with reference to other, established authorities on the subject. They also need to demonstrate that they understand that their argument is situated among other, related opinions on the same subject. Teach your writers some of the common ways literary essayists often include outside sources by citing other literary critics and either agreeing with or talking back to their claims or by using a nonfiction text to provide context on a theme or time period.

Possible structures for an essay using outside source material include:

| Structure | Example |
|---|---|
| Idea<br><br>Context (nonfiction text or literary criticism)<br><br>Evidence from the literary text<br><br>Implications or conclusions | In *The Hunger Games*, President Snow evolves as a Muammar Qaddafi-like figure. Both leaders are ruthless, long-lasting, and hard to displace.<br><br>• History of Qaddafi's dictatorship, especially the qualities of being ruthless, long-lasting, and hard to displace<br><br>• Evidence of Snow being like Qaddafi<br><br>• Implications that Snow is not such an exaggeration but that dictators exist today who oppress their people to maintain power; also implications for resistance |

Whatever source material they bring in, encourage your writers to revisit strategies for analyzing this evidence and connecting it back to the thesis statement.

### Bend II, Session 7: Preparing for Publication: A Celebration

As students get their pieces ready for publication, remind them of the editing work they have done in past units of study. Distribute the craft section of the Argument Writing Checklist and encourage students to use these with partners to make appropriate changes. Citations will surely present ongoing difficulties. As you teach more sophisticated ways of bringing in text evidence, students may have trouble incorporating the text gracefully. You will want to have plenty of examples up in the room and perhaps even a citation cheat sheet that has several models that students can keep in their folders. You may choose to include several reminders, including how to indent a longer passage to set it off from the rest of the text, how to embed a citation within a sentence, using ellipses to indicate text that has been left out, and how to preserve the tense of a passage. Likely, students will need reminders of how to properly punctuate citations as well.

If you are teaching students to incorporate outside sources, or even if you know they will only be citing the literary texts that are under discussion in their work, you may want to take this opportunity to teach them how to create a bibliography or a works cited page. If students are drafting and revising on the computer and you have Internet access for your class, talk to your school librarian or technology teacher to find out if your school subscribes to NoodleTools. This is an easy online way to create accurate MLA or Chicago-style bibliographies. You can, of course, also teach students these conventions more formally,

## Argument Writing Checklist (continued)

| | Grade 7 | NOT YET | STARTING TO | YES! | Grade 8 | NOT YET | STARTING TO | YES! |
|---|---|---|---|---|---|---|---|---|
| **Craft** | I used words purposefully to affect meaning and tone. | ☐ | ☐ | ☐ | I intended to affect my reader in particular ways—to make the reader think, realize, or feel a particular way—and I chose language to do that. | ☐ | ☐ | ☐ |
| | I chose precise words and used metaphors, images, or comparisons to explain what I meant. | ☐ | ☐ | ☐ | I consistently used comparisons, analogies, vivid examples, anecdotes, or other rhetorical devices to help readers follow my thinking and grasp the meaning and significance of a point or a piece of evidence. | ☐ | ☐ | ☐ |
| | I included domain-specific, technical vocabulary relevant to my argument and audience and defined these terms when appropriate. | ☐ | ☐ | ☐ | I varied my tone to match the different purposes of different sections of my argument. | ☐ | ☐ | ☐ |
| | I used a formal tone, but varied it appropriately to engage the reader. | ☐ | ☐ | ☐ | | | | |
| | **Conventions** | | | | **Conventions** | | | |
| **Spelling** | I matched the spelling of technical vocabulary to that found in resources and text evidence. I spelled material in citations correctly. | ☐ | ☐ | ☐ | I spelled technical vocabulary and literary vocabulary accurately. I spelled materials in citations according to sources, and spelled citations accurately. | ☐ | ☐ | ☐ |
| **Punctuation and Sentence Structure** | I varied my sentence structure, sometimes using simple and sometimes using complex sentence structure. | ☐ | ☐ | ☐ | I used different sentence structures to achieve different purposes throughout my argument. | ☐ | ☐ | ☐ |
| | I used internal punctuation appropriately within sentences and when citing sources, including commas, dashes, parentheses, colons, and semicolons. | ☐ | ☐ | ☐ | I used verb tenses that shift when needed, (as in when moving from a citation back to my own writing), deciding between active and passive voice where appropriate. | ☐ | ☐ | ☐ |
| | | | | | I used internal punctuation effectively, including the use of ellipses to accurately insert excerpts from sources. | ☐ | ☐ | ☐ |

through your own modeling and with the help of the *Chicago Manual of Style* or another guidebook that students can access. Either way, the important thing is that you are explicit about how to use these reference resources properly, so kids can return to them in the future.

Students should decide which essay they want to take to publication—the first essay they drafted using one text or the comparative essay they drafted in the second bend. To celebrate this writing work, you may decide to have students present in small groups of students with similar themes. Or you may decide to group students with a range of themes to give them exposure to different big ideas that emerged from texts. Either way, encourage students to compliment the writer's thinking and idea development at the end of each reading. After all students have presented, you might gather them in the meeting area for a toast with a glass of sparkling water and snack as you lead them in recapping some of the most important takeaways from the unit.

# Fantasy
## *Writing within Literary Traditions*

## RATIONALE/INTRODUCTION

By now, it is likely that your students have been exposed to narrative writing in different contexts and different years. If they grew up in a Project school, they will have well-honed skills in writing focused, meaningful personal narrative, fiction, and even memoir. If students are new to workshop teaching, they will have experiences from the sixth-grade unit *Personal Narrative: Crafting Powerful Life Stories* to draw from, and from the seventh-grade unit, *Writing Realistic Fiction: Symbolism, Syntax, and Truth*. Before beginning this unit, it is important to remind yourself (and your students!) that narrative writing is narrative writing. That is, the skills and strategies they applied to crafting personal narratives in sixth grade or fiction stories in seventh will pay off in big ways for them now, despite the fact that they are writing fantasy.

It benefits writers enormously to have an opportunity to return to a genre such as narrative, working in it once again, this time with greater control, incorporating strategies learned earlier with greater finesse. When writers work more than once in a genre, they can progress from doing as they're told toward working with independence, using all they know to accomplish their own big goals. By now, your students will know a thing or two about how to create a story arc, establishing conflict that builds and is resolved at the end. They know how to show, not tell, and elaborate and how to move a story forward through a blend of dialogue, action, and description. The more students return to narrative genres, the more extensive their understanding and use of craft will be. They'll grasp how to shift perspective, incorporate symbolism and metaphor, create atmospheric settings, and develop minor characters. You'll want to look at your students' prior fiction stories to see what they're ready to learn next and plan for some differentiated small-group work to support and challenge your diverse writers. You'll be able to tackle challenges if you expect them; you can then predict the small groups you'll teach to help students with structure, character development, and theme.

This unit will also afford you the opportunity to emphasize reading–writing connections and the rigorous work called for in the seventh- and eighth-grade CCSS for reading literature. You will teach students to read through the lens of writers—analyzing short stories, novels, and even picture books for writing craft moves they can use. If they've read any fantasy, perhaps they'll take note of the descriptions of fantastical worlds, the insertion of magical objects or characters, the use of symbolism to guide readers toward interpretations, and so forth. Even if their fiction reading hasn't included fantasy, they can still notice how an author sets the stage for the world of a story—how she uses places, objects, and symbols to create an atmosphere and tone and to illustrate big meanings. Their observations will enrich their understanding of *how* writers develop themes, characters, and settings in fantasy.

In many ways, fantasy fiction is one of the most challenging genres you can teach students. What makes this unit such a joy to teach is also what makes it a challenge: students love to write fantasy and think of it as the easiest genre to write because they believe (mistakenly) that anything goes. This can result in pieces that are ten and even twenty pages long; pieces that read as one long, convoluted summary. Students will throw in magical characters, worlds, even multiple plotlines with armies from warring nations doing battle. Almost anything they have ever read or seen in movies will land in the same muddied piece. As you read pieces like this, you'll find yourself sighing and asking, "What happened to all they learned about finely crafted narratives?" Throughout this write-up, we'll offer concrete ways to battle this problem, helping students develop plans for challenging yet attainable goals.

## A SUMMARY OF THE BENDS IN THE ROAD FOR THIS UNIT

**In Bend I (Collecting and Developing Ideas for Fantasy Fiction: Writing Stories that Have Depth and Significance)**, you will teach students to generate possible story ideas while drawing upon students' past experience generating ideas for realistic fiction stories. Students will begin by rehearsing, which involves thinking about a lot of possible story ideas, generating possible stories, and then, once one has the gist of an idea, thinking deeply about the setting, the characters, and the various ways the story might spin out. When writing a fantasy story, the need for rehearsal is amplified. You will teach students that the question a fantasy fiction writer needs to ask is not just, "What would make a great story?" but also, "How can I keep my fantasy story grounded in the real world?"

**In Bend II (Drafting and Revising: Crafting a Compelling Fantasy Fiction Story)**, you will teach students how to draft from inside the fantasy world of their stories, writing to make the unrealistic feel realistic. From there, you will teach them to revise with an eye on craft. Among other things, students will develop meaning and significance through showing, not telling, and they will attend to symbolism and the use of "expert" vocabulary appropriate for their fantasy world.

**In Bend III (Editing and Publishing: Preparing the Fantasy Story for Readers)**, you will help students put the finishing touches on their pieces. This bend—and the unit—will end with a culminating celebration of their stories and of your and their hard work!

## GETTING READY

If you opt to pair this unit with a reading workshop unit on fantasy reading, we suggest you launch the reading unit just a few days, if not a full week, before the writing work. This way, students will have the opportunity to immerse themselves in the genre as readers, which will not only orient them to its elements, but also create a vision for the writing they'll be doing themselves.

Whether you opt to go this route or to teach this unit as an unpaired writing unit, you will want to gather examples of the genre that are accessible to students. This is important with every unit, of course, but doubly so with fantasy. A majority of students' experiences with fantasy comes from reading novels and watching movies, which often leaves the impression that fantasy stories are only of the epic variety. To combat this viewpoint, you will want to offer students lots of exposure to fun and compelling fantasy stories that are of a smaller scale. Gather up armfuls of picture books and short story collections with short, finely crafted fantasy stories containing streamlined plots that represent a variety of cultures. Don't be put off by the reading level of the picture books. Although your students will likely have much higher reading levels, their fantasy writing skills will more closely match a lower-leveled fantasy book. In addition to being invaluable coteachers in this unit, these mentor texts also give students an opportunity to look closely at stories from different cultures—an important Common Core standard for middle-schoolers. Some of the Project's favorite fantasy mentor texts include picture books such as *Merlin and the Dragons, Stranger in the Mirror, Raising Dragons*, and *The Rain Babies*, as well as short stories from anthologies such as *Fire and Wings, But That's Another Story*, and *A Glory of Unicorns*.

As you plan to launch your unit, here's a suggestion we first learned from Jane Yolen: fantasy writers either must be keen observers of the world or researchers or both. This may sound odd, considering that much of what the fantasy writer writes is make-believe. Yet when you stop and remember that all fantasy is based in some reality—fantasy landscapes are based on earthly ones, fantasy creatures are based on real ones—it should come as no surprise that Yolen writes, "All the fantasy authors I know own research volumes on wildlife, wildflowers, insects, and birds." You might consider creating a small basket of photographs, geologic guides, and nonfiction books on animals and the environment. These will serve as inspiration for your students' writing that is based in realism—or at least grounded in the believable. You might also consider other resources, such as baby name books (to help students choose names for characters that are laden with significance and history) or dictionaries (which can be helpful when looking up the etymology of words), as well as anything else you can imagine that will support and inspire your young writers. Another favorite book, and one you will want to have on the shelf with easy access for you and your students alike is Gail Carson Levine's *Writing Magic*—a book she has written for children about writing fantasy.

Finally, a few days before you officially launch the unit, you might consider doing a quick fantasy writing on-demand. You might say to your students, "Our next unit is going to be fantasy, and I would love to know what you already know about writing fantasy stories. Would you please write a fantasy Small Moment story that incorporates everything you know about writing strong narratives and everything you know about fantasy?" Give students one period to try this. You can then collect the pieces and look at them with an eye first and foremost on what they know about or are approximating in narrative writing. The Learning Progression for Narrative Writing will be an invaluable resource in this work. Secondly, you will want to see what students already know about how fantasy writing should go. Prepare to be shocked! Students often know more than we do about the genre, and many a teacher finds herself furiously revising her unit plans after seeing all that her students already know and can do.

## BEND I: COLLECTING AND DEVELOPING IDEAS FOR FANTASY FICTION: WRITING STORIES THAT HAVE DEPTH AND SIGNIFICANCE

*"All fantasy should have a solid base in reality."*

—Sir Max Beerbohm

The above quote comes as a shock to many novice fantasy writers. Isn't fantasy all about making everything up? Anything goes? In fact, most fantasy is allegorical—real-life stories and lessons cloaked in fantastical settings, characters, quests, or all of the above. When you teach students to collect ideas for fantasy stories, you will do yourself and your students a favor by following two simple guidelines: keep fantasy stories grounded in some way in the real world, and move *quickly* through the collecting section of this unit. Both of these guidelines will keep students' ideas for projects realizable.

### Bend I, Session 1: Finding Inspiration for Fantasy Writing in Real-Life Events

With this in mind, almost any ideas that worked with realistic fiction idea gathering can be recast and used in this unit. On the first day of the unit, you might teach students that writers often look at their own lives and imagine how events and issues could be turned into fantasy stories. Then suggest that they can do this, too. A student with a sick parent might create a fantasy story in which the hero must go on a quest to find the magical potion to save the ailing queen, for example. A student who's recently been caught in a fight between two friends might write a fantasy story in which the main character is charged with the task of settling an old dispute between two neighboring communities—and longtime rivals. The possibilities are endless, and students will have a fun time turning their own (perhaps everyday) life stories, friends, and environments into fantasy-based creations.

You'll want to allow students the time to imagine, to linger in the possibilities, but not so much time that they don't get started writing story blurbs. It's important that you convey to students that they are collecting not a list of possible story ideas, but rather a short description of how a story might go, including possible main characters, problem, and resolution. Therefore, your teaching might sound something like, "Today I want to teach you that fantasy writers gather ideas for the fantastical from the ordinary. They look at the people, events, and issues around them, letting these spark ideas for fantasy stories. Then, they jot a quick blurb of how that story might go." Of course, the ideas students ultimately choose will change and develop as their writing progresses, but it is essential that students have mostly formed ideas for ways their stories could go before they begin writing, because this will set them up for success.

### Bend I, Session 2: Generating Ideas for Fantasy by Considering Setting

You could teach students that fantasy writers often consider settings to develop possible story ideas. The settings can be ones in our world ("What would happen if Fin were sitting in math class and an elf popped out of his pencil case?"), built upon portals to another world ("Fin opens his backpack to find himself transported into a castle made entirely of school supplies"), or else based entirely in a fantasy world ("Fin lives in a village in a thatched cottage where everyone rides unicorns"). Students can then use these settings to imagine possible story ideas that might play out there, as well as characters that might inhabit the settings. While some of your students will have no difficulty drumming up ideas for a fantasy story, imagining twisting plots and complicated characters, others will need the inspiration that comes from these first two days of idea-generating strategies. Then, too, your more visual kids will thrive on this day, because the invitation to imagine setting to enter a story world will be right up their alley.

Perhaps during the day's share, you might suggest that students revisit their notebooks, particularly their essay work, to see what life ideas they can find that matter most to them. Justice, kindness, peace, and other big world ideas and issues can be particularly potent sources of inspiration in an allegorical genre. You can teach students to think of possible fantasy story ideas that build off of these topics. For example, if a student is passionate about the environment, she might craft a story idea that revolves around a magical forest that is slowly dying after being pillaged for its magical plants by an evil dragon. Perhaps a young peasant girl must slay the dragon to spare the forest.

It is worth noting that the gathering stage is often an ideal time for you to offer suggestions of ways that students might simplify their story arcs. You can cut some of those epic and novel-length story ideas off at the pass by teaching and conferring into single-arc story lines with only one or two main characters and only a couple of obstacles, rather than a never-ending series of obstacles. For example, you might channel a student who wants to write a story about a prince who, faced with the potential loss of his kingdom, engages in more than twenty years of battles and quests, until with the help of magicians he finally regains his crown, to choose one episode from his epic storyline—perhaps the day when the prince won the crown in one moment of magical valor.

A note of caution: many students will want to leap, both feet forward, into drafting their stories in their notebooks rather than collecting several ideas to choose from and giving each one enough attention to warrant a thoughtful final choice. This can only lead to thin stories, heavy on plot, light on craft and structure, and almost always too exhaustively long to revise. Encourage these students to do what Carl Anderson has said: "Date around a few ideas, before getting married." The notebook is a great place to explore lots of different ideas before settling on one.

**Bend I, Session 3: Developing the Story: Shaping Fantastical Yet Believable Characters, Settings, and Plots**

After students have collected a good handful of possible fantasy story blurbs, you will want to guide them to choose an idea to turn into a draft and ultimately publish. You may find it simplest to pull out old charts you have from previous units that instruct students in the fine art of choosing a story (or seed) idea. Or you might opt to add to their repertoire of idea choosing strategies. For example, you could teach students that some fantasy writers choose their story ideas based on the messages they want to send out into the world—based on how they would like their readers to live differently. Or you could suggest that sometimes writers choose their ideas based on what they think is the most compelling—or even just the most fun—to write.

Whether you revisit an old chart or offer a new repertoire, you'll word your teaching point something like this: "Today I want to teach you that after fantasy writers have mulled over and written blurbs of a few possible ideas, they settle on just one to develop into a full-fledged story. They might pick the story idea with the most compelling message or pick the one that is simply the most fun to write. Once writers have chosen an idea, they begin to develop aspects of it by writing long about the characters, the setting, or the plot." The idea here is that students quickly choose a story to commit to before beginning the important work of developing it.

As you model how to do this, you will certainly want to rely on the narrative teaching you have done earlier, or if you are an eighth-grade teacher, on the narrative teaching students had in seventh grade. For example, you might model thinking through your own main character's internal and external traits, imagining what she has to learn, what may become hurdles, what the character longs for most, and with what and whom your character surrounds herself. All of these considerations will position students to develop characters that have depth and emotion—not just a fantastical shell.

Students will have spent a little time thinking about setting as a way to generate an idea for a story, but you could suggest (perhaps during the mid-workshop teaching) that fantasy writers often write long about the settings for their stories. As students do this, you might point out that settings are often laden with meaning—that they can reflect what is going on inside a character's head or establish a tone for the journey on which the character is embarking. (This, too, students should remember from prior narrative units.) Although students will be engaged in writing work, the nature of it supports the analysis work of Reading Standard RL.7.3: "Analyze how particular elements of a story or drama interact (e.g., how setting shapes the characters or plot)." In this case, however, students will be analyzing not already written texts, but their own creations as they put them onto the page.

**Bend I, Session 4: Planning a Story Idea**

By now, students will be ready for a key step in the process of fantasy writing: planning. They have a story idea in mind (with a blurb that describes it), a sense of some of the characters that will embody the story, and an image of the world in which these characters live. Now it's time for students to put this all together into a plan that they will follow as they write. It's important to convey what you consider the qualities of an effective plan so that they have a crystal clear understanding of how to make their own. You might say,

"Today I want to teach you that once writers have a story idea, full of characters and a world they have started to develop, they take time to make a plan for how their story will go. Specifically, they come up with a compelling opening scene, an idea of how the story will end, and a clear path that leads from the beginning to that ending. Oftentimes this means trying out several versions of how their story will go before deciding on the best option." Of course, it isn't, in fact, the case that all fiction writers work off of a clear plan, from opening to final scene, as they write. However, for the purpose of setting students up for success, you'll want to suggest that this is the case.

Again, it will help students to see you doing this planning work yourself, so be prepared to model with your own fantasy story, doing so in ways that students might replicate themselves, with no one part too complicated or overdrawn. You could then give that planning strategy a decidedly fantastical bent by referencing one of your fantasy mentor texts, such as "Family Monster," and showing students how, if there's to be magic in a story, it needs to be introduced at the beginning of the story to establish the story's "rules," as well as to introduce tension and suspense right at the start of the plot. Creating both a plan for how a story will unfold and a way to introduce magical elements and characters up front sets your writers up to meet Standard W.7.3a/W.8.3a: "Engage and orient the reader by establishing a context and point of view and introducing a narrator and/or characters; organize an event sequence that unfolds naturally and logically."

We recommend that you encourage students to recycle a planning strategy they used with some success either at the start of the seventh-grade year, during the unit *Writing Realistic Fiction: Symbolism, Syntax, and Truth* or, if they are eighth-graders, in a prior upper grade or middle school fiction unit: story booklets, timelines, or even a simple story mountain. You may want to limit students to story ideas with two or three well-developed scenes as a way to combat the desire to write complicated narratives that in the span of a unit can only be realistically (and not well) handled through summary.

It cannot be stressed enough how *crucial* it is that students not only plan how their stories will go, but that you keep a keen eye on those plans. This is the stage when many a well-intentioned student's fantasy writing piece has spun out of control. Plan to check in frequently with students during this time—perhaps moving from table to table or else having students leave their notebooks out on their desks while they head to gym, during which time you read over each one to ensure that no student has gone too far astray.

You might also suggest that students help each other assess their writing plans. Partners might share plans with each other to discover what does and doesn't seem doable about a plan and to consider other ways the story may go in instances where a particular plot point seems incongruent with the rest of the story or outside the rules of the world that the student has created. (This simply means that if the student has established a world in which animals can talk, that remains consistent. It can't then be that a nontalking animal exists—unless there's a reason for this anomaly.) These partner discussions will not only act as support to your writers, but it will also set them up to address Speaking and Listening Standard 1, which is expected of both seventh- and eighth-grade students.

You might also consider pulling a small group of advanced writers, who can handle more intricate plans, to teach them to do a double-decker plan: one line for plot points and the other line for the deeper meaning or internal storyline or the learning journey the character is on.

## BEND II: DRAFTING AND REVISING: CRAFTING A COMPELLING FANTASY FICTION STORY

Now that they have spent some time planning, you will want students to move rather quickly through drafting and on to the revision process, once again with the goal to keep kids from getting bogged down in epic story creations. Our suggestion, then, is that you plan to teach only one drafting minilesson, moving quickly to revision so that students are incorporating the qualities of good writing you are teaching, even if some are still in the midst of drafting.

### Bend II, Session 1: Fast-Drafting

In addition to reminding your students of all the effective narrative writing strategies they've learned by referring to past charts and possibly even past writing pieces, you will want to teach students that the best way to write the strongest draft is to get lost in writing it, much as they get lost in books that they read. Your goal here is to convey that writers draft their best work when they are able to block everything out, almost entering the world that they are creating on the page. Your hope is that students are so caught up in the world of their invented stories that they may even miss your call to the carpet for the teaching share!

You might include in your teaching point the specific tip that students can focus their imaginations, either by closing their eyes and envisioning the characters moving through the world of their story, or else perhaps storytelling to a partner, directly before they write. Coach them to imagine all the sights, sounds, and even smells that will bring their stories to life, making these as concrete and *real* for readers as possible. Then it will be time for students to do what they have been itching to do all along—write! Encourage them to keep their story plans beside them as they begin to draft, writing one scene at a time and referring to the plans as often as needed.

If you opt to devote two days of instruction to drafting, you might, on Day Two, teach students that writers pay special attention to conflict as they draft, making things harder and harder for the main character, in particular. Some writing teachers have referred to this as "torturing your character." Students will already know from prior fiction units that conflict is at the heart of a good story, and this is especially the case in a fantasy story, in which ordinary, unlikely heroes must overcome all sorts of sinister things and towering challenges to set things right again—to save the day.

Your mid-workshop teaching point might be a quick reminder to students that for there to be conflict, there must be action, and for there to be action, characters must do things. They must speak and move and challenge others. This may seem like an obvious tip, but for many novice (and even experienced) writers, getting characters to be active is often a difficult task. If a student creates a story about an awkward boy who pines all day for the beautiful village girl, but never *does* anything about it, the reader will soon lose interest. For readers to be as invested in reading a story as students are in writing them, there must be action. As part of this, you can remind students that they can use a blend of "narrative techniques, such as dialogue, pacing, description, and reflection, to develop experiences, events, and/or characters" (CCSS.W.8.3b). (The seventh-grade version of this standard is almost identical.)

## Bend II, Session 2: Revising Fantasy Stories in Ways that Up the Stakes

The possibilities for revision are endless, in part because students are often so invested in their fantasy stories that they are willing to try more and work harder. There are dizzying teaching opportunities here! You will, of course, want to be a close observer of your students' drafts to assess what your students are most ready to learn as well as what they most need to learn. The Learning Progression for Narrative Writing and the Common Core State Standards will be helpful guides in this work.

One revision technique we especially like is writing to make the unrealistic feel realistic, thus forcing readers to suspend disbelief. If you opt to teach this one, you might word your teaching point like this: "Today I want to teach you that the more specific fantasy writers are in their descriptions of key characters, settings, and objects, the more believable these elements become. If a writer wants to describe a table that begins to float, for example, she could make that unlikely scenario more believable to readers by describing it in concrete detail":

Lyssa watched in shock as the round cherry wood table—the one under which she'd counted seventeen pieces of gum stuck to its underside—suddenly began to vibrate under her fingers. Lyssa's marble composition notebook slid off the table's shiny surface as the table rose one foot, then two feet above the library's linoleum floor.

Point out to students that it's the details that do all the work here. By describing this table with such precision, the author conveys to us that this is a table her character knows well—intimately. This is one that Lyssa has sat at so many times that she knows exactly how many pieces of gum are stuck to its underside. We trust, then, that when she sees it rise in the air, this is, in fact, happening.

You could extend this instruction today during a mid-workshop teaching point in which you remind students that if they plan to include magic in their stories, it is essential to introduce the magic early on in the story. There are several reasons for this: first, doing so establishes the rules of the story; right from the start, readers understand that magic is a part of this story, this world. Second, introducing elements of magic early on in a story foreshadows what's to come and thus builds tension; when we know that a wicked creature has special powers to destroy, we read on the edge of our seats, wondering when that creature and those powers will emerge—and who will suffer. And finally, on a related note, the early introduction of magic means that readers will not be thrown off course (or less likely to buy in) when magic occurs later. If a student plans to have a hero use a magic stone to cast a protective spell, the first time we hear of this stone should not be when the dragon is about to breathe his fiery breath. Readers need to know of the stone's existence, and of its power, so that they are on board when the hero produces it.

Although the focus of today's teaching is specific to fantasy writing, the tips you're offering might as easily apply to any form of narrative writing. Just replace *magic* with *special situation*. In any narrative account, the reader needs to know up front what sort of story or world he is entering. This doesn't mean there won't be surprising twists and turns along the way, but all good narratives introduce whatever information the reader needs to know to be oriented to the story—from beginning to end.

## Bend II, Session 3: Revising to Show, Not Tell

Of course, one of the most important revision moves is one that student have learned again and again over the years—to develop meaning and significance in stories through showing, not telling. Chances are, students have learned to stop, identify, and then stretch out the heart of the story—even to use scissors and tape to elaborate on these crucial moments. However, many students get so lost in the fun and magic of fantasy that they can soon lose track of the heart of their story.

If you opt to teach the "show, don't tell" strategy, you'll want to phrase your teaching point as a reminder: "Today I want to remind you that all narrative writers make sure to show, not just tell, when they write. Fantasy writers know the importance of showing to pull their readers into the fun, fantastical elements of their story—and especially when they are writing the heart of their story." You'll want to follow this up with a reminder—perhaps in a mid-workshop teaching point—that just as they did in their personal narratives, students should aim to write with a balance of action, thought, dialogue, and description, letting their fantasy stories unfold bit by bit (W.7.3b, W.8.3b).

## Bend II, Session 4: Revising to Highlight Symbolism and Meaning

On another day, you might teach students that they can revise on the lookout for physical elements of their story—for settings and objects—that they can turn into symbols to convey deeper meanings. The magic stone can come to represent the bravery the young hero must show, despite her fears. It is small, but strong—just as our hero is. The dark night can stand for the fear the hero is grappling with before the dawn comes. Once students have identified objects and elements of setting that can stand for something important, they'll want to spend a little time describing these with care, choosing words and details that alert readers to the fact that this is more than just a stone, more than just a dark night.

As part of this day, perhaps during the mid-workshop or share, you might take the opportunity to develop your kids' "expert" vocabulary, tying this to the symbol work you did earlier. Fantasy writers often spotlight archaic, medieval words such as *saddlebags* and *abode* or borrow from Latin or Greek or other forms of etymology to create new words for their imagined world and characters (L.7.6, L.8.6). Often, these words bear meaning; they aren't chosen on a whim. Your writers may want to use dictionaries or use Internet searches to make use of established "expert vocabulary" or to create their own meaning-laden words (L.7.4c, L.8.4c).

## Bend II, Session 5: Revising with a Partner

Now is a useful time to encourage students to work in partnerships; there is nothing like two sets of eyes to discover new and interesting—or tried and true—ways to revise. You might teach students that because fantasy can be intricate, fantasy writers often seek one another out when they are looking to revise, relying on their shared understanding of the genre. Specifically, fantasy writers look together to be sure that each section of the story is easy to follow. They make sure that the scenes create a cohesive whole, that the images and characters are as clear and compelling as they can be, and that the rules of the story are evident to the reader. They check that the plot is well developed, with loose ends tied up, and above all, that the story is fun and engaging. Partners can swap stories and put Post-it notes on parts that need more attention. Then they can talk about what they discovered and plan next possible steps.

You may also want to suggest, perhaps during a mid-workshop teaching point, that fantasy writers turn to mentor texts for help during revision. Students can look at whatever titles you have available in your room—or to whatever mentor text you've chosen to use during this unit—to get ideas for ways to lift the level of their own stories. Perhaps they'll notice how a mentor author chooses character names that relate to the larger meaning of her story or how the author manages to tie up the trouble at the end in a way that feels both believable and exciting. They might notice more technical craft moves that fantasy authors regularly employ. What can they notice about sentence length and variation? When do fantasy authors use longer or shorter sentences? (Most authors use longer sentences when they are describing things or slowing action down and shorter sentences when there is action.) What do they notice about the author's use of dialogue? How does the author make different characters speak differently? Word choice? Punctuation? Speech habits? How do fantasy stories that they love the most tend to start? How do they tend to end? Students can study and emulate all of these things as they revise.

If you are itching to teach additional revision lessons, you might refer to books written by adult writers of fantasy for ideas. Books such as *How to Write Science Fiction and Fantasy*, by Orson Scott Card (2001), *The Complete Guide to Writing Fantasy, Vol. 1: Alchemy with Words*, by Darin Park and Tom Dullemond (2006), and *Writing Science Fiction & Fantasy*, by Gardner Dozois (1993), are full of strategies that you can modify into teaching points your students will grasp, ones that translate into the types of skills you want your students to learn.

## BEND III: EDITING AND PUBLISHING: PREPARING THE FANTASY STORY FOR READERS

There is a natural bridge from revision to editing in mentor text work. You can guide students to look at mentor texts for editing help as well. You can show students to attend to the punctuation usage employed in longer sentences (commas, dashes, colons)—as well the way fantasy writers choose to spell words (even made-up words) with conventional spelling in mind. In this final bend, your students will put the finishing touches on their fantasy stories and publish their work for the world.

### Bend III, Session 1: Editing for Punctuation

By seventh or eighth grade, your students will have had years of practice with punctuation, but they may benefit from a reminder about how to revise their drafts with punctuation in mind. Your teaching point might sound something like, "Today I want to teach you that fantasy writers, like all fiction writers, use punctuation to influence how readers read and understand their work." You might examine an excerpt of dialogue from a mentor text, for example, asking students how the meaning of the dialogue might change if you replaced the periods with exclamation marks. You might show examples of how a writer might break up a long passage with commas, slowing down the action, or connect a series of short sentences with dashes to create a sense of urgency. You might also remind students how to check for common punctuation problems, such as missing apostrophes in possessives or unnecessary apostrophes in plural nouns.

## Bend III, Session 2: Using Standard Conventions in Unconventional Worlds

One of the great challenges for fantasy writers is to create worlds that are fantastical and wonderfully imaginative, yet are still grounded in reality, so that readers feel comfortable immersing themselves in those worlds. You might teach students that fantasy writers often help readers feel more at home in these worlds, with their unusual character and place names, by using conventional capitalization, punctuation, and spelling. This helps to make sure that readers do not get distracted from the story because they are confused by the unusual conventions, and it gives students the opportunity to "demonstrate command of the conventions of standard English capitalization, punctuation, and spelling when writing" (L.7.2, L.8.2).

You might ask students to work with a partner, reading each other's work with an ey for the use of conventions. Suggest to partners that as they read, they check each other's work for the following:

- Use of initial capital letters for all character and place names.
- Inclusion of letters that are commonly used in English. Avoid using unusual punctuation or symbols in names and words to make them look foreign.
- Inclusion of letter combinations that are similar to those in English. Readers should be able to pronounce invented words that begin with *th-* or *sk-*, for example, but they may stumble over those beginning with *pq-* or *kz-*.

## Bend III, Session 3: Publishing and Celebrating

When students move to publishing, you might opt to have them publish their books as picture books—since so much of fantasy writing lends itself nicely to visuals. Some teachers choose this unit to have students create a class anthology of short stories. This is especially apropos if you did a lot of short story work with your students.

No matter how you publish, you will no doubt want to think of a fitting celebration for this unit. You could invite your students to come to the publishing party dressed as one of the characters from their stories and to read aloud to one another, or to an audience, dressed as fairies, elves, wizards, and dragons!

Part Two: Differentiating Instruction for Individuals and Small Groups: If . . . Then . . . Conferring Scenarios

THERE IS NO GREATER CHALLENGE, when teaching writing, than to learn to confer well. And conferring well is a big deal. It matters. If you can pull your chair alongside a student, study what he or she has been doing, listen to the student's own plans, and then figure out a way to spur that youngster on to greater heights, that ability means that you will always be able to generate minilessons, mid-workshop teaching points, and share sessions that have real-world traction because these are really conferences-made-large.

However, knowing conferring matters doesn't make it easier to master. Even if you know that learning to confer well is important, even if you devote yourself to reading about the art of conferring, you are apt to feel ill-prepared for the challenges that you encounter.

I remember Alexandra, tall with long brown hair and a thick Russian accent. I'd pull up beside her after the minilesson, notebook in hand, ready to execute the perfect conference. We'd talk, I'd research, and without fail, every time, I'd be left with the same terrifying realization: "She's already doing everything! I don't know what to teach her." In an attempt to preserve my own integrity, I'd leave her with a compliment. Despite having joined our class mid-year, despite the challenge of mastering a new language and adapting to a new culture, Alexandra implemented anything and everything I hoped she would as a writer. I thought, "What should she do next?" I was stuck.

Then there was a student I'll call Matthew, who in truth, represents many others across my years as a teacher. It felt as if I was always conferring with him—modeling, pulling him into small groups, implementing all the scaffolds I knew of—and yet he didn't make the progress I hoped for. In reality, it felt like nothing worked. As I'd sit beside him, looking over his work, I couldn't help but wonder what was happening. Why was my teaching passing him over? What do I teach him, right now in this conference, when his writing needs *everything*?

If you have had conferences like these and end up wondering what's wrong, know that you aren't alone. Teachers across the world find that conferring well is a challenge. Most of us have, at one time or another, written questions on our hands, or on cue cards, that we want to remember to ask. Many of us have mantras that we repeat to ourselves, over and over. "Teach the writer, not the writing." "It's a good conference if the writer leaves, wanting to write." "Your job is to let this student teach you how to help."

Many of the books on conferring will help you understand the architecture of a conference. You'll learn to research first, then to compliment, then to give critical feedback and/or to teach. You'll learn tips about each part of a conference. When researching, follow more than one line of inquiry. If you ask "What are you working on?" and hear about the student's concerns with one part of the writing, don't jump to teaching that part of the writing until you generate a second line of inquiry—whether it's "What do you plan to do next?" or "How do you feel about this piece?" or "If you were going to revise this, what might you do?" There are similar tips that you'll learn about other aspects of conferring too.

But you will no doubt feel as if there is another kind of help that you need. You will probably want help knowing not only *how* to confer, but also knowing *what* to teach.

Visiting hundreds of schools has given me a unique perspective on that question, a perspective that may be difficult to come by when you are in one classroom, with one set of students with very particular needs.

After working in so many schools, with so many youngsters, I've begun to see patterns. I notice that when X is taught, students often need Y or Z. I meet one Matthew in Chicago and another in Tulsa, Oklahoma. I met Alexandras in Seattle and Shanghai. And I've begun to realize that, despite the uniqueness of each student, there are familiar ways they struggle and predictable ways in which a teacher can help with those struggles. Those ways of helping come from using all we know about learning progressions, writing craft, language development, and grade-specific standards to anticipate and plan for the individualized instruction that students are apt to need.

The charts that follow are designed to help you feel less empty-handed when you confer. I've anticipated some of the most common struggles you will see as you teach narrative, opinion, and information writing through the units of study in this series and I've named a bit about those struggles in the "If . . ." column of the charts. When you identify a student (or a group of students) who resembles the "If . . ." that I describe, then see if perhaps the strategy I suggest might help. That strategy is described in the column titled "After acknowledging what the student is doing well, you might say . . ." Of course, you will want to use your own language. What I've presented is just one way your teaching might go!

Often you will want to leave the writer with a tangible artifact of your work together. This will ensure that he or she remembers the strategy you've worked on and next time you meet with the student, it will allow you to look back and see what you taught the last time you worked together. It will be important for you to follow up on whatever the work is that you and the youngster decide upon together. Plan to check back in, asking a quick "How has the work we talked about been going for you? Can you show me where you've tried it?"

Some teachers choose to print the "Leave the writer with . . ." column onto reams of stickers or label paper (so they can be easily placed in students' notebooks). You also might choose to print them out on plain paper and tape them onto the writer's desk as a reminder (see the CD-ROM for this chart in reproducible format). I hope these charts will help you anticipate, spot, and teach into the challenges your writers face during the independent work portion of your writing workshop.

# Narrative Writing

| If . . . | After acknowledging what the student is doing well, you might say . . . | Leave the writer with . . . |
|---|---|---|
| **Structure and Cohesion** | | |
| **The writer is new to the writing workshop or this particular genre of writing.**<br><br>This writer struggles because narrative is a new genre for her—or she has been taught to write in ways that are different than those you are teaching. She may display certain skill sets (i.e., the ability to craft a strong plotline or to write with elaborate descriptive details) but lacks the vision of what she is being asked to produce. Most often, this means that she has not yet come to understanding the concept of a small, focused moment that is then elaborated upon. Her story is probably long and unfocused and is usually dominated by summary, not storytelling. | Someone famously once said, "You can't hit a target if you don't know what that target is." This is especially true for writers. They can't write well if they don't have a vision, a mental picture, of what they hope to produce. Today I want to teach you that one way writers learn about the kinds of writing they hope to produce is by studying mentor texts. They read a mentor text once, enjoying it as a story. Then, they read it again, this time asking, "How does this kind of story seem to go?" They label what they notice and then try it in their own writing. | Writers use mentor texts to help them imagine what they hope to write. They:<br><br>• Read the text and enjoy it as a good story.<br><br>• Reread the text and ask, "How does this kind of story seem to go?"<br><br>• Annotate what they notice. (It can be helpful to do this right on the text with arrows pointing to the various things you see!)<br><br>• Try to do some of what they noticed in their own writing. |
| **The writer seems to paragraph randomly or not much at all.**<br><br>When you read this writer's piece, you are struck by the paragraphing. It may be that he seems to be paragraphing in haphazard ways, as if he knows he should be creating paragraphs but does not know why or when. Alternatively, this writer may not paragraph often enough, making the piece of writing difficult to follow. Regardless of the issue, it is likely that this student would benefit from learning about some of the *reasons* narrative writers paragraph and then trying out a few different alternatives in his own writing. | When I first read your piece, I was struck by all the beautiful writing you have. Once in a while, though, I felt like I couldn't enjoy what you were attempting to do as a writer (perhaps point to a particular place where the writer tried to create tension or show a time change), because you didn't use paragraphs. It can be hard for a reader to take in all that we do as writers, and paragraphs act like signals that say, "Pause. Take this in. Something just happened or is about to happen."<br><br>Today I want to teach you a few of the main reasons story writers use paragraphs. Specifically, writers often start new paragraphs when a new event is starting, when their story is switching to a new time or place, when a new character speaks, or when a very important part needs to be emphasized. | Make a new paragraph here:<br><br>• Very important part needs emphasis<br><br>• New event<br><br>• New time<br><br>• New place<br><br>• New character speaks |

| If . . . | After acknowledging what the student is doing well, you might say . . . | Leave the writer with . . . |
|---|---|---|
| **The story lacks tension.**<br><br>This writer's story is flat and lacks the tension or conflict that suggests she has considered the issues her character is dealing with or what her story is really about. The story reads like a chronological retelling of events, without a sense that the writer has considered pacing—speeding up less important parts and slowing down parts that draw the reader in or reveal important aspects of the character's struggle. It may be that the character has no struggle at all, and that there is a simple problem and quick solution. This writer would benefit from a study of story structure, noting the ways authors build tension throughout a story. | What I want to teach you today is that any good story—the stories that resonate with us and stay in our hearts long after we've finished reading them—involve some sort of struggle. Most often, this struggle surrounds something that a character wants. Today I want to teach you how to uncover what your character wants and then build a story where that want is revealed, the character encounters trouble, she attempts to get what is wanted, and the tension builds to a climactic moment before a resolution is revealed. Even the most complex stories often have this simple structure underneath them:<br><br>1. Someone really wants something.<br><br>2. Someone encounters trouble.<br><br>3. Someone tries, tries, tries (often with one or two failed attempts). | To create edge-of-the-seat tension, try this formula:<br><br>1. Someone really wants something.<br><br>2. Someone encounters trouble.<br><br>3. Someone tries, tries, tries (often with one or two failed attempts). |
| **The beginning of the piece is lacking story elements or does not hint at larger issues or tension.**<br><br>The writer may have written a beginning that introduces basic plot elements, such as the characters and the setting, but the beginning lacks depth. Perhaps the writer does not suggest a larger conflict or does not suggest character flaws or struggles. | I've heard it said about movie scripts that the problem has to be revealed within the first ten minutes or so, otherwise the audience loses interest. It's the same with the beginning of a narrative piece. In the beginning, you have a short window to draw readers into the world of your story, to get them hooked so they just have to keep on reading. To get readers hooked, writers usually reveal three things right away: One, who the characters are and what they struggle with; two, where the story takes place and what kind of a place it is, and three, what are some of the larger issues at play. In the beginning, writers also often give clues about what the story is really, really about. | In the beginning, writers often reveal:<br><br>• Who the characters are and what they struggle with<br><br>• Where the story takes place and what kind of a place it is<br><br>• Some of the larger issues at play |
| **The ending of the piece seems incomplete or incongruous with the rest of the piece.**<br><br>The piece either ends abruptly, without bringing closure to major plot developments, or ends in a way that feels out of sync with the overall message or meaning of the piece. For example, the ending may feel rushed or too breezy or simplistic, as if the writer has "run out of steam." | Many writers agree that the ending of a story is perhaps the most important part, but it can be the hardest to write. The ending is the part where you bring your message home, where you get to leave your reader with exactly the feelings and understandings you want your story to convey. When you are trying to find the best ending to your story, it can help to try several versions of your ending on for size. In fact, this is just the kind of thing writers return to their notebooks to do, even if they've since moved on to drafting outside of the notebook. It helps to start by asking yourself, "What is my story really, really about?" and "What feelings or thoughts do I want readers to have at the end of my story?" Finally, ask yourself, "Have I tied up most of the loose ends and brought closure to most of the issues I created in my story?" | To find the best possible ending to a narrative piece, writers ask themselves:<br><br>• What is my story really, really about?<br><br>• What feelings or thoughts do I want readers to have at the end of my story?<br><br>• Have I tied up most of the loose ends and brought closure to most of the issues I created in my story? |

| If . . . | After acknowledging what the student is doing well, you might say . . . | Leave the writer with . . . |
|---|---|---|
| **The writer is ready to learn about the use of flashbacks and flash-forwards.**<br><br>This student has a well-structured piece that is ordered chronologically. It may be that the student is trying to incorporate information that would most efficiently be included in the narrative through the use of a flashback or a flash-forward. Alternatively, the writer's narrative may be fine as it is, but this student is ready to learn about alternative narrative structures and to experiment with those in her writing. Then too, the writer may have a meaning or theme that she is attempting to convey, and you sense that playing with time would help her to do this (for instance, perhaps she is trying to show that a moment is really about how she has always longed for her father's attention and the piece would be all the more powerful if she was able to flash-back to a time in her childhood when she eagerly awaited his arrival at an important event, or flash-forward to the moment she sees him walk through the doors at her big recital). | When we first teach narrative writing to students, we teach them to tell a story chronologically (first this happened, then this happened, and so on). As students mature, they are often ready to learn about new and different ways of structuring a story. You are at this point. Today I want to teach you that writers often use flashbacks or flash-forwards in their stories. They flash-back to a particular memory or have their character flash-forward and imagine the future, and they usually do this to show a deep desire the character has or to reinforce something important to the story. | Writers bring out the heart of their stories by embedding flashbacks or flash-forwards into the sequence of events. They make these shifts in time clear to their reader by using phrases like:<br><br>• "Thinking back to that day . . ."<br><br>• "I remember when . . ."<br><br>• "I imagined myself, four years later . . ."<br><br>• "Suddenly my mind flashed forward, picturing . . ." |
| **Elaboration** | | |
| **The writer has elaborated, but in seemingly haphazard ways.**<br><br>This writer has elaborated in one or multiple places across his text (perhaps using description or by slowing down the action in a particular scene), but it is unclear that he has chosen to elaborate for any purpose. That is, the writer may have stopped to describe a shiny, red apple that glinted in the sunlight, but the apple doesn't seem to have any real significance in the story. Alternatively, he may have extensively documented the dialogue between characters, but it is unclear how their conversation relates to what the story is really about. This writer has some tools for elaborating but needs to be more purposeful in using them, specifically, learning to elaborate on the parts of his story that relate back to the theme, message, or lesson he hopes to convey. | You know that writers elaborate, and you have a variety of techniques to do this—dialogue, internal thinking, descriptive details, slowing down the action, even figurative language. Today I want to teach you that elaboration is something writers do *purposefully*, for a reason. Elaboration is a way to make readers stop in their tracks and notice something, and writers usually want readers to stop and notice parts of the story that relate back to a larger theme or message they are trying to convey. In other words, writers elaborate on parts of their story that connect to what the story is *really* about. One way they do this is by rereading their story and asking, "Which moments relate to what my story is about? Where do I want readers to stop and linger?" They circle these parts and elaborate on them, making them larger and more powerful. | Writers don't just elaborate anywhere. They expand the parts of their story that relate back to the **theme, message**, or **lesson** they are trying to convey. |

| If . . . | After acknowledging what the student is doing well, you might say . . . | Leave the writer with . . . |
|---|---|---|
| **The writer has created a story that is sparse, with little elaboration.**<br><br>The writer has written a story that is short, with one or more parts that need elaboration. She has conveyed the main outline of an event (this happened, then this happened, then this happened), but there is no sense that she has expanded on any one particular part. | You have gotten skilled at telling what happens, but you write with just the bare-bones sequence. As writers, we want to bulk up our stories in specific, purposeful places—the places where we want to convey something important or where we want our reader right along with us, picturing every moment. Today I want to teach you that you can go back to your story and circle places where something particularly important is going on, places worth lingering in. These might include places where you want your reader to picture the setting, where you want to create tension, where something important is happening, or where there is an opportunity to show what the story is really about. Then, writers bulk up these sections using narrative techniques like description, dialogue, internal thinking, and the addition of small, meaningful actions. | Writers return to particularly significant portions of their story. These might include places where:<br><br>• They are establishing setting<br>• They want to create tension<br>• Something important is happening<br>• The scene ties back to the theme of their story<br><br>They can elaborate using all they know about narrative technique, by including:<br><br>• Descriptive details<br>• Dialogue<br>• Internal thinking<br>• Small, meaningful actions |
| **The writer has written the external story but not the internal story.**<br><br>This writer has captured the events of a story precisely, and likely has done a fine job of moving the story along at an appropriate pace. There is no sense, however, that the writer has considered anything beyond the external series of events. In other words, the writer has not clarified a lesson, theme, or emotional experience he wishes to convey to readers. The internal story is missing. This is often evident when, as each event occurs, the main character is swept along in the series of events with little to no response. For instance, he may get into trouble or get into a fight with his friends with little emotional response. The reader is left wondering what the main character is feeling and thinking throughout the story, and as a result, the story lacks depth. | Oftentimes when we go to write stories, we focus on the plot events. We carefully map out the story (this happens, then this happens, then this happens), but we forget that what makes stories powerful and memorable is the *internal* story. What I mean by this is that each story has a plotline (the series of events that occur) and an internal storyline (the main characters' responses and reactions to the events that occur). This helps readers to step into the shoes of the main character, and also helps them to understand what the story is *really* about. | Writers tell not just what happened in a story—the **actions**—but also how the character felt about each of these events—the **reactions**. |

| If . . . | After acknowledging what the student is doing well, you might say . . . | Leave the writer with . . . |
|---|---|---|
| **The writer relies on dialogue and internal thinking to show what a character is thinking and feeling and is ready for new techniques to achieve the same effect.**<br><br>This writer knows that a character's internal struggle drives any good narrative. In an attempt to convey the character's emotions to the reader, she has included an abundance of dialogue and internal thinking. This writer would benefit from a lesson that broadens her repertoire of techniques—learning subtler, more nuanced ways that authors show emotion. | You understand the need to convey your characters' thought and feelings to your reader, and you have done so effectively through the use of dialogue and internal thinking. Today I want to teach you another way you can reveal your characters' thoughts and feelings—through the use of small, meaningful actions. Writers know that having a character twist her hair or fiddle with a penny in her pocket or stare blankly out a window can give readers as much insight into that person's feelings as what the character says and thinks. | Writers rely on **tiny actions** to reveal **big emotions**. |
| **The writer is not making use of literary devices.**<br><br>This writer is successfully using a variety of narrative techniques but is not implementing literary devices. He has a clear sense of the meaning behind his story, as well as the places where this meaning might be emphasized or further revealed. | I think you are ready for a new challenge. You are humming along, using all that you know about narrative technique to elaborate, show what your story is really about, and make the story come alive for your reader. But I've noticed that you haven't yet tried to use more sophisticated techniques—namely, literary devices. Today I wanted to remind you about a few of the literary devices that writers use most often and give you some strategies for trying them. Specifically, I want to teach you that writers use literary devices—such as comparisons, repetition, and symbolism—to highlight important messages in their story. This often involves trying out a whole score of techniques in their notebooks, playing around with a scene or sentence a bit, until they find something that works. | Writers use literary devices to reveal meaning to a reader. They know that these complex narrative techniques rarely just come to them—voila!—and magically work perfectly. Instead, writers need to try a few different options and versions before settling on the revisions they'll include in their drafts. They might experiment with:<br><br>• Comparisons such as metaphors and similes<br>• Repetition<br>• Symbolism |
| **Language Conventions** | | |
| **The student is struggling with spelling, halting her progress.**<br><br>This student struggles with spelling and either does not make an effort to get help (for instance, by consulting a peer or using a dictionary) or simply barrels on, seemingly unaware of the spelling mistakes she makes. Either way, the quality of her writing is affected by the fact that it is riddled with errors. You do not want to stifle this students' writing stamina, but you do want to help her develop an increased awareness of spelling and learn to use resources to help her as she writes. | I can see that you are working very hard on this story in an attempt to say all that you want to say about the characters and the issues. Certainly the content and meaning of your story are paramount. I noticed, though, that in some parts your message doesn't come across fully, because some of the words aren't spelled exactly right. Don't worry. You're not alone in your issues with spelling. Mark Twain once said, "The English alphabet is a pure insanity. It can hardly spell any word in the language with any large degree of certainty." If Mark Twain struggled with spelling, you know you're in good company. Writers aren't expected to just know how to spell every single word they want to write. They use plenty of tools to make sure their spelling is correct. Of course, they could consult a dictionary. I often use my smart phone, or look up the word on a dictionary website. Sometimes, I ask one of my friends, who is a better speller than I. | Quick and Easy Tools to Check Spelling<br><br>• Smart phone<br>• Dictionary website<br>• A friend<br>• Classroom resources (word bank, dictionary) |

| If . . . | After acknowledging what the student is doing well, you might say . . . | Leave the writer with . . . |
|---|---|---|
| **The writer constructs short, simple sentences and is ready to learn to punctuate longer, more complex sentences using median punctuation.**<br><br>This writer is using short, simple sentences through his writing. It may be that this is all he is attempting, and he needs to be made aware of, and then taught how to construct, more complex sentences. Alternatively, he may be attempting to form more complex sentences but misusing commas or dashes, culminating in run-on, overly convoluted sentences. This writer needs help understanding the various roles commas play in sentence composition. | I've noticed that you've been trying to write longer, more sophisticated sentences, similar to the kinds you use when you speak. This is a big transition for writers, and I thought I'd give you a bit of support. Today I want to teach you that writers often rely on commas to string together longer sentences. Commas help readers know where to pause and help the sentence make sense. Writers use commas in lists, to separate two or more adjectives, before (and sometimes after) names of people, and to separate two strong clauses that are also separated by a conjunction. | Use Commas:<br><br>To separate items in a list:<br><br>• I want to eat breakfast, go for a walk, and then start my homework.<br><br>To separate adjectives:<br><br>• She pushed back her long, curly hair.<br><br>Before and after names of people:<br><br>• George, my best friend, is always there for me.<br><br>• "Don't do that, Julianna!"<br><br>To separate two strong clauses that are separated by a conjunction:<br><br>• I worked hard to make my teacher happy, but she always seemed to find something wrong with my work.<br><br>• He was walking rapidly down the street, and then he spotted her sitting on a bench. |

# Information Writing

| If . . . | After acknowledging what the student is doing well, you might say . . . | Leave the writer with . . . |
|---|---|---|
| **Structure and Cohesion** | | |
| **The writer has not established a clear organizational structure.**<br><br>This writer is struggling with organization. The book may be a jumble of information about a larger topic, with no clear subheadings or internal organization. Or the writer may have a table of contents, but the some of the chapters contain information unrelated to the chapter titles or to the broader topic. | One of the most important things information writers do is organize their writing by grouping related ideas and information. They help their reader to understand the way their writing is organized with formatting, such as headings, subheadings, text features, and bold words. Doing this is like creating little signs that say, "Hey, reader, I'm about to start talking about a new part of my topic!"<br><br>Also, it's important to name what the upcoming part of your writing will be about, then to write about just that subtopic in that section. | <u>One Subtopic</u><br><br>Information about that subtopic<br><br>Ideas about that subtopic<br><br>More information about that subtopic<br><br>More ideas about that subtopic<br><br>~~Unrelated or tangential information or ideas~~ |
| **There is no logical order to the sequence of information.**<br><br>The writer has a clearly structured piece of writing and is ready to consider the logical order of information both within and across sections. That is, she is ready to think strategically about how to place her chapters or sections and how to place information within each chapter. In doing so, she will consider audience, as well as the strength of each part of her writing. | As a middle school writer, it's important to organize your information into chapters, but it's not enough to stop there when thinking about organization. Middle school writers must organize with more purpose. Experienced information writers ask themselves, "Which part of my text should come first? Which should come second? Third?" They think about what order makes the most sense for their particular topic. They might decide to organize their information from least to most important, from weakest to strongest, or in chronological order. Or they might think about ways to order their information to build tension or to sustain readers' interest, such as writing about a problem related to the information and then later writing about how the problem was solved. | Information writers sort their information **logically**.<br><br>• They might put the sections in order from least to most important, weakest to strongest, or chronologically.<br><br>• They might think about ways to order their information to build tension or sustain readers' interest. |

| If . . . | After acknowledging what the student is doing well, you might say . . . | Leave the writer with . . . |
| --- | --- | --- |
| **The writer is ready to experiment with alternative organizing structures.**<br><br>This writer may have a relatively strong organizational structure to his information piece, but you sense there are better options or more challenging avenues he might take. Then, too, he may have tried to organize his piece one way, but the topic does not lend itself well to the structure he has chosen. In either instance, he is ready to broaden his repertoire in regard to organizational structure and study mentor texts to imagine alternative ways his text might go. | One of the greatest things about informational writing is that there are so many different ways a text can go. If we were to lay out a few different books on the same topic, we would find dozens of different ways the authors chose to organize them. Some authors, like Betsy and Giulio Maestro, write chronologically. Others, like Seymour Simon, write about different sections of a topic, and some authors, like Bobby Kalman, use pros and cons or questions and answers to organize their information. The options are endless.<br><br>When writers are looking to challenge themselves and try out some new ways of organizing their writing, they study mentor texts. One way to study an information text is to read, asking, "How does this author structure and organize his information?" Then, you can try out the same structure with your own writing. | Information writers study mentor texts and ask, "How does this author structure and organize his information?" Then, they try the same with their own writing. |
| **The writer has chosen a topic that is too broad.**<br><br>This writer has chosen a topic that is broad, such as the Middle East or teen activism, and has likely created a table of contents that suggests the product will be more of an all-about book. In an attempt to make her writing more sophisticated, and the processes of crafting an information piece more demanding, you can teach her to narrow her topic a bit. | I was looking at your topic choice earlier and thought to myself, "She is ready for a challenge!" You chose a topic that is very broad, very big. I'll bet you have a lot to say about your topic. But when information writers want to push themselves, when they want to craft a text that is more sophisticated, they narrow the topic. Narrowing your topic will probably make your book more interesting, and, though it seems counterintuitive, it might even help you have more to say. Today I'm going to teach you how to narrow your topic by asking, "What is *one part* of this subject I can write a lot about?"<br><br>You can also consider *ideas* when narrowing your topic. The most sophisticated information writers, like Malcolm Gladwell, usually have a big idea, or a thesis, about the information they are teaching. You can ask yourself, "What do I believe about this topic that I want others to know or believe?" | Writers challenge themselves by narrowing their topics. They might ask:<br><br>• "What is *one part* of this subject I can write a lot about?"<br><br>• "What do I believe about this topic that I want others to know or believe?" |

| If . . . | After acknowledging what the student is doing well, you might say . . . | Leave the writer with . . . |
|---|---|---|
| **The writer does not use transition words and phrases to help readers to understand how the text is organized or how information fits together.**<br><br>Information in the piece is mostly well organized in that like information is grouped together and there seems to be a logic to the placement of information. However, the writer uses few or no transition words to signify relationships between pieces of information and/or ideas. Alternatively, the writer may use some transition words, but they are fairly low-level and do not demonstrate the sophisticated thinking and organization called for by the Common Core Standards for middle school writers. | It looks like your text is chock-full of rich information. You are ready for the next step, which is to add some of those words and phrases that help readers to understand how information fits together. As information writing gets more sophisticated, it tends to include more than just fact after fact. It has ideas, examples, comparisons, and more. Readers need a way to understand how all of these fit together. Writers might use phrases like *for instance* and *such as* to tell readers that an example is coming. They might use phrases like *because of* or *as a result* to show a cause-and-effect relationship. The phrases *unlike, despite, on the other hand*, and *in contrast to* are all used to signify conflicting information.<br><br>Let's look at our class piece to see if we can find any places that might benefit from adding one of these phrases.<br><br>As a final tip, it might help to analyze your work for transition words at the end of each chapter or section you draft. Make a quick note of how many you used in each chapter. If you have fewer than five, chances are there are places where you could help your reader by adding more. | <u>Common Transition Words and Phrases</u><br><br>Giving an Example<br><br>• For instance<br><br>• Such as<br><br>Cause/Effect<br><br>• Because of<br><br>• As a result<br><br>Conflicting Information<br><br>• Unlike<br><br>• Despite<br><br>• On the other hand<br><br>• In contrast to<br><br>I used _____ transition words in this chapter. |
| **The introduction to the piece is lacking or weak.**<br><br>The writer may state the topic in the introduction and perhaps has even attempted to draw the reader in with an interesting quote or fact. However, the writer does not forecast the structure of the text by telling readers about the subtopics he will cover or otherwise suggest how the text will unfold.<br><br>Alternatively, the writer does not include much in the way of background information or place the topic in a larger context. | As you know, good information writing is like good teaching. Before taking a course on a topic, it often helps if the person taking the course understands the parts of the course and generally how the course will go. It's the same with information writing. As the writer, it helps if you set up your reader to learn by explaining the parts of your text and giving a sense of how your text is organized. In some texts, writers do this by including a table of contents. You might also do this by writing about it in your introduction. You might say, "This text about the beginnings of the American Revolution contains chapters on how the events in several different cities, including Philadelphia, Boston, and New York, led to the start of the revolution." | <u>Introductions Pull Readers In</u><br><br>• Give a bit of information about the topic.<br><br>• Give an interesting fact, story, or statistic to interest and orient your reader.<br><br>• Forecast the way the piece will go by telling the reader about its sections and the way it is organized. |
| **The conclusion is lacking or weak.**<br><br>The writer may either end the piece abruptly or end with a breezy, light tone. The writer may share her feelings about the topic. The writer is ready to adopt a more formal, sophisticated tone and learn more nuanced (and more subtle) ways of pulling readers in and providing closure. | In stories, writers use introductions to pull their readers in. Their conclusions, or endings, usually give the reader some closure. Information writing isn't much different. Writers use introductions to *pull* readers in, often by giving them a little information on the topic, just as a tour guide might do at the start of a tour. Then, they give their reader a sense of closure by wrapping things up with a conclusion. In this conclusion, they might restate important ideas, offer a final insight, or leave readers with something to mull over. Some writers might even make a plea for change or suggest possibilities for further study.<br><br>Some writers find that using an essay structure in the conclusion to an information text works well. | Conclusions give readers closure and wrap things up. Possible ways to conclude are:<br><br>• Restate important ideas and tell why the information matters.<br><br>• Leave readers with something to mull over.<br><br>• Make a plea for change.<br><br>• Suggest possibilities for further study. |

| If . . . | After acknowledging what the student is doing well, you might say . . . | Leave the writer with . . . |
|---|---|---|
| **Elaboration** | | |
| **Each section is short and needs elaboration.**<br><br>This writer has attempted to group his information, but each section is short. For example, he may have listed one or two facts related to a specific subsection but is stuck for what to add next. | Information writers need to be able to say a lot about each part of their topic, or to elaborate. There are a few things you can do to make each part of your book chock-full of information.<br><br>Be sure to use plenty of examples. To do this, it might be helpful to use prompts like, "It's also important to know this because . . ." and "Also . . ." and "What this means is . . ."<br><br>Another thing that might help you to say more is to consider using different organizational structures to teach about the topic more fully. You might think about making a comparison or a list of pros and cons. Or you might include some stories, some parts that are structured like mini-essays, or even some how-to sections. | <u>Writers Elaborate</u><br><br>1. They check to make sure they have at least six or seven pieces of information for each subtopic. If not, they consider cutting that section and starting a new one.<br><br>2. They use prompts such as "It's also important to know . . ." and "Also . . ." and "What this means is . . ." to say more about a particular piece of information.<br><br>3. They elaborate by using different organizational structures. |
| **The writer elaborates by adding fact after fact.**<br><br>This writer has elaborated but has done so by adding fact upon fact upon fact. As a result, her writing reads like a list, rather than a cohesive section of text. The writer has made little or no attempt to make her writing lively or interesting. This writer would benefit from learning to add a bit of her own voice into her information, relying on her own ability to synthesize and make sense of these facts for the reader. | You have tackled the first step in information writing—gathering the information needed to support various subtopics. Here's the thing, though. Writers don't *just* list facts for reader. It is also their job to take these facts and make something of them, to help explain why they are important. This is one way writers make sure their writing is interesting for the reader. Writers often use phrases like "What this really means is . . . ," "This shows . . . ," "All of this is important because . . . ," and "The implications of this are . . ." to help readers understand the information they've put forth. | Information writers don't just list fact after fact. They distill their writing for readers, adding their own ideas about the information. Phrases that can help are:<br><br>• "In other words . . ."<br><br>• "What this really means is . . ."<br><br>• "This shows . . ."<br><br>• "All of this is important because . . ." |
| **The writer does not elaborate on information from outside sources.**<br><br>The writer has included information from outside sources, such as quotes, facts, or statistics, but does not elaborate on this information for his reader. As a result, his writing is often very short, hopping from interesting fact to interesting fact. | I love all the research you have included in your information piece. It really shows that you are an expert on this topic. One way to show you are an expert, to show all you know about your topic, is by including outside information like quotes, facts, and statistics. Another way to be an expert and teach your readers (the way I'm going to teach you today) is by elaborating on, or saying more about, those facts. Today I want to teach you that writers don't just plop information into their writing. Instead, they explain what it means to their readers by using phrases like "What this means is . . ." or "In other words . . ." | Writers don't just plop information into their writing. Instead, they explain what it means to their readers by using phrases like "What this means is . . ." or "In other words . . ." |

| If . . . | After acknowledging what the student is doing well, you might say . . . | Leave the writer with . . . |
|---|---|---|
| **The writer does not credit outside sources in her writing.**<br><br>The writer's bibliography is lacking or weak or is not the correct format specified for her grade level. Alternatively, the writer has included a bibliography but does not credit sources in the body of the text. | I can tell that you are the kind of information writer who knows how important it is to lean heavily on information from credible sources. But what is just as important is to acknowledge the authors of the sources you use. In fact, acknowledging other writers actually makes your writing more credible because it shows you have done your research. It's also so important to give published authors credit if you use their ideas, to avoid possible issues with plagiarism. To give credit to an author right in the body of your text, you can use phrases like, "According to (so and so, or such and such text) . . ." or "The author/text _____ posits that . . ." Be sure to give the specific name of the author and the text. | Phrases to use when crediting outside sources:<br><br>According to . . .<br><br>The author/text _____ posits that . . .<br><br>A major claim made in the text/by the author_____ is . . . |
| **The writer does not incorporate domain-specific vocabulary.**<br><br>This writer has written about a topic but has done so without incorporating domain-specific vocabulary. It may be that the writer simply glossed over terms such as *caravan* or *brigade* (because he did not understand them or know how to incorporate them into his own writing) or used simpler language in place of complex vocabulary. Alternatively, the writer included some domain-specific vocabulary but did not give consideration to how those words should be defined. | As an information writer, it's important that you come across as an expert on your topic. Readers expect to learn something new, and one way to teach them something new is by using technical, expert vocabulary. Today I want to teach you that writers don't just toss these words into their writing. Instead, they learn what they mean, and then they make decisions about how to define them for readers. They consider which words are so important they should be defined within the text, perhaps in an appositive phrase set off by commas, or which words might be better defined in a sidebar or a text box. Finally, information writers decide whether the entire piece could use a technical glossary of terms. | Information writers us expert vocabulary (and define it for their readers, too). They can:<br><br>• Say the word and then explain what it means.<br><br>*Example:* Loyalists were people who remained loyal to the king during the American Revolution.<br><br>• Tuck the definition into the sentence using two commas.<br><br>*Example:* Loyalists, people who remained loyal to the king during the American Revolution, fought throughout the war. |
| **Language Conventions** | | |
| **The writer incorporates quotes, facts, and statistics, but does so awkwardly.**<br><br>This writer uses quotes, facts, statistics, and other outside information to elaborate on the sections of her information text. The information is well organized, and the facts and quotes are generally well placed, but they often sound awkward. It is not clear that the writer understands how to move from her words to the words and examples of an author or experts, and she needs help with ways to do this more fluently. | Quotes, facts, and statistics are incredibly important in information writing because they tell a reader that, yes, I have done my research and know a lot about my topic! Today I want to teach you how to take quotes, facts, and statistics and make them sound like a part of your writing. You can do this by using transitional phrases like *for instance*, *one example*, or *according to*. | Writers use transitional phrases to introduce quotes, facts, and statistics.<br><br>*Example:* Sharks aren't that dangerous. *One example* of this is basking sharks. People in the Hamptons often see them and they are slow-moving and harmless. *According to* Science-Facts.com, "more people die of alligator attacks than shark attacks." |

| If . . . | After acknowledging what the student is doing well, you might say . . . | Leave the writer with . . . |
|---|---|---|
| **The writer struggles with spelling, particularly domain-specific vocabulary words.**<br><br>Many of technical terms and names are misspelled, or the writer frequently asks for spelling assistance from peers or a teacher, inhibiting writing volume. | One thing that is so important when writing to teach others is to correctly spell the words that are the most important to the topic. I recommend making a list of the most important words to your topic—such as technical terms, names, and places—and then double-checking their spelling using one of your sources. Keep this list right next to you as you write. Then you'll make sure to spell these words correctly, and you won't get stopped in your tracks, having to check on how to spell these words all the time. I'll bet before long you won't need to consult your list at all. | Terms important to my study:<br><br>• _____<br>• _____<br>• _____<br>• _____<br>• _____ |

# Argument Writing

| If . . . | After acknowledging what the student is doing well, you might say . . . | Leave the writer with . . . |
|---|---|---|
| **Structure and Cohesion** | | |
| **The introduction does not forecast the structure of the essay.** <br><br> The writer has made a claim and supported it with reasons, but there is no forecasting statement early on in the essay that foreshadows the reasons to come. Instead, it seems as if the writer thought of and wrote about one reason, then, when reaching the end of the first body paragraph, thought, "What's another reason?" and then raised and elaborated upon that reason. He would benefit from learning to plan for the overarching structure of his argument and forecast that structure in the introduction. | You have learned to make a claim in your essay and to support that claim with reasons. As essayists, though, it's important to preplan how our essay will go, and to let the reader know how our writing will be organized from the very beginning. This is called *forecasting*. Today I want to teach you that opinion writers forecast how their writing will go. They do this by stating their claim in the introduction and then adding on, "I think this because . . ." Then they list the reasons that they will write about in the body of their piece. | Writers use the introduction to forecast how their opinion pieces will go. <br><br> 1. State your claim. <br><br> 2. Tell your reader why your claim is true. <br> • "One reason this is true is because . . ." <br> • "Another reason this is true is because . . ." <br> • "A third reason this is true is because . . ." |
| **The writer's introduction and/or conclusion feel formulaic.** <br><br> The writer has stated her thesis up front and forecasted the reasons to come in the essay. She has probably done something similar in her conclusion—wrapping up the essay by recapping her opinion and reasons. Though there is nothing wrong with this, the essay feels formulaic and dull. This writer would benefit from learning a few techniques to make her introduction and conclusion a place where she can grab a reader's attention, shed light on important issues, and appeal to her audience. | You have done everything that a teacher would ask a student to do when writing an introduction and conclusion. You have stated your thesis and told the reasons you have for it. But here's the thing. Once essay writers have mastered the basics, they are ready to take a next step. That next step often means asking themselves, "What should my readers take away from this essay? What thoughts, feelings or ideas do I want to leave them with?" Then, once they've answered those questions, they know there are a few special techniques they can use to get their message across. | When writers want to draw their readers in or leave them with something to think about, they . . . <br><br> 1. Tell the story of someone who would benefit from the lessons or themes they are writing about <br><br> 2. Discuss how the theme or message relate to a larger audience <br><br> 3. Call for the audience to help with the cause <br><br> 4. Tell a small story to illustrate the importance of the issue |

| If . . . | After acknowledging what the student is doing well, you might say . . . | Leave the writer with . . . |
|---|---|---|
| **The writer's supports overlap.**<br><br>In this instance, the writer has developed supporting reasons that are overlapping or overly similar. While this may pose few problems now, the writer will struggle when the time comes for him to find examples to support each reason (because the examples he uses are apt to be the same!). | Sometimes, when writers develop supporting reasons for their thesis, they find that one or more of them overlap. What I mean by this is that they basically say the same thing! Today I want to teach you that writers look at their supporting reasons with a critical eye, checking to see if any overlap. One way they do this is by listing the evidence they'll use for each body paragraph. If some of the evidence is the same, then the reasons are probably too similar. | Are your supporting reasons too similar? Test them out to find out.<br><br>Reason/Support#1:_____<br><br>    Evidence: _____<br><br>    Evidence: _____<br><br>Reason/Support#2:_____<br><br>    Evidence: _____<br><br>    Evidence: _____<br><br>Reason/Support#3:_____<br><br>    Evidence: _____<br><br>    Evidence: _____ |
| **The writer's supports are not parallel or equal in weight.**<br><br>This writer has developed a thesis and supports. While all the supports may support the writer's overall claim, they are not parallel. For instance, when arguing that *The Lightning Thief* teaches readers that friendship has the power to right wrongs in people's lives, the writer may have suggested that this is because (A) Annabeth helps Percy become the hero he is, (B) Grover helps Percy deal with his self-doubt, and (C) in one scene, Percy helps Annabeth. In this instance, Support C refers to one particular scene, while Supports A and B are far larger and will be supported by evidence from across the text. For C to be parallel to A and B, the writer would need to make a larger statement about Percy that incorporates evidence from across the text. For instance, she might write, "Percy helps heal Annabeth's pain." | As a writer, you want each part of your essay to be about equal in weight. What I mean by this is that all your supports should prove your overall claim *and* they should be something you can elaborate on with several examples. Today I want to teach you that writers look back over their supports and ask, "Are these equal in size?" One way to test out this question is by checking to see if they can give two to three examples for each support. If they can't, they have to revise the supporting reason to make it larger. | Do you have examples to prove each of your supports?<br><br>Reason/Support#1:_____<br><br>    Evidence: _____<br><br>    Evidence: _____<br><br>Reason/Support#2:_____<br><br>    Evidence: _____<br><br>    Evidence: _____<br><br>Reason/Support#3:_____<br><br>    Evidence: _____<br><br>    Evidence: _____ |

| If . . . | After acknowledging what the student is doing well, you might say . . . | Leave the writer with . . . |
|---|---|---|
| **The writer has developed a thesis that is complex and nuanced, but lacks the skills to organize an essay that supports it.**<br><br>Whether writing about a text or the world, this writer has developed a thesis that is complex. The last thing you want to do is ask this writer to simplify his thinking, but it is clear that you will need to teach him some alternative structures for supporting a thesis (beyond the classic reason/way/part five-paragraph essay). This writer would benefit from learning that essays come in many shapes and sizes and that essayists often "try on" several organizational structures before deciding on the one that works best for them. | As a writer and a thinker, you have grown in tremendous ways. It used to be that you developed theses that were safe and easy to support (like "Dogs make great friends" or "Percy is a brave character"). Now your thinking is stronger, but this brings new challenges. When a thesis is more complex, it requires a more complex structure to support it! Today I want to teach you a few organizational structures that essayists often use and show you how writers "try on" different structures for size. They might try giving examples from across a text or across a period of time. They might try supporting an idea with context, evidence, and then a bit about the implications. They might support the idea by comparing and contrasting. They also might support their thesis with support from several different texts or sources. Other times, they need to make up their own structure! | Idea/Thesis<br><br>• "At first . . . "<br>• "Then . . . "<br>• "Later on . . ."<br><br>Idea/Thesis<br><br>• Context surrounding the idea<br>• Evidence to support the idea<br>• Implications or conclusions regarding what you have just argued<br><br>Idea/Thesis<br><br>• How two texts/people/etc. treat this idea in similar ways<br>• How two texts/people/etc. treat this idea in different ways<br><br>Idea/Thesis<br><br>• Support from source/text #1<br>• Support from source/text #2<br>• Support from source/text #1, #2, or #3<br><br>Or make up an organizational structure all your own! |
| **The writer needs help incorporating counterargument into her essay.**<br><br>The writer is ready to consider counterargument but needs help doing it well. She may have written something like, "Not everyone agrees, but . . ." or may have gone further and mentioned the opposing argument that others might make. She is ready to learn that argument writers not only address alternative views in their essay, but work to debunk them. | You are doing one of the hardest things there is to do when you are working to write an argument. You are imagining the people who might disagree with your claim and are trying to see a point of view that is different from your own. Today I want to show you how to raise the level of that work by teaching you to use counterarguments to *make your own argument stronger*! One way to do this is by showing that there are flaws or gaps or problems in the counterargument. Thought prompts can help you get started. | Expose the flaws, gaps, and problems in the counterargument! Then, prove that your point of view is correct.<br><br>You might try a few of these sentence starters:<br><br>• "This argument overlooks . . ."<br>• "This argument isn't showing the full story."<br>• "Some people argue that . . . , but . . ."<br>• "While it's easy to assume that . . . , this is incorrect because . . ." |

| If . . . | After acknowledging what the student is doing well, you might say . . . | Leave the writer with . . . |
|---|---|---|
| **The writer has a thesis and supports, but there is no evidence that he has considered a logical order for his supporting paragraphs.**<br><br>The writer has developed a thesis and supports but would benefit from considering different ways he might order the supports in his essay. Perhaps he begins with one of his weaker body paragraphs or ends with one that is not particularly strong. Alternatively, his argument might flow better if ordered chronologically, in order of importance, or in a way where one body paragraph builds on the next. This writer is ready to learn that structuring an essay is not simply about listing supports one by one. Instead, essayists carefully consider the order in which they will give evidence, considering an order that will be most logical and persuasive. | You have developed body paragraphs that solidly support your thesis, and this is a huge step. I have a tip for you, a way that essayists play with their body paragraphs to make them even more powerful. When essayists try to convince somebody of something, they know it is really important to consider the order of their reasons. Essayists know it is important to convince readers of their idea early on, but at the same time, they want to conclude with something powerful. One trick is to start off with the second most powerful support you have, put the weaker one in the middle, and save the best for last. That way you leave on a strong foot! | Take a look at this quick picture if you're having trouble remembering!<br><br>Opening<br><br>#2<br><br>#3<br><br>#1<br><br>Closing |
| **Elaboration** | | |
| **The writer is struggling to elaborate.**<br><br>The writer has an opinion as well as several reasons to support that opinion, but most statements are made without elaboration. The writer may have created a long list of reasons to support her opinion. Alternatively, she may have written sparsely by simply stating each piece of evidence in one simple sentence. This might result in three very short supporting paragraphs. This writer needs help finding more to say to support her claim and convince her reader. | You already know that when you state a claim you need to support it with evidence. But essayists don't stop there. They know that part of their job as writers is to convince others to agree with their opinion. To do that, essayists provide a variety of strong evidence and then unpack and explain how that evidence supports their thesis. They might use facts, statistics, definitions, quotes, stories, or examples in their supporting paragraphs. Then, thought prompts can help them explain how that evidence connects to their thesis. | Opinion writers support their thesis using:<br><br>• Facts<br><br>• Statistics<br><br>• Definitions<br><br>• Quotes<br><br>• Stories<br><br>• Examples<br><br>• And more. . .<br><br>Then they unpack their evidence using thought prompts like:<br><br>• "This proves/shows . . ."<br><br>• "This is an example of how . . ."<br><br>• "This demonstrates . . ."<br><br>• "From this we can infer . . ."<br><br>• "This teaches us . . ." |

| If . . . | After acknowledging what the student is doing well, you might say . . . | Leave the writer with . . . |
|---|---|---|
| **The writer has chosen evidence for each body paragraph, but it does not all support his claim.**<br><br>This writer has elaborated on his supports with a variety of evidence, but not all of this evidence matches the point he is trying to make. It may be that the evidence is unwieldy and unfocused and that the writer would benefit from learning to angle information to support a particular point. It may also be that a quote or statistic or example does not connect directly to the claim. Either way, this writer needs help rereading his piece with a critical lens, checking to be sure that each sentence he has written helps to further his claim. | As a writer, you know it is important to support a claim with plenty of evidence. Today I want to teach you that as writers try out different pieces of evidence, they ask themselves, "Does this really support the idea I am writing about?" and "Can I show how this proves what I'm trying to say?" They keep the parts of the evidence that support their idea and get rid of the rest. If it takes too much defending or explaining to show how the evidence supports their thesis, writers usually find it is best to go in search of better evidence. | When deciding on the evidence they'll include, opinion writers ask:<br><br>• "Does this support the idea I am writing about?"<br><br>• "Can I show how this proves what I'm trying to say?"<br><br>If the answer is *yes*, they keep the evidence! If not, they cut it and go in search of better evidence. |
| **The writer has included a variety of details and evidence, but it has swamped her piece.**<br><br>This writer is attempting to be convincing and knows that details matter. Her writing is full of examples and quotes, but she has not been discerning about what she will include. For instance, if the author uses a powerful word or sentence, the student may have quoted an entire paragraph or two and put it into her essay. She may not understand that writers take liberties with the evidence they include, cutting the parts that are less effective and including only those that hammer home a point. | Today I want to teach you that essayists choose only the most compelling pieces of evidence. This often mean cutting quotes apart and retelling or citing only small episodes. One thing writers do is reread each piece of evidence and underline the parts that really, truly support their thesis. Then they cut the rest. Sometimes this means they are only keeping a word or a sentence that an author has used. | Reread your evidence. What words, sentences, and examples *best* support what you are trying to say? Underline the most powerful parts (this often means cutting a lot!) and use only those in your essay. |

| If . . . | After acknowledging what the student is doing well, you might say . . . | Leave the writer with . . . |
|---|---|---|
| **When writing about reading, the writer is ready to analyze the craft moves an author makes and use those to support his argument.**<br><br>The writer has a variety of evidence that supports his claim well. He knows how to make use of quotations, paraphrasing, retelling, and the like. This writer is ready to take the next step: consider the craft moves an author has made and use those to support his argument. | As writers, we know that every word we choose is for a purpose. We might want to shock readers or draw their attention. We might want to set a mood or create tension. We might even use craft moves, such as symbolism, comparisons, and other figurative language, to convey a big message or idea in our writing. As essayists, we can study the words, examples, and illustrations that authors include and ask, "What does this author want me to think, feel, or know?" Then, we can use what we notice as evidence to further support our claim. This works if we are writing about a text in a literary essay or if we are using a text as evidence in a research-based essay. | What does this author want me to **think**, **feel**, or **know**? We might find out by studying:<br><br>• Word choice<br>• Example choice<br>• Illustration or picture choice<br><br>When looking at an author's choices, it can be helpful to keep in mind that authors often want to:<br><br>• Make us feel a certain emotion<br>• Recognize the importance of something they are discussing<br>• Side with them on an issue |
| **Language Conventions** | | |
| **The writer uses a casual, informal tone when writing.**<br><br>This writer's opinion piece may have a lively, fun feel to it, but she writes as if she is talking to a friend. She might start with a question ("Have you ever heard about . . . ?") or an exclamatory statement meant to bring readers on board with her opinion ("Can you believe . . . ???!!!!!") These writers often use talking to their audience as their main form of persuasion ("Thanks for reading my essay. Never buy cosmetics that have been tested on animals!") and would benefit from learning new, more nuanced and academic ways of appealing to readers. | When we are trying to get somebody to agree with us about something, we are much more convincing when we sound like an expert. Today I want to teach you one thing that opinion writers often do. They often write as if they are experts (even if they are not). They make themselves sound like experts by addressing those who might disagree with them, citing research, and using phrases that make them sound confident in their opinions. A few of these include "While some say . . . , what they neglect to realize is . . . ," "Research shows . . . ," and "It is clear that . . . ." | When trying to get someone to agree with your viewpoint, talk like an expert. Here are some things to try:<br><br>Address those who might disagree with you and say why their viewpoint in inaccurate:<br><br>• "While some say . . . , what they neglect to realize is . . . ."<br><br>Cite research that supports your argument:<br><br>• "Research shows . . . ."<br>• "According to sources . . . ."<br><br>Sound confident about your opinion:<br><br>• "It is clear that . . . ."<br>• "What this means is . . . ." |

| If . . . | After acknowledging what the student is doing well, you might say . . . | Leave the writer with . . . |
|---|---|---|
| **The writer struggles to punctuate correctly when quoting, especially when using only part of a quote from a text.**<br><br>This writer knows the basics of quoting but is struggling to extend that knowledge to accommodate places where he wants to use only part of a quote. Alternatively, it may be that he only has one way of quoting ("In the text ___, it says . . .") and would benefit from a larger repertoire of ways to incorporate others' words into his own writing. | The great news is that you've got the most important part down—using evidence that proves your point and convinces your audience. But sometimes quoting can get tricky when we are only citing a small part of a text (especially if it isn't a complete sentence!), and other times we find ourselves using the same phrase again and again to introduce a quote. Let me teach you the golden rules of quoting:<br><br>1. You have to put the quote into a complete sentence that makes sense grammatically.<br><br>2. Punctuation goes inside quotation marks, not directly after it.<br><br>3. Make sure you tell the reader where the quote came from and any information they need to understand why you've included it. | A few examples that can help you craft your own, complex quotes:<br><br>• As the researcher claimed, "Chocolate milk has even more sugar and calories in it than soda."<br><br>• "Furthermore," the researcher claimed, "students drink it under the assumption that it's good for them."<br><br>• Chocolate milk is not actually good for you. This is just an "assumption" that students have, according to the researcher. |